£6.25

# Cascades

*Cascades consultants:*
John Mannion, Head of English at Elliott School, Wandsworth
Sheena Davies, Head of English at Bishopbriggs High School,
Glasgow
Adrian Jackson, Advisory Teacher for English
Geoff Fox, Lecturer at the University of Exeter School of
Education, and a National Curriculum Advisor

# My Family
# and Other Animals

GERALD DURRELL

# *My Family and Other Animals*

Collins Educational

*An imprint of* HarperCollins*Publishers*

www.CollinsEducation.com
On-line support for schools and colleges

© Gerald M. Durrell 1956

ISBN 000 330318 7

First published in Great Britain by Rupert Hart-Davis 1956
Published in *Cascades* in 1997 by Collins Educational
Reprinted 2000

You might also like to visit
www.fireandwater.co.uk
The book lover's website

Printed and bound in China

Cover design by Carla Turchini
Cover photograph by Reinhard Siegl, Tony Stone Images
Commissioning Editor: Helen Clark

## ABOUT THE AUTHOR

Gerald Durrell was born in 1925 in India. After living in various parts of Europe, his family later settled on the island of Corfu, where he became fascinated by animals. As an adult, he took part in many animal-collecting expeditions all over the world, about which numerous television programmes were made. His brother, the novelist Lawrence Durrell, encouraged him to write about his experiences. After Gerald's first book, *The Overloaded Ark*, became a bestseller in 1953, Gerald went on to write 36 more books. In 1964 he founded the Jersey Wildlife Preservation Trust. He helped to prevent such creatures as the Mauritius pink pigeon and the Rodrigues fruit-bat from becoming extinct. Gerald Durrell received the OBE in 1982. He died in 1995.

Other KS4 titles in the *Cascades* series that you might enjoy:

### *The Loved One* — EVELYN WAUGH

A satirical look at the Americans' attitude to death in post-war Los Angeles. Dennis Barlow wants to be a screenwriter, but he is working in a pets' cemetery. He visits Whispering Glades, a cemetery for human beings, and falls in love with Aimée, a cosmetician. But she is in love with the chief embalmer and can't decide between the two of them.

ISBN 000 330092 7

### *A Welsh Childhood* — ALICE THOMAS ELLIS

The affectionate memoirs of the author's childhood in North Wales, and her later life there with her children. The book is both poignant and humorous, and contains haunting memories and amusing anecdotes.

ISBN 000 330094 3

### *Spies I Have Known* — DORIS LESSING

In this collection of short stories, the reactions of people to each other and to the various situations in which they find themselves, are explored as the reader gets a fascinating glimpse of the characters' lives. The stories cover a range of genres and subjects.

ISBN 000 330309 8

### *Ticket to Prague* — JAMES WATSON

From the highly successful author of *Talking in Whispers*, this is the story of the relationship between teenager Amy Douglas and a mysterious old Czech man, Josef. The pair travel from an old people's home in Britain to post-Communist Prague, where the past comes back to haunt Josef. This is a story of friendship and loyalty, as well as a passionate plea for reconciliation.

ISBN 000 330313 6

*For further information, please call 0141 306 3484*

TO MY MOTHER

IT IS A MELANCHOLY OF MINE OWN, COMPOUNDED OF MANY SIMPLES, EXTRACTED FROM MANY OBJECTS, AND INDEED THE SUNDRY CONTEMPLATION OF MY TRAVELS, WHICH, BY OFTEN RUMINATION, WRAPS ME IN A MOST HUMOROUS SADNESS.     AS YOU LIKE IT.

# Contents

# The Speech for the Defence

Why, sometimes I've believed as many as six impossible things before
breakfast.'
                The White Queen – *Alice Through the Looking-Glass*

This is the story of a five-year sojourn that I and my family
made on the Greek island of Corfu. It was originally intended
to be a mildly nostalgic account of the natural history of the
island, but I made a grave mistake by introducing my family
into the book in the first few pages. Having got themselves on
paper, they then proceeded to establish themselves and invite
various friends to share the chapters. It was only with the
greatest difficulty, and by exercising considerable cunning,
that I managed to retain a few pages here and there which
I could devote exclusively to animals.

I have attempted to draw an accurate and unexaggerated
picture of my family in the following pages; they appear as
I saw them. To explain some of their more curious ways,
however, I feel that I should state that at the time we were
in Corfu the family were all quite young: Larry, the eldest,
was twenty-three; Leslie was nineteen; Margo eighteen; while
I was the youngest, being of the tender and impressionable
age of ten. We have never been very certain of my mother's
age, for the simple reason that she can never remember her
date of birth; all I can say is that she was old enough to have
four children. My mother also insists that I explain that she is
a widow for, as she so penetratingly observed, you never know
what people might think.

In order to compress five years of incident, observation, and
pleasant living into something a little less lengthy than the

*Encyclopaedia Britannica*, I have been forced to telescope, prune, and graft, so that there is little left of the original continuity of events. Also I have been forced to leave out many happenings and characters that I would have liked to describe.

It is doubtful if this would have been written without the help and enthusiasm of the following people. I mention this so that blame can be laid in the right quarter.

My grateful thanks, then, to:

Dr Theodore Stephanides. With typical generosity, he allowed me to make use of material from his unpublished work on Corfu, and supplied me with a number of dreadful puns, some of which I have used.

My family. They, after all, unconsciously provided a lot of the material, and helped me considerably during the writing of the book by arguing ferociously and rarely agreeing about any incident on which I consulted them.

My wife, who pleased me by laughing uproariously when reading the manuscript, only to inform me that it was my spelling that amused her.

Sophie, my secretary, who was responsible for the introduction of commas and the ruthless eradication of the split infinitive.

I should like to pay a special tribute to my mother, to whom this book is dedicated. Like a gentle, enthusiastic, and understanding Noah, she has steered her vessel full of strange progeny through the stormy seas of life with great skill, always faced with the possibility of mutiny, always surrounded by the dangerous shoals of overdraft and extravagance, never being sure that her navigation would be approved by the crew, but certain that she would be blamed for anything that went wrong. That she survived the voyage is a miracle, but survive it she did, and, moreover, with her reason more or less intact. As my brother Larry rightly points out, we can be proud of the way we have brought her up; she is a credit to us. That she has reached that happy Nirvana where nothing shocks or startles is exemplified by the fact that one week-end recently, when all alone in the house, she was treated to the sudden arrival of a series of crates containing two pelicans, a scarlet ibis, a vulture, and eight monkeys. A lesser mortal might have quailed at such a contingency, but not Mother. On Monday morning I found her in the garage being pursued round and round by an irate pelican which she was trying to feed with sardines from a tin.

'I'm glad you've come, dear,' she panted; 'this pelican is a *little* difficult to handle.'

When I asked her how she *knew* the animals belonged to me, she replied: 'Well, of course I knew they were yours, dear; who else would send pelicans to me?'

Which goes to show how well she knows at least one of her family.

Lastly, I would like to make a point of stressing that all the anecdotes about the island and the islanders are absolutely true. Living in Corfu was rather like living in one of the more flamboyant and slapstick comic operas. The whole atmosphere and charm of the place was, I think, summed up neatly on an Admiralty map we had, which showed the island and the adjacent coastline in great detail. At the bottom was a little inset which read:

CAUTION: As the buoys marking the shoals are often out of position, mariners are cautioned to be on their guard when navigating these shores.

# PART I

There is a pleasure sure
In being mad, which none but madmen know.
      DRYDEN, *The Spanish Friar, II, i*

# The Migration

July had been blown out like a candle by a biting wind that
ushered in a leaden August sky. A sharp, stinging drizzle fell,
billowing into opaque grey sheets when the wind caught it.
Along the Bournemouth sea-front the beach-huts turned blank
wooden faces towards a greeny-grey, froth-chained sea that
leapt eagerly at the cement bulwark of the shore. The gulls
had been tumbled inland over the town, and they now drifted
above the house-tops on taut wings, whining peevishly. It was
the sort of weather calculated to try anyone's endurance.

Considered as a group my family was not a very prepos-
sessing sight that afternoon, for the weather had brought
with it the usual selection of ills to which we were prone.
For me, lying on the floor, labelling my collection of shells,
it had brought catarrh, pouring it into my skull like cement,
so that I was forced to breathe stertorously through open
mouth. For my brother Leslie, hunched dark and glowering
by the fire, it had inflamed the convolutions of his ears so
that they bled delicately but persistently. To my sister Margo
it had delivered a fresh dappling of acne spots to a face that
was already blotched like a red veil. For my mother there was
a rich, bubbling cold, and a twinge of rheumatism to season
it. Only my eldest brother, Larry, was untouched, but it was
sufficient that he was irritated by our failings.

It was Larry, of course, who started it. The rest of us felt too
apathetic to think of anything except our own ills, but Larry
was designed by Providence to go through life like a small,
blond firework, exploding ideas in other people's minds, and
then curling up with cat-like unctuousness and refusing to take
any blame for the consequences. He had become increasingly

irritable as the afternoon wore on. At length, glancing moodily round the room, he decided to attack Mother, as being the obvious cause of the trouble.

'Why do we stand this bloody climate?' he asked suddenly, making a gesture towards the rain-distorted window. 'Look at it! And, if it comes to that, look at us . . . Margo swollen up like a plate of scarlet porridge . . . Leslie wandering around with fourteen fathoms of cotton wool in each ear . . . Gerry sounds as though he's had a cleft palate from birth . . . And look at you: you're looking more decrepit and hag-ridden every day.'

Mother peered over the top of a large volume entitled *Easy Recipes from Rajputana*.

'Indeed I'm not,' she said indignantly.

'You *are*,' Larry insisted; 'you're beginning to look like an Irish washerwoman . . . and your family looks like a series of illustrations from a medical encyclopaedia.

Mother could think of no really crushing reply to this, so she contented herself with a glare before retreating once more behind her book.

'What we need is sunshine,' Larry continued; 'don't you agree, Les? . . . Les . . . *Les!*'

Leslie unravelled a large quantity of cotton wool from one ear.

'What d'you say?' he asked.

'There you are!' said Larry, turning triumphantly to Mother, 'it's become a major operation to hold a conversation with him. I ask you, what a position to be in! One brother can't hear what you say, and the other one can't be understood. Really, it's time something was done. I can't be expected to produce deathless prose in an atmosphere of gloom and eucalyptus.'

'Yes dear,' said Mother vaguely.

'What we all need,' said Larry, getting into his stride again, 'is sunshine . . . a country where we can *grow*.'

'Yes, dear, that would be nice,' agreed Mother, not really listening.

'I had a letter from George this morning – he says Corfu's wonderful. Why don't we pack up and go to Greece?'

'Very well, dear, if you like,' said Mother unguardedly.

Where Larry was concerned she was generally very careful not to commit herself.

'When?' asked Larry, rather surprised at this cooperation.

Mother, perceiving that she had made a tactical error, cautiously lowered *Easy Recipes from Rajputana*.

'Well, I think it would be a sensible idea if you were to go

6

on ahead, dear, and arrange things. Then you can write and tell me if it's nice, and we all can follow,' she said cleverly.

Larry gave her a withering look.

'You said *that* when I suggested going to Spain,' he reminded her, 'and I sat for two interminable months in Seville, waiting for you to come out, while you did nothing except write me massive letters about drains and drinking-water, as though I was the Town Clerk or something. No, if we're going to Greece, let's all go together.'

'You do *exaggerate*, Larry,' said Mother plaintively; 'anyway, I can't go just like that. I have to arrange something about this house.'

'Arrange? Arrange what, for heaven's sake? Sell it.'

'I can't do that, dear,' said Mother, shocked.

'Why not?'

'But I've only just bought it.'

'Sell it while it's still untarnished, then.'

'Don't be ridiculous, dear,' said Mother firmly; 'that's quite out of the question. It would be madness.'

So we sold the house and fled from the gloom of the English summer, like a flock of migrating swallows.

We all travelled light, taking with us only what we considered to be the bare essentials of life. When we opened our luggage for Customs inspection, the contents of our bags were a fair indication of character and interests. Thus Margo's luggage contained a multitude of diaphanous garments, three books on slimming, and a regiment of small bottles each containing some elixir guaranteed to cure acne. Leslie's case held a couple of roll-top pullovers and a pair of trousers which were wrapped round two revolvers, an air-pistol, a book called *Be Your Own Gunsmith*, and a large bottle of oil that leaked. Larry was accompanied by two trunks of books and a brief-case containing his clothes. Mother's luggage was sensibly divided between clothes and various volumes on cooking and gardening. I travelled with only those items that I thought necessary to relieve the tedium of a long journey: four books on natural history, a butterfly net, a dog, and a jam-jar full of caterpillars all in imminent danger of turning into chrysalids. Thus, by our standards fully equipped, we left the clammy shores of England.

France rain-washed and sorrowful, Switzerland like a Christmas cake, Italy exuberant, noisy, and smelly, were passed, leaving only confused memories. The tiny ship

7

throbbed away from the heel of Italy out into the twilit sea, and as we slept in our stuffy cabins, somewhere in that tract of moon-polished water we passed the invisible dividing-line and entered the bright looking-glass world of Greece. Slowly this sense of change seeped down to us, and so, at dawn, we awoke restless and went on deck.

The sea lifted smooth blue muscles of wave as it stirred in the dawn-light, and the foam of our wake spread gently behind us like a white peacock's tail, glinting with bubbles. The sky was pale and stained with yellow on the eastern horizon. Ahead lay a chocolate-brown smudge of land, huddled in mist, with a frill of foam at its base. This was Corfu, and we strained our eyes to make out the exact shapes of the mountains, to discover valleys, peaks, ravines, and beaches, but it remained a silhouette. Then suddenly the sun shifted over the horizon, and the sky turned the smooth enamelled blue of a jay'e eye. The endless, meticulous curves of the sea flamed for an instant and then changed to a deep royal purple flecked with green. The mist lifted in quick lithe ribbons, and before us lay the island, the mountains as though sleeping beneath a crumpled blanket of brown, the folds stained with the green of olive-groves. Along the shore curved beaches as white as tusks among tottering cities of brilliant gold, red, and white rocks. We rounded the northern cape, a smooth shoulder of rust-red cliff carved into a series of giant caves. The dark waves lifted our wake and carried it gently towards them, and then, at their very mouths, it crumpled and hissed thirstily among the rocks. Rounding the cape, we left the mountains, and the island sloped gently down, blurred with the silver and green iridescence of olives, with here and there an admonishing finger of black cypress against the sky. The shallow sea in the bays was butterfly blue, and even above the sound of the ship's engines we could hear, faintly ringing from the shore like a chorus of tiny voices, the shrill, triumphant cries of the cicadas.

# 1

# The Unsuspected Isle

We threaded our way out of the noise and confusion of the Customs shed into the brilliant sunshine on the quay. Around us the town rose steeply, tiers of multi-coloured houses piled haphazardly, green shutters folded back from their windows, like the wings of a thousand moths. Behind us lay the bay, smooth as a plate, smouldering with that unbelievable blue.

Larry walked swiftly, with head thrown back and an expression of such regal disdain on his face that one did not notice his diminutive size, keeping a wary eye on the porters who struggled with his trunks. Behind him strolled Leslie, short, stocky, with an air of quiet belligerence, and then Margo, trailing yards of muslin and scent. Mother, looking like a tiny, harassed missionary in an uprising, was dragged unwillingly to the nearest lamp-post by an exuberant Roger, and was forced to stand there, staring into space, while he relieved pent-up feelings that had accumulated in his kennel. Larry chose two magnificently dilapidated horse-drawn cabs, had the luggage installed in one, and seated himself in the second. Then he looked round irritably.

'Well?' he asked. 'What are we waiting for?'

'We're waiting for Mother,' explained Leslie. 'Roger's found a lamp-post.'

'Dear God!' said Larry, and then hoisted himself upright in the cab and bellowed. 'Come *on*, Mother, come on. Can't the dog wait?'

'Coming, dear,' called Mother passively and untruthfully, for Roger showed no signs of quitting the post.

'That dog's been a damned nuisance all the way,' said Larry.

'Don't be so impatient,' said Margo indignantly; 'the dog can't help it . . . and anyway, we had to wait an hour in Naples for *you*.'

'My stomach was out of order,' explained Larry coldly.

'Well, presumably *his* stomach's out of order,' said Margo triumphantly. 'It's six of one and a dozen of the other.'

'You mean half a dozen of the other.'

'Whatever I mean, it's the same thing.'

At this moment Mother arrived, slightly dishevelled, and we had to turn our attentions to the task of getting Roger into the cab. He had never been in such a vehicle, and treated it with suspicion. Eventually we had to lift him bodily and hurl him inside, yelping frantically, and then pile in breathlessly after him and hold him down. The horse, frightened by this activity, broke into a shambling trot, and we ended in a tangled heap on the floor of the cab with Roger moaning loudly underneath us.

'What an entry,' said Larry bitterly. 'I had hoped to give an impression of gracious majesty, and this is what happens . . . we arrive in town like a troupe of medieval tumblers.'

'Don't keep *on*, dear,' Mother said soothingly, straightening her hat; 'we'll soon be at the hotel.'

So our cab clopped and jingled its way into the town, while we sat on the horsehair seats and tried to muster the appearance of gracious majesty Larry required. Roger, wrapped in Leslie's powerful grasp, lolled his head over the side of the vehicle and rolled his eyes as though at his last gasp. Then we rattled past an alley-way in which four scruffy mongrels were lying in the sun. Roger stiffened, glared at them and let forth a torrent of deep barks. The mongrels were immediately galvanized into activity, and they sped after the cab, yapping vociferously. Our pose was irretrievably shattered, for it took two people to restrain the raving Roger, while the rest of us leaned out of the cab and made wild gestures with magazines and books at the pursuing horde. This only had the effect of exciting them still further, and at each alley-way we passed their numbers increased, until by the time we were rolling down the main thoroughfare of the town there were some twenty-four dogs swirling about our wheels, almost hysterical with anger.

'Why doesn't somebody *do* something?' asked Larry, raising his voice above the uproar. 'This is like a scene from *Uncle Tom's Cabin*.'

'Why don't *you* do something, instead of criticizing?' snapped Leslie, who was locked in combat with Roger.

Larry promptly rose to his feet, snatched the whip from our astonished driver's hand, made a wild swipe at the herd of dogs, missed them, and caught Leslie across the back of the neck.

'What the hell d'you think you're playing at?' Leslie snarled, twisting a scarlet and angry face towards Larry.

'Accident,' explained Larry airily. 'I'm out of practice . . . it's so long since I used a horse-whip.'

'Well, watch what you're bloody well doing,' said Leslie loudly and belligerently.

'Now, now, dear, it was an accident,' said Mother.

Larry took another swipe at the dogs and knocked off Mother's hat.

'You're more trouble than the dogs,' said Margo.

'Do be careful, dear,' said Mother, clutching her hat; 'you might hurt someone. I should put the whip down.'

At that moment the cab shambled to a halt outside a doorway over which hung a board with Pension Suisse inscribed on it. The dogs, feeling that they were at last going to get to grips with this effeminate black canine who rode in cabs, surrounded us in a solid panting wedge. The door of the hotel opened and an ancient be-whiskered porter appeared and stood staring glassily at the turmoil in the street. The difficulties of getting Roger out of the cab and into the hotel were considerable, for he was a heavy dog, and it took the combined efforts of the family to lift, carry, and restrain him. Larry had by now forgotten his majestic pose and was rather enjoying himself. He leapt down and danced about the pavement with the whip, cleaving a path through the dogs, along which Leslie, Margo, Mother, and I hurried, bearing the struggling, snarling Roger. We staggered into the hall, and the porter slammed the front door and leant against it, his moustache quivering. The manager came forward, eyeing us with a mixture of apprehension and curiosity. Mother faced him, hat on one side of her head, clutching in one hand my jam-jar of caterpillars.

'Ah!' she said, smiling sweetly, as though our arrival had been the most normal thing in the world. 'Our name's Durrell. I believe you've got some rooms booked for us?'

'Yes, madame,' said the manager, edging round the still grumbling Roger; 'they are on the first floor . . . four rooms and a balcony.'

11

'How nice,' beamed Mother; 'then I think we'll go straight up and have a little rest before lunch.'

And with considerable majestic graciousness she led her family upstairs.

Later we descended to lunch in a large and gloomy room full of dusty potted palms and contorted statuary. We were served by the be-whiskered porter, who had become the head waiter simply by donning tails and a celluloid dicky that creaked like a convention of crickets. The meal, however, was ample and well cooked, and we ate hungrily. As coffee was served, Larry sat back in his chair with a sigh.

'That was a passable meal,' he said generously. 'What do you think of this place, Mother?'

'Well, the *food's* all right, dear,' said Mother, refusing to commit herself.

'They seem a helpful crowd,' Larry went on. 'The manager himself shifted my bed nearer the window.'

'He wasn't very helpful when I asked for paper,' said Leslie.

'Paper?' asked Mother. 'What did you want paper for?'

'For the lavatory ... there wasn't any in there,' explained Leslie.

'Shhh! Not at the table,' whispered Mother.

'You obviously don't look,' said Margo in a clear and penetrating voice; 'they've got a little box full by the pan.'

'Margo, dear!' exclaimed Mother, horrified.

'What's the matter? Didn't you see the little box?'

Larry gave a snort of laughter.

'Owing to the somewhat eccentric plumbing system of the town,' he explained to Margo kindly, 'that little box is provided for the ... er ... debris, as it were, when you have finished communing with nature.'

Margo's face turned scarlet with a mixture of embarrassment and disgust.

'You mean ... you mean ... that was ... My God! I might have caught some foul disease,' she wailed, and, bursting into tears, fled from the dining-room.

'Most insanitary,' said Mother severely; 'it really is a *disgusting* way to do things. Quite apart from the mistakes one can make, I should think there's a danger of getting typhoid.'

'Mistakes wouldn't happen if they'd organize things properly,' Leslie pointed out, returning to his original complaint.

'Yes, dear; but I don't think we ought to discuss it now. The best thing we can do is to find a house as soon as possible, before we all go down with something.

Upstairs Margo was in a state of semi-nudity, splashing disinfectant over herself in quantities, and Mother spent an exhausting afternoon being forced to examine her at intervals for the symptoms of the diseases which Margo felt sure she was hatching. It was unfortunate for Mother's peace of mind that the Pension Suisse happened to be situated in the road leading to the local cemetery. As we sat on our small balcony overhanging the street an apparently endless succession of funerals passed beneath us. The inhabitants of Corfu obviously believed that the best part of a bereavement was the funeral, for each seemed more ornate than the last. Cabs decorated with yards of purple and black crêpe were drawn by horses so enveloped in plumes and canopies that it was a wonder they could move. Six or seven of these cabs, containing the mourners in full and uninhibited grief, preceded the corpse itself. This came on another cart-like vehicle, and was ensconced in a coffin so large and lush that it looked more like an enormous birthday cake. Some were white, with purple, black-and-scarlet, and deep blue decorations; others were gleaming black with complicated filigrees of gold and silver twining abundantly over them, and glittering brass handles. I had never seen anything so colourful and attractive. This, I decided, was really the way to die, with shrouded horses, acres of flowers, and a horde of most satisfactorily grief-stricken relatives. I hung over the balcony rail watching the coffins pass beneath, absorbed and fascinated.

As each funeral passed, and the sounds of mourning and the clopping of hooves died away in the distance, Mother became more and more agitated.

'I'm sure it's an epidemic,' she exclaimed at last, peering down nervously into the street.

'Nonsense, Mother; don't fuss,' said Larry airily.

'But dear, so *many* of them . . . it's unnatural.'

'There's nothing unnatural about dying . . . people do it all the time.'

'Yes, but they don't die like flies unless there's something wrong.'

'Perhaps they save 'em up and bury 'em in a bunch,' suggested Leslie callously.

'Don't be silly,' said Mother. 'I'm sure it's something to do with the drains. It can't be healthy for people to have *those* sort of arrangements.'

13

'My God!' said Margo sepulchrally, 'then I suppose I'll get it.'

'No, no, dear; it doesn't follow,' said Mother vaguely; 'it might be something that's not catching.'

'I don't see how you can have an epidemic unless it's something catching,' Leslie remarked logically.

'Anyway,' said Mother, refusing to be drawn into any medical arguments, 'I think we ought to find out. Can't you ring up the health authorities, Larry?'

'There probably aren't any health authorities here,' Larry pointed out, 'and even if there were, I doubt if they'd tell me.'

'Well,' Mother said with determination, 'there's nothing for it. We'll have to move. We must get out of the town. We must find a house in the country *at once.*'

The next morning we started on our house-hunt, accompanied by Mr Beeler, the hotel guide. He was a fat little man with cringing eyes and sweat-polished jowls. He was quite sprightly when we set off, but then he did not know what was in store for him. No one who has not been house-hunting with my mother can possibly imagine it. We drove around the island in a cloud of dust while Mr Beeler showed us villa after villa in a bewildering selection of sizes, colours, and situations, and Mother shook her head firmly at them all. At last we had contemplated the tenth and final villa on Mr Beeler's list, and Mother had shaken her head once again. Brokenly Mr Beeler seated himself on the stairs and mopped his face with his handkerchief.

'Madame Durrell,' he said at last, 'I have shown you every villa I know, yet you do not want any. Madame, what is it you require? What is the matter with these villas?'

Mother regarded him with astonishment.

'Didn't you *notice?*' she asked. 'None of them had a bathroom.'

Mr Beeler stared at Mother with bulging eyes.

'But Madame,' he wailed in genuine anguish, 'what for you want a bathroom . . . Have you not got the sea?'

We returned in silence to the hotel.

By the following morning Mother had decided that we would hire a car and go out house-hunting on our own. She was convinced that somewhere on the island there lurked a villa with a bathroom. We did not share Mother's belief, and so it was a slightly irritable and argumentative group that she herded down to the taxi-rank in the main square. The taxi-drivers, perceiving our innocent appearance, scrambled from inside their cars and flocked round us like vultures, each trying to out-shout his compatriots. Their voices grew louder and louder, their eyes flashed, they clutched each other's arms and ground their teeth at one another, and then they laid hold of us as though they would tear us apart. Actually, we were being treated to the mildest of mild altercations, but we were not used to the Greek temperament, and to us it looked as though we were in danger of our lives.

'Can't you *do* something, Larry?' Mother squeaked, disentangling herself with difficulty from the grasp of a large driver.

'Tell them you'll report them to the British consul,' suggested Larry, raising his voice above the noise.

'Don't be silly, dear,' said Mother breathlessly. 'Just explain that we don't understand.'

Margo, simpering, stepped into the breach.

'We English,' she yelled at the gesticulating drivers; 'we no understand Greek.'

'If that man pushes me again I'll poke him in the eye,' said Leslie, his face flushed red.

'Now, now, dear,' panted Mother, still struggling with the driver who was propelling her vigorously towards his car; 'I don't think they mean any harm.'

At that moment everyone was startled into silence by a voice that rumbled out above the uproar, a deep, rich, vibrant voice, the sort of voice you would expect a volcano to have,.

'Hoy!' roared the voice, 'whys donts yous have someones who can talks your own language?'

Turning, we saw an ancient Dodge parked by the kerb, and behind the wheel sat a short, barrel-bodied individual, with ham-like hands and a great, leathery, scowling face surmounted by a jauntily-tilted peaked cap. He opened the door of the car, surged out on to the pavement, and waddled across to us. Then he stopped, scowling even more ferociously, and surveyed the group of silent cab-drivers.

'Thems been worrying yous?' he asked Mother.

'No, no,' said Mother untruthfully; 'it was just that we had difficulty in understanding them.'

'Yous wants someones who can talks your own language,' repeated the new arrival; 'thems bastards ... if yous will excuses the words ... would swindles their own mothers. Excuses me a minute and I'll fix thems.'

He turned on the drivers a blast of Greek that almost swept them off their feet. Aggrieved, gesticulating, angry, they were herded back to their cars by this extraordinary man. Having given them a final and, it appeared, derogatory blast of Greek, he turned to us again.

'Wheres yous wants to gos?' he asked, almost truculently.

'Can you take us to look for a villa?' asked Larry.

'Sure, I'll takes yous anywheres. Just yous says.'

'We are looking,' said Mother firmly, for a villa with a bathroom. Do you know of one?'

The man brooded like a great, sun-tanned gargoyle, his black eyebrows twisted into a knot of thoughtfulness.

'Bathrooms?' he said. 'Yous wants a bathrooms?'

'None of the ones we have seen so far had them,' said Mother.

'Oh, I knows a villa with a bathrooms,' said the man. 'I was wondering if its was goings to be bigs enough for yous.'

'Will you take us to look at it, please?' asked Mother.

'Sure, I'll takes yous. Gets into the cars.'

We climbed into the spacious car, and our driver hoisted his bulk behind the steering-wheel and engaged his gears with a terrifying sound. We shot through the twisted streets on the outskirts of the town, swerving in and out among the loaded donkeys, the carts, the groups of peasant women, and innumerable dogs, our horn honking a deafening warning. During this our driver seized the opportunity to engage us in conversation. Each time he addressed us he would crane his massive head round to see our reactions, and the car would swoop back and forth across the road like a drunken swallow.

'Yous English? Thought so ... English always wants bathrooms ... I gets a bathroom in my house ... Spiro's my name, Spiro Hakiaopulos ... they alls calls me Spiro Americano on accounts of I lives in America ... Yes, spent eight years in Chicago ... That's where I learnt my goods English ... Wents there to makes moneys ... Then after eight years I says: "Spiros," I says, "yous mades enough ..." sos I comes backs to Greece ... brings this car ... best ons the islands ... no one else gets a car like this ... All the English tourists knows me, theys all asks for me when theys comes here ... They knows theys wonts be swindled ... I likes the English ... best kinds of peoples ... Honest to Gods, ifs I wasn't Greek I'd likes to be English.'

We sped down a white road covered in a thick layer of silky dust that rose in a boiling cloud behind us, a road lined with prickly pears like a fence of green plates each cleverly balanced on another's edges, and splashed with knobs of scarlet fruit. We passed vineyards where the tiny, stunted vines were laced in green leaves, olive-groves where the pitted trunks made a hundred astonished faces at us out of the gloom of their own shadow, and great clumps of zebra-striped cane that fluttered their leaves like a multitude of green flags. At last we roared to the top of a hill, and Spiro crammed on his brakes and brought the car to a dust-misted halt.

'Theres you ares,' he said, pointing with a great stubby forefinger; 'that's the villa with the bathrooms, likes you wanted.'

Mother, who had kept her eyes firmly shut throughout the drive, now opened them cautiously and looked. Spiro was pointing at a gentle curve of hillside that rose from the glittering sea. The hill and the valleys around it were an eiderdown of olive-groves that shone with a fish-like gleam where the breeze touched the leaves. Half-way up the slope, guarded by a group of tall, slim cypress-trees, nestled a small strawberry-pink villa, like some exotic fruit lying in the greenery. The cypress-trees undulated gently in the breeze, as if they were busily painting the sky a still brighter blue for our arrival.

# 2

# The Strawberry-Pink Villa

The villa was small and square, standing in its tiny garden with an air of pink-faced determination. Its shutters had been faded by the sun to a delicate creamy-green, cracked and bubbled in places. The garden, surrounded by tall fuchsia hedges, had the flower-beds worked in complicated geometrical patterns, marked with smooth white stones. The white cobbled paths, scarcely as wide as a rake's head, wound laboriously round beds hardly larger than a big straw hat, beds in the shape of stars, half-moons, triangles, and circles, all overgrown with a shaggy tangle of flowers run wild. Roses dropped petals that seemed as big and smooth as saucers, flame-red, moon-white, glossy, and unwrinkled; marigolds like broods of shaggy suns stood watching their parent's progress through the sky. In the low growth the pansies pushed their velvety, innocent faces through the leaves, and the violets drooped sorrowfully under their heart-shaped leaves. The bougainvillaea that sprawled luxuriously over the tiny front balcony was hung, as though for a carnival, with its lantern-shaped magenta flowers. In the darkness of the fuchsia hedge a thousand ballerina-like blooms quivered expectantly. The warm air was thick with the scent of a hundred dying flowers, and full of the gentle, soothing whisper and murmur of insects. As soon as we saw it, we wanted to live there – it was as though the villa had been standing there waiting for our arrival. We felt we had come home.

Having lumbered so unexpectedly into our lives, Spiro now took over complete control of our affairs. It was better, he explained, for him to do things, as everyone knew him, and he would make sure we were not swindled.

'Donts you worrys yourselfs about anything, Mrs Durrells,' he had scowled; 'leaves everythings to me.'

So he would take us shopping, and after an hour's sweating and roaring he would get the price of an article reduced by perhaps two drachmas. This was approximately a penny; it was not the cash, but the principle of the thing, he explained. The fact that he was Greek and adored bargaining was, of course, another reason. It was Spiro who, in discovering that our money had not yet arrived from England, subsidized us, and took it upon himself to go and speak severely to the bank manager about his lack of organization. That it was not the poor manager's fault did not deter him in the least. It was Spiro who paid our hotel bill, who organized a cart to carry our luggage to the villa, and who drove us out there himself, his car piled high with groceries that he had purchased for us.

That he knew everyone on the island, and that they all knew him, we soon discovered was no idle boast. Wherever his car stopped, half a dozen voices would shout out his name, and hands would beckon him to sit at the little tables under the trees and drink coffee. Policemen, peasants, and priests waved and smiled as he passed; fishermen, grocers, and café-owners greeted him like a brother. 'Ah, Spiro!' they would say, and smile at him affectionately as though he was a naughty but lovable child. They respected his honesty, his belligerence, and above all they adored his typically Greek scorn and fearlessness when dealing with any form of Governmental red tape. On arrival, two of our cases containing linen and other things had been confiscated by the Customs on the curious grounds that they were merchandise. So, when we moved out to the strawberry-pink villa and the problem of bed-linen arose, Mother told Spiro about our cases languishing in the Customs, and asked his advice.

'Gollys, Mrs Durrells,' he bellowed, his huge face flushing red with wrath; 'whys you never tells me befores? Thems bastards in the Customs. I'll take you down theres tomorrows and fix thems: I knows thems alls, and they knows *me*. Leaves everythings to me – I'll fix thems.'

The following morning he drove Mother down to the Customs shed. We all accompanied them, for we did not want to miss the fun. Spiro rolled into the Customs-house like an angry bear.

'Wheres these peoples things?' he inquired of the plump little Customs man.

'You mean their boxes of merchandise?' asked the Customs official in his best English.

'Whats you think I means?'

'They are here,' admitted the official cautiously.

'We've comes to takes thems,' scowled Spiro; 'gets thems ready.'

He turned and stalked out of the shed to find someone to help carry the luggage, and when he returned he saw that the Customs man who had taken the keys from Mother was just lifting the lid of one of the cases. Spiro, with a grunt of wrath, surged forward, and slammed the lid down on the unfortunate man's fingers.

'Whats fors you open it, you sonofabitch?' he asked, glaring.

The Customs official, waving his pinched hand about, protested wildly that it was his duty to examine the contents.

'Dutys?' said Spiro with fine scorn. 'Whats you means, dutys? Is it your dutys to attacks innocent foreigners, eh? Treats thems like smugglers, eh? Thats what you calls dutys?'

Spiro paused for a moment, breathing deeply, then he picked up a large suitcase in each great hand and walked towards the door. He paused and turned to fire his parting shot.

'I knows you, Christaki, sos donts you go talkings about dutys to me. I remembers when you was fined twelve thousand drachmas for dynamitings fish. I won't have any criminal talkings to *me* about dutys.'

We rode back from the Customs in triumph, all our luggage intact and unexamined.

'Thems bastards thinks they owns the islands,' was Spiro's comment. He seemed quite unaware of the fact that he was acting as though he did.

Once Spiro had taken charge he stuck to us like a burr. Within a few hours he had changed from taxi-driver to our champion, and within a week he was our guide, philosopher, and friend. He became so much a member of the family that very soon there was scarcely a thing we did, or planned to do, in which he was not involved in some way. He was always there, bull-voiced and scowling, arranging things we wanted done, telling us how much to pay for things, keeping a watchful eye on us all, and reporting to Mother anything he thought she should know. Like a great, brown, ugly angel he watched over us as tenderly as though we were slightly weak-minded children. Mother he frankly adored, and he would sing her praises in a loud voice wherever we happened to be, to her acute embarrassment.

'You oughts to be carefuls whats you do,' he would tell us, screwing up his face earnestly; 'we donts wants to worrys your mothers.'

'Whatever for, Spiro?' Larry would protest in well-simulated astonishment. 'She's never done anything for us ... why should we consider her?'

'Gollys, Master Lorrys, donts *jokes* like that,' Spiro would say in anguish.

'He's quite right, Spiro,' Leslie would say very seriously; 'she's really not much good as a mother, you know.'

'Donts says that, *donts says that*,' Spiro would roar. 'Honest to Gods, if I hads a mother likes yours I'd gos down every mornings and kisses her feets.'

So we were installed in the villa, and we each settled down and adapted ourselves to our surroundings in our respective ways. Margo, merely by donning a microscopic swim-suit and sun-bathing in the olive-groves, had collected an ardent band of handsome peasant youths who appeared like magic from an apparently deserted landscape whenever a bee flew too near her or her deckchair needed moving. Mother felt forced to point out that she thought this sun-bathing was rather *unwise*.

'After all, dear, that costume doesn't cover an awful lot, does it?' she pointed out.

'Oh, Mother, don't be so old-fashioned,' Margo said impatiently. 'After all, you only die once.'

This remark was as baffling as it was true, and successfully silenced Mother.

It had taken three husky peasant boys half an hour's sweating and panting to get Larry's trunks into the villa, while Larry bustled round them, directing operations. One of the trunks was so big it had to be hoisted in through the window. Once they were installed, Larry spent a happy day unpacking them, and the room was so full of books that it was almost impossible to get in or out. Having constructed battlements of books round the outer perimeter, Larry would spend the whole day in there with his typewriter, only emerging dreamily for meals. On the second morning he appeared in a highly irritable frame of mind, for a peasant had tethered his donkey just over the hedge. At regular intervals the beast would throw out its head and let forth a prolonged and lugubrious bray.

'I ask you! Isn't it laughable that future generations should be deprived of my work simply because some horny-handed

idiot has tied that stinking beast of burden near my window?'
Larry asked.

'Yes, dear,' said Mother; 'why don't you move it if it disturbs
you?'

'My dear Mother, I can't be expected to spend my time
chasing donkeys about the olive-groves. I threw a pamphlet on
Christian Science at it; what more do you expect me to do?'

'The poor thing's tied up. You can't expect it to untie itself,'
said Margo.

'There should be a law against parking those loathsome
beasts anywhere near a house. Can't one of you go and
move it?'

'Why should we? It's not disturbing us,' said Leslie.

'That's the trouble with this family,' said Larry bitterly: 'no
give and take, no consideration for others.'

'*You* don't have much consideration for others,' said Margo.

'It's all your fault, Mother,' said Larry austerely; 'you
shouldn't have brought us up to be so selfish.'

'I like that!' exclaimed Mother. 'I never did anything of
the sort!'

'Well, we didn't get as selfish as this without *some* guidance,'
said Larry.

In the end, Mother and I unhitched the donkey and moved
it farther down the hill.

Leslie meanwhile had unpacked his revolvers and startled
us all with an apparently endless series of explosions while
he fired at an old tin can from his bedroom window. After a
particularly deafening morning, Larry erupted from his room
and said he could not be expected to work if the villa was going
to be rocked to its foundations every five minutes. Leslie,
aggrieved, said that he had to practise. Larry said it didn't
sound like practice, but more like the Indian Mutiny. Mother,
whose nerves had also been somewhat frayed by the reports,
suggested that Leslie practise with an empty revolver. Leslie
spent half an hour explaining why this was impossible. At
length he reluctantly took his tin farther away from the house
where the noise was slightly muffled but just as unexpected.

In between keeping a watchful eye on us all, Mother was
settling down in her own way. The house was redolent with
the scent of herbs and the sharp tang of garlic and onions,
and the kitchen was full of a bubbling selection of pots, among
which she moved, spectacles askew, muttering to herself. On
the table was a tottering pile of books which she consulted
from time to time. When she could drag herself away from the

kitchen, she would drift happily about the garden, reluctantly pruning and cutting, enthusiastically weeding and planting.

For myself, the garden held sufficient interest; together Roger and I learnt some surprising things. Roger, for example, found that it was unwise to smell hornets, that the peasant dogs ran screaming if he glanced at them through the gate, and that the chickens that leapt suddenly from the fuchsia hedge, squawking wildly as they fled, were unlawful prey, however desirable.

This doll's-house garden was a magic land, a forest of flowers through which roamed creatures I had never seen before. Among the thick, silky petals of each rose-bloom lived tiny, crab-like spiders that scuttled sideways when disturbed. Their small, translucent bodies were coloured to match the flowers they inhabited: pink, ivory, wine-red, or buttery-yellow. On the rose-stems, encrusted with greenflies, lady-birds moved like newly painted toys; lady-birds pale red with large black spots; lady-birds apple-red with brown spots; lady-birds orange with grey-and-black freckles. Rotund and amiable, they prowled and fed among the anaemic flocks of greenfly. Carpenter bees, like furry, electric-blue bears, zigzagged among the flowers, growling fatly and busily. Humming-bird hawk-moths, sleek and neat, whipped up and down the paths with a fussy efficiency, pausing occasionally on speed-misty wings to lower a long, slender proboscis into a bloom. Among the white cobbles large black ants staggered and gesticulated in groups round strange trophies: a dead caterpillar, a piece of rose-petal, or dried grass-head fat with seeds. As an accompaniment to all this activity there came from the olive-groves outside the fuchsia hedge the incessant shimmering cries of the cicadas. If the curious, blurring heat-haze produced a sound, it would be exactly the strange, chiming cries of these insects.

At first I was so bewildered by this profusion of life on our very doorstep that I could only move about the garden in a daze, watching now this creature, now that, constantly having my attention distracted by the flights of brilliant butterflies that drifted over the hedge. Gradually, as I became more used to the bustle of insect life among the flowers, I found I could concentrate more. I would spend hours squatting on my heels or lying on my stomach watching the private lives of the creatures around me, while Roger sat nearby, a look of resignation on his face. In this way I learnt a lot of fascinating things.

I found that the little crab-spiders could change colour just as successfully as any chameleon. Take a spider from a wine-red rose, where he had been sitting like a bead of coral, and place him in the depths of a cool white rose. If he stayed there – and most of them did – you would see his colour gradually ebb away, as though the change had given him anaemia, until, some two days later, he would be crouching among the white petals like a pearl.

I discovered that in the dry leaves under the fuchsia hedge lived another type of spider, a fierce little huntsman with the cunning and ferocity of a tiger. He would stalk about his continent of leaves, eyes glistening in the sun, pausing now and then to raise himself up on his hairy legs to peer about. If he saw a fly settle to enjoy a sun-bath he would freeze; then, as slowly as a leaf growing, he would move forward, imperceptibly, edging nearer and nearer, pausing occasionally to fasten his life-line of silk to the surface of the leaves. Then, when close enough, the huntsman would pause, his legs shift minutely as he got a good purchase, and then he would leap, legs spread out in a hairy embrace, straight on to the dreaming fly. Never did I see one of these little spiders miss its kill, once it had manoeuvred into the right position.

All these discoveries filled me with a tremendous delight, so that they had to be shared, and I would burst suddenly into the house and startle the family with the news that the strange, spiky black caterpillars on the roses were not caterpillars at all, but the young of lady-birds, or with the equally astonishing news that lacewing-flies laid eggs on stilts. This last miracle I was lucky enough to witness. I found a lacewing-fly on the roses and watched her as she climbed about the leaves, admiring her beautiful, fragile wings like green glass, and her enormous liquid golden eyes. Presently she stopped on the surface of a rose-leaf and lowered the tip of her abdomen. She remained like that for a moment and then raised her tail, and from it, to my astonishment, rose a slender thread, like a pale hair. Then, on the very tip of this stalk, appeared the egg. The female had a rest, and then repeated the performance until the surface of the rose-leaf looked as though it was covered with a forest of tiny club moss. The laying over, the female rippled her antennae briefly and flew off in a mist of green gauze wings.

Perhaps the most exciting discovery I made in this multi-coloured Lilliput to which I had access was an earwig's nest. I had long wanted to find one and had searched everywhere without success, so the joy of stumbling upon one unexpectedly was overwhelming, like suddenly being given a wonderful present. I moved a piece of bark and there beneath it was the nursery, a small hollow in the earth that the insect must have burrowed out for herself. She squatted in the middle of it, shielding underneath her a few white eggs. She crouched over them like a hen, and did not move when the flood of sunlight struck her as I lifted the bark. I could not count the eggs, but there did not seem to be many, so I presumed that she had not yet laid her full complement. Tenderly I replaced her lid of bark.

From that moment I guarded the nest jealously. I erected a protecting wall of rocks round it, and as an additional precaution I wrote out a notice in red ink and stuck it on a pole nearby as a warning to the family. The notice read: 'BEWAR – EARWIG NEST – QUIAT PLESE.' It was only remarkable in that the two correctly spelt words were biological ones. Every hour or so I would subject the mother earwig to ten minutes' close scrutiny. I did not dare examine her more often for fear she might desert her nest. Eventually the pile of eggs beneath her grew, and she seemed to have become accustomed to my lifting off her bark roof. I even decided that she had begun to recognize me, from the friendly way she waggled her antennae.

To my acute disappointment, after all my efforts and constant sentry duty, the babies hatched out during the night. I felt that, after all I had done, the female might have held up the hatching until I was there to witness it. However, there they were, a fine brood of young earwigs, minute, frail, looking as though they had been carved out of ivory. They moved gently under their mother's body, walking between her legs, the more venturesome even climbing on to her pincers. It was a heart-warming sight. The next day the nursery was empty: my wonderful family had scattered over the garden. I saw one of the babies some time later: he was bigger, of course, browner and stronger, but I recognized him immediately. He was curled up in a maze of rose-petals, having a sleep, and when I disturbed him he merely raised his pincers irritably over his back. I would have liked to think that it was a salute, a cheerful greeting, but honesty compelled me to admit that it was nothing more than an earwig's warning to a potential enemy. Still, I excused him. After all, he had been very young when I last saw him.

I came to know the plump peasant girls who passed the garden every morning and evening. Riding side-saddle on their slouching, drooping-eared donkeys, they were shrill and colourful as parrots, and their chatter and laughter echoed among the olive-trees. In the mornings they would smile and shout greetings as their donkeys pattered past, and in the evenings they would lean over the fuchsia hedge, balancing precariously on their steeds' backs, and smiling, hold out gifts for me – a bunch of amber grapes still sun-warmed, some figs black as tar striped with pink where they had burst their seams with ripeness, or a giant water-melon, with an inside like pink ice. As the days passed, I came gradually to understand them. What had at first been a confused babble became a series of recognizable separate sounds. Then, suddenly, these took on meaning, and slowly and haltingly I started to use them myself; then I took my newly acquired words and strung them into ungrammatical and stumbling sentences. Our neighbours were delighted, as though I had conferred some delicate compliment by trying to learn their language. They would lean over the hedge, their faces screwed up with concentration, as I groped my way through a greeting or a simple remark, and when I had successfully concluded they would beam at me, nodding and smiling, and clap their hands. By degrees I learnt their names, who was related to whom, which were married and which hoped to be, and other details. I learnt where their little cottages were among the olive-groves, and should Roger and I chance to pass that way the entire family, vociferous and pleased, would tumble out to greet us, to bring a chair, so that I might sit under their vine and eat some fruit with them.

Gradually the magic of the island settled over us as gently and clingingly as pollen. Each day had a tranquillity, a timelessness, about it, so that you wished it would never end. But then the dark skin of night would peel off and there would be a fresh day waiting for us, glossy and colourful as a child's transfer and with the same tinge of unreality.

# 3

# The Rose-Beetle Man

In the morning, when I woke, the bedroom shutters were luminous and barred with gold from the rising sun. The morning air was full of the scent of charcoal from the kitchen fire, full of eager cock-crows, the distant yap of dogs, and the unsteady, melancholy tune of the goat-bells as the flocks were driven out to pasture.

We ate breakfast out in the garden, under the small tangerine-trees. The sky was fresh and shining, not yet the fierce blue of noon, but a clear milky opal. The flowers were half-asleep, roses dew-crumpled, marigolds still tightly shut. Breakfast was, on the whole, a leisurely and silent meal, for no member of the family was very talkative at that hour. By the end of the meal the influence of the coffee, toast, and eggs made itself felt, and we started to revive, to tell each other what we intended to do, why we intended to do it, and then argue earnestly as to whether each had made a wise decision. I never joined in these discussions, for I knew perfectly well what I intended to do, and would concentrate on finishing my food as rapidly as possible.

'*Must* you gulp and slush your food like that?' Larry would inquire in a pained voice, delicately picking his teeth with a match-stick.

'Eat it slowly, dear,' Mother would murmur; 'there's no hurry.'

No hurry? With Roger waiting at the garden gate, an alert black shape, watching for me with eager brown eyes? No hurry, with the first sleepy cicadas starting to fiddle experimentally among the olives? No hurry, with the island waiting, morning cool, bright as a star, to be explored? I could hardly expect the family to understand this point of view, however, so I would slow down until I felt that their attention had been attracted elsewhere, and then stuff my mouth again.

Finishing at last, I would slip from the table and saunter towards the gate, where Roger sat gazing at me with a questioning air. Together we would peer through the wrought-iron gates into the olive-groves beyond. I would suggest to Roger that perhaps it wasn't worth going out today. He would wag his stump in hasty denial, and his nose would butt at my hand. No, I would say, I really didn't think we ought to go out. It looked as though it was going to rain, and I would peer up into the clear, burnished sky with a worried expression. Roger, ears cocked, would peer into the sky too, and then look at me imploringly. Anyway, I would go on, if it didn't look like rain now it was almost certain to rain later, and so it would be much safer just to sit in the garden with a book. Roger, in desperation, would place a large black paw on the gate, and then look at me, lifting one side of his upper lip, displaying his white teeth in a lop-sided, ingratiating grin, his stump working itself into a blur of excitement. This was his trump card, for he knew I could never resist his ridiculous grin. So I would stop teasing him, fetch my matchboxes and my butterfly net, the garden gate would creak open and clang shut, and Roger would be off through the olive-groves swiftly as a cloud-shadow, his deep bark welcoming the new day.

In those early days of exploration Roger was my constant companion. Together we ventured farther and farther afield, discovering quiet, remote olive-groves which had to be investigated and remembered, working our way through a maze of blackbird-haunted myrtles, venturing into narrow valleys where the cypress-trees cast a cloak of mysterious, inky shadow. He was the perfect companion for an adventure, affectionate without exuberance, brave without being belligerent, intelligent, and full of good-humoured tolerance for my eccentricities. If I slipped when climbing a dew-shiny bank, Roger appeared suddenly, gave a snort that sounded like suppressed laughter, a quick look over, a rapid lick of commiseration, shook himself, sneezed and gave me his lop-sided grin. If I found something that interested me – an ant's nest, a caterpillar on a leaf, a spider wrapping up a fly in swaddling clothes of silk – Roger sat down and waited until I had finished examining it. If he thought I was taking too long, he shifted nearer, gave a gentle, whiny yawn, and then sighed deeply and started to wag his tail. If the matter was of no great importance, we would move on, but if it was something absorbing that had to be pored over, I had only to frown at Roger and he would realize it was going to be a long job. His ears would droop, his tail slow down and stop, and he would slouch off to the nearest bush, fling himself down in the shade, giving me a martyred look as he did so.

During these trips Roger and I came to know and be known by a great number of people in various parts of the surrounding countryside. There was, for example, a strange, mentally defective youth with a round face as expressionless as a puffball. He was always dressed in tattered shirt, shiny blue serge trousers that were rolled up to the knee, and on his head the elderly remains of a bowler hat without a brim. Whenever he saw us he came hurrying through the olives, raised his absurd hat politely, and wished us good day in a voice as childish and sweet as a flute. He would stand, watching us without expression, nodding at any remark I happened to make, for ten minutes or so. Then, raising his hat politely, he would go off through the trees. Then there was the immensely fat and cheerful Agathi, who lived in a tiny tumbledown cottage high up the hill. She was always sitting outside her house with a spindle of sheep's wool, twining and pulling it into coarse thread. She must have been well over seventy, but her hair was still black and lustrous, plaited carefully and wound round a pair of polished cow's horns, an ornament that some of the older peasant women adopted. As she sat in the sun, like a great black toad with a scarlet head-dress draped over the cow's horns, the bobbin of wool would rise and fall, twisting like a top, her fingrs busy unravelling and plucking, and her drooping mouth with its hedge of broken and discoloured teeth wide open as she sang, loudly and harshly, but with great vigour.

It was from Agathi that I learnt some of the most beautiful and haunting of the peasant songs. Sitting on an old tin in the sun, eating grapes or pomegranates from her garden, I would sing with her, and she would break off now and then to correct my pronunciation. We sang (verse by verse) the gay, rousing song of the river, *Vangeliò*, and of how it dropped from the mountains, making the gardens rich, the fields fertile, and the trees heavy with fruit. We sang, rolling our eyes at each other in exaggerated coquetry, the funny little love-song called 'Falsehood', 'Lies, lies,' we warbled, shaking our heads, 'all lies, but it is my fault for teaching you to go round the countryside telling people I love you.' Then we would strike a mournful note and sing, perhaps, the slow, lilting song called 'Why are you leaving me?' We were almost overcome by this one, and would wail out the long, soulful lyrics, our voices quavering. When we came to the last bit, the most heart-rending of all, Agathi would clasp her hands to her great breasts, her black eyes would become misty and sad, and her chins would tremble with emotion. As the last discordant notes of our duet faded away, she would turn to me, wiping her nose on the corner of her head-dress.

'What fools we are, eh? What fools, sitting here in the sun, singing. And of love, too! I am too old for it and you are too young, and yet we waste our time singing about it. Ah, well, let's have a glass of wine, eh?'

Apart from Agathi, the person I liked best was the old shepherd Yani, a tall, slouching man with a great hooked nose like an eagle, and incredible moustaches. I first met him one hot afternoon when Roger and I had spent an exhausting hour trying to dig a large green lizard out of its hole in a stone wall. At length, unsuccessful, sweaty, and tired, we had flung ourselves down beneath five little cypress-trees that cast a neat square of shadow on the sun-bleached grass. Lying there, I head the gentle, drowsy tinkling of a goat-bell, and presently the herds wandered past us, pausing to stare with vacant yellow eyes, bleat sneeringly, and then move on. The soft sound of the bells, and of their mouths ripping and tearing at the undergrowth, had a soothing effect on me, and by the time they had drifted slowly past and the shepherd appeared I was nearly asleep. He stopped and looked at me, leaning heavily on his brown olive-wood stick, his little black eyes fierce under his shaggy brows, his big boots planted firmly in the heather.

'Good afternoon,' he greeted me gruffly; 'you are the foreigner . . . the little English lord?'

By then I was used to the curious peasant idea that all English people were lords, and I admitted that that's who I was. He turned and roared at a goat which had reared on to its hind legs and was tearing at a young olive, and then turned back.

'I will tell you something, little lord,' he said; 'it is dangerous for you to lie here, beneath these trees.'

I glanced up at the cypresses, but they seemd safe enough to me, and so I asked why he thought they were dangerous.

'Ah, you may *sit* under them, yes. They cast a good shadow, cold as well-water; but that's the trouble, they tempt you to sleep. And you must never, for any reason, sleep beneath a cypress.'

He paused, stroked his moustache, waited for me to ask why, and then went on:

'Why? Why? Because if you did you would be changed when you woke. Yes, the black cypresses, they are dangerous. While you sleep, their roots grow into your brains and steal them, and when you wake up you are mad, head as empty as a whistle.'

I asked whether it was only the cypress that could do this, or did it apply to other trees.

'No, only the cypress,' said the old man, peering up fiercely at the trees above me as though to see whether they were listening; 'only the cypress is the thief of intelligence. So be warned, little lord, and don't sleep here.'

He nodded briefly, gave another fierce glance at the dark blades of the cypress, as if daring them to make some comment, and then picked his way carefully through the myrtle-bushes to where his goats grazed scattered about the hill, their great udders swinging like bagpipies beneath their bellies.

I got to know Yani very well, for I was always meeting him during my explorations, and occasionally I visited him in his little house, when he would ply me with fruit, and give me advice and warnings to keep me safe on my walks.

Perhaps one of the most weird and fascinating characters I met during my travels was the Rose-beetle Man. He had a fairy-tale air about him that was impossible to resist, and I used to look forward eagerly to my infrequent meetings with him. I first saw him on a high, lonely road leading to one of the remote mountain villages. I could hear him long before I could see him, for he was playing a rippling tune on a shepherd's pipe, breaking off now and then to sing a few words in a curious, nasal voice. As he rounded the corner both Roger and I stopped and stared at him in amazement.

He had a sharp, fox-like face with large, slanting eyes of such a dark brown that they appeared black. They had a weird, vacant look about them, and a sort of bloom such as one finds on a plum, a pearly covering almost like a cataract. He was short and slight, with a thinness about his wrists and neck that argued a lack of food. His dress was fantastic, and on his head was a shapeless hat with a very wide, floppy brim. It had once been bottle-green, but was now speckled and smeared with dust, wine-stains, and cigarette burns. In the

31

band were stuck a fluttering forest of feathers: cock-feathers, hoopoe-feathers, owl-feathers, the wing of a kingfisher, the claw of a hawk, and a large dirty white feather that may have come from a swan. His shirt was worn and frayed, grey with sweat, and round the neck dangled an enormous cravat of the most startling blue satin. His coat was dark and shapeless, with patches of different hues here and there; on the sleeve a bit of white cloth with a design of rosebuds; on the shoulder a triangular patch of wine-red and white spots. The pockets of this garment bulged, the contents almost spilling out: combs, balloons, little highly coloured pictures of the saints, olive-wood carvings of snakes, camels, dogs and horses, cheap mirrors, a riot of handkerchiefs, and long twisted rolls of bread decorated with seeds. His trousers, patched like his coat, drooped over a pair of scarlet *charouhias*, leather shoes with upturned toes decorated with a large black-and-white pompon. This extraordinary character carried on his back bamboo cages full of pigeons and young chickens, several mysterious sacks, and a large bunch of fresh green leeks. With one hand he held his pipe to his mouth, and in the other a number of lengths of cotton, to each of which was tied an almond-size rose-beetle, glittering golden green in the sun, all of them flying round his hat with desperate, deep buzzings, trying to escape from the thread tied firmly round their waists. Occasionally, tired of circling round and round without success, one of the beetles would settle for a moment on his hat, before launching itself off once more on its endless merry-go-round.

When he saw us the Rose-beetle Man stopped, gave a very exaggerated start, doffed his ridiculous hat, and swept us a low bow. Roger was so overcome by this unlooked-for attention that he let out a volley of surprised barks. The man smiled at us, put on his hat again, raised his hands, and waggled his long, bony fingers at me. Amused and rather startled by this apparition, I politely bade him good day. He gave another courtly bow. I asked him if he had been to some fiesta. He nodded his head vigorously, raised his pipe to his lips and played a lilting little tune on it, pranced a few steps in the dust of the road, and then stopped and jerked his thumb over his shoulder, pointing back the way he had come. He smiled, patted his pockets, and rubbed his forefinger and thumb together in the Greek way of expressing money. I suddenly realized that he must be dumb. So, standing in the middle of the road, I carried on a conversation with him and he replied with a varied and very clever pantomime. I asked what

32

the rose-beetles were for, and why he had them tied with pieces of cotton. He held his hand out to denote small boys, took one of the lengths of cotton from which a beetle hung, and whirled it rapidly round his head. Immediately the insect came to life and started on its planet-like circling of his hat, and he beamed at me. Pointing up at the sky, he stretched his arms out and gave a deep nasal buzzing, while he banked and swooped across the road. Aeroplane, any fool could see that. Then he pointed to the beetles, held out his hand to denote children, and whirled his stock of beetles round his head so that they all started to buzz peevishly.

Exhausted by his explanation, he sat down by the edge of the road, played a short tune on his flute, breaking off to sing in his curious nasal voice. They were not articulate words he used, but a series of strange gruntings and tenor squeaks, that appeared to be formed at the back of his throat and expelled through his nose. He produced them, however, with such verve and such wonderful facial expressions that you were convinced the curious sounds really meant something. Presently he stuffed his flute into his bulging pocket, gazed at me reflectively for a moment and then swung a small sack off his shoulder, undid it, and, to my delight and astonishment, tumbled half a dozen tortoises into the dusty road. Their shells had been polished with oil until they shone, and by some means or other he had managed to decorate their front legs with little red bows. Slowly and ponderously they unpacked their heads and legs from their gleaming shells and set off down the road, doggedly and without enthusiasm. I watched them, fascinated; the one that particularly took my fancy was quite a small one with a shell about the size of a tea-cup. It seemed more sprightly than the others, and its shell was a paler colour – chestnut, caramel, and amber. Its eyes were bright and its walk was as alert as any tortoise's could be. I sat contemplating it for a long time. I convinced myself that the family would greet its arrival at the villa with tremendous enthusiasm, even, perhaps, congratulating me on finding such an elegant specimen. The fact that I had no money on me did not worry me in the slightest, for I would simply tell the man to call at the villa for payment the next day. It never occurred to me that he might not trust me. The fact that I was English was sufficient, for the islanders had a love and respect for the Englishman out of all proportion to his worth. They would trust an Englishman where they would not trust each other. I asked the Rose-beetle Man the price of the little tortoise. He held up both hands, fingers spread out. However, I hadn't watched the peasants transacting business for nothing. I shook my head firmly and held up two fingers, unconsciously imitating the man. He closed his eyes in horror at the thought, and held up nine fingers; I held up three; he shook his head, and after some thought held up six fingers; I, in return, shook my head and held up five. The Rose-beetle Man shook his head, and sighed deeply and sorrowfully, so we sat in silence and stared at the tortoises crawling heavily and uncertainly about the road, with the curious graceless determination of babies. Presently the Rose-beetle Man indicated the little tortoise and held up six fingers again. I shook my head and held up five. Roger yawned loudly; he was thoroughly bored by this silent bargaining. The Rose-beetle Man picked up the reptile and showed me in pantomime how smooth and lovely its shell was, how erect its head, how pointed its nails. I remained implacable. He shrugged, handed me the tortoise, and held up five fingers.

Then I told him I had no money, and that he would have to come the next day to the villa, and he nodded as if it were the most natural thing in the world. Excited by owning this new pet, I wanted to get back home as quickly as possible in order to show it to everyone, so I said good-bye, thanked him, and hurried off along the road. When I reached the place where I had to cut down through the olive-groves, I stopped and examined my acquisition carefully. He was undoubtedly the finest tortoise I had ever seen, and worth, in my opinion, at least twice what I had paid for him. I patted his scaly head with my finger and placed him carefully in my pocket. Before diving down the hillside I glanced back. The Rose-beetle Man was still in the same place on the road, but he was doing a little jig, prancing and swaying, his flute warbling, while in the road at his feet the tortoises ambled to and fro, dimly and heavily.

The new arrival was duly christened Achilles, and turned out to be a most intelligent and lovable beast, possessed of a peculiar sense of humour. At first he was tethered by a leg in the garden, but as he grew tamer we let him go where he pleased. He learned his name in a very short time, and we had only to call out once or twice and then wait patiently for a while and he would appear, lumbering along the narrow cobbled paths on tip-toe, his head and neck stretched out eagerly. He loved being fed, and would squat regally in the sun while we held out bits of lettuce, dandelions, or grapes for him. He loved grapes as much as Roger did, so there was always great rivalry. Achilles would sit mumbling the grapes in his mouth, the juice running down his chin, and Roger would lie nearby, watching him with agonized eyes, his mouth drooling saliva. Roger always had his fair share of the fruit, but even so he seemed to think it a waste to give such delicacies to a tortoise. When the feeding was over, if I didn't keep an eye on him, Roger would creep up to Achilles and lick his front vigorously in an attempt to get the grape-juice that the reptile had dribbled down himself. Achilles, affronted at such a liberty, would snap at Roger's nose, and then, when the licks became too overpowering and moist, he would retreat into his shell with an indignant wheeze, and refuse to come out until we had removed Roger from the scene.

But the fruit that Achilles liked best were wild strawberries. He would become positively hysterical at the mere sight of them, lumbering to and fro, craning his head to see if you were going to give him any, gazing at you pleadingly with his tiny boot-button eyes. The very small strawberries he could devour at a gulp, for they were only the size of a fat pea. But if you gave him a big one, say the size of a hazel nut, he behaved in a way that I have never seen another tortoise emulate. He would grab the fruit and, holding it firmly in his mouth, would stumble off at top speed until he reached a safe and secluded spot among the flower-beds, where he would drop the fruit and then eat it at leisure, returning for another one when he had finished.

As well as developing a passion for strawberries, Achilles also developed a passion for human company. Let anyone come into the garden to sit and sun-bathe, to read or for any other reason, and before long there would be a rustling among the sweet williams, and Achilles's wrinkled and earnest face would be poked through. If you were sitting in a chair, he contented himself with getting as close to your feet as possible, and there he would sink into a deep and peaceful sleep, his head drooping out of his shell, his nose resting on the ground. If, however, you were lying on a rug, sun-bathing, Achilles would be convinced that you were lying on the ground simply in order to provide him with amusement. He would surge down the path and on to the rug with an expression of bemused good humour on his face. He would pause, survey you thoughtfully, and then choose a portion of your anatomy on which to practise mountaineering. Suddenly to have the sharp claws of a determined tortoise embedded in your thigh as he

35

tries to lever himself up on to your stomach is not conducive to relaxation. If you shook him off and moved the rug it would only give you temporary respite, for Achilles would circle the garden grimly until he found you again. This habit became so tiresome that, after many complaints and threats from the family, I had to lock him up whenever we lay in the garden. Then one day the garden gate was left open and Achilles was nowhere to be found. Search-parties were immediately organized, and the family, who up till then had spent most of their time openly making threats against the reptile's life, wandered about the olive-groves shouting, 'Achilles ... strawberries, Achilles ... Achilles ... strawberries ...' At length we found him. Ambling along in his usual detached manner, he had fallen into a disused well, the wall of which had long since disintegrated, and the mouth of which was almost covered by ferns. He was, to our regret, quite dead. Even Leslie's attempts at artificial respiration, and Margo's suggestion of forcing strawberries down his throat (to give him, as she explained, something to live for), failed to get any response. So, mournfully and solemnly, his corpse was buried in the garden under a small strawberry plant (Mother's suggestion). A short funeral address, written and read in a trembling voice by Larry, made the occasion a memorable one. It was only marred by Roger, who, in spite of all my protests, insisted on wagging his tail throughout the burial service.

Not long after Achilles had been taken from us I obtained another pet from the Rose-beetle Man. This time it was a pigeon. He was still very young and had to be force-fed on bread-and-milk and soaked corn. He was the most revolting bird to look at, with his feathers pushing through the wrinkled scarlet skin, mixed with the horrible yellow down that covers baby pigeons and makes them look as though they have been peroxiding their hair. Owing to his repulsive and obese appearance, Larry suggested we called him Quasimodo and, liking the name without realizing the implications, I agreed. For a long time after he could feed himself, and when all his feathers had grown, Quasimodo retained a sprig of yellow down on his head which gave him the appearance of a rather pompous judge wearing a wig several sizes too small.

Owing to his unorthodox upbringing and the fact that he had no parents to teach him the facts of life, Quasimodo became convinced that he was not a bird at all, and refused to fly. Instead he walked everywhere. If he wanted to get on to a table, or a chair, he stood below it, ducking his head and cooing in a rich contralto until someone lifted him up. He was always eager to join us in anything we did, and would even try to come for walks with us. This, however, we had to stop, for either you carried him on your shoulder, which was risking an accident to your clothes, or else you let him walk behind. If you let him walk, then you had to slow down your own pace to suit his, for should you get too far ahead you would hear the most frantic and imploring coos and turn round to find Quasimodo running desperately after you, his tail wagging seductively, his iridescent chest pouted out with indignation at your cruelty.

Quasimodo insisted on sleeping in the house; no amount of coaxing or scolding would get him to inhabit the pigeon-loft I had constructed for him. He preferred to sleep on the end of Margo's bed. Eventually, however, he was banished to the drawing-room sofa, for if Margo turned over in bed at night Quasimodo would wake, hobble up the bed, and perch on her face, cooing loudly and lovingly.

It was Larry who discovered that Quasimodo was a musical pigeon. Not only did he like music, but he actually seemed to recognize two different varieties, the waltz and the military march. For ordinary music he would waddle as close to the gramophone as possible and sit there with pouting chest, eyes half-closed, purring softly to himself. But if the tune was a waltz he would move round and round the machine, bowing, twisting, and cooing tremulously. For a march, on the other hand – Sousa for preference – he drew himself up to his full height, inflated his chest, and stamped up and down the room, while his coo became so rich and throaty that he seemed in danger of strangling himself. He never attempted to perform these actions for any other kind of music except marches and waltzes. Occasionally, however, if he had not heard any music for some time, he would (in his enthusiasm at hearing the gramophone) do a march for a waltz, or vice versa, but he invariably stopped and corrected himself half-way through.

One sad day we found, on waking Quasimodo, that he had duped us all, for there among the cushions lay a glossy white egg. He never quite recovered from this. He became embittered, sullen, and started to peck irritably if you attempted to pick him up. Then he laid another egg, and his nature changed completely. He, or rather she, became wilder and wilder, treating us as though we were her worst enemies, slinking up to the kitchen door for food as if she feared for her life. Not even the gramophone would tempt her back into the house. The last time I saw her she was sitting in an olive-tree, cooing in the most pretentious and coy manner, while further along the branch a large and very masculine-looking pigeon twisted and cooed in a perfect ecstasy of admiration.

For some time the Rose-beetle Man would turn up at the villa fairly regularly with some new addition to my menagerie: a frog, perhaps, or a sparrow with a broken leg. One afternoon Mother and I, in a fit of extravagant sentimentalism, bought up his entire stock of rose-beetles and, when he had left, let them all go in the garden. For days the villa was full of rose-beetles, crawling on the beds, lurking in the bathroom, banging against the lights at night, and falling like emeralds into our laps.

The last time I saw the Rose-beetle Man was one evening when I was sitting on a hill-top overlooking the road. He had obviously been to some fiesta and had been plied with much wine, for he swayed to and fro across the road, piping a melancholy tune on his flute. I shouted a greeting, and he waved extravagantly without looking back. As he rounded the corner he was silhouetted for a moment against the pale lavender evening sky. I could see his battered hat with the fluttering feathers, the bulging pockets of his coat, the bamboo cages full of sleepy pigeons on his back, and above his head, circling drowsily round and round. I could see the dim specks that were the rose-beetles. Then he rounded the curve of the road and there was only the pale sky with a new moon floating in it like a silver feather, and the soft twittering of his flute dying away in the dusk.

# 4

# A Bushel of Learning

Scarcely had we settled into the Strawberry-pink Villa before Mother decided that I was running wild, and that it was necessary for me to have some sort of education. But where to find this on a remote Greek island? As usual when a problem arose, the entire family flung itself with enthusiasm into the task of solving it. Each member had his or her own idea of what was best for me, and each argued with such fervour that any discussion about my future generally resulted in an uproar.

'Plenty of time for him to learn,' said Leslie; 'after all, he can read, can't he? I can teach him to shoot, and if we bought a boat I could teach him to sail.'

'But, dear, that wouldn't *really* be much use to him later on,' Mother pointed out, adding vaguely, 'unless he was going into the Merchant Navy or something.'

'I think it's essential that he learns to dance,' said Margo, 'or else he'll grow up into one of these awful tongue-tied hobbledehoys.'

'Yes, dear; but that sort of thing can come *later*. He should be getting some sort of grounding in things like mathematics and French . . . and his spelling's appalling.'

'Literature,' said Larry, with conviction, 'that's what he wants, a good solid grounding in literature. The rest will follow naturally. I've been encouraging him to read some good stuff.'

'But don't you think Rabelais is a little *old* for him?' asked Mother doubtfully.

'Good, clean fun,' said Larry airily; 'it's important that he gets sex in its right perspective now.'

'You've got a mania about sex,' said Margo primly; 'it doesn't matter what we're discussing, you always have to drag it in.'

'What he wants is a healthy, outdoor life; if he learnt to shoot and sail . . .' began Leslie.

'Oh, stop talking like a bishop . . . you'll be advocating cold baths next.'

'The trouble with you is you get in one of these damned supercilious moods where you think you know best, and you won't even listen to anyone else's point of view.'

'With a point of view as limited as yours, you can hardly expect me to listen to it.'

'Now, now, there's no sense in fighting,' said Mother.

'Well, Larry's so bloody unreasonable.'

'I like that!' said Larry indignantly; 'I'm far and away the most reasonable member of the family.'

'Yes, dear, but fighting doesn't solve the problem. What we want is someone who can teach Gerry and who'll encourage him in his interests.'

'He appears to have only one interest,' said Larry bitterly, 'and that's this awful urge to fill things with animal life. I don't think he ought to be encouraged in *that*. Life is fraught with danger as it is . . . I went to light a cigarette only this morning and a damn' great bumble-bee flew out of the box.'

'It was a grasshopper with me,' said Leslie gloomily.

'Yes, I think that sort of thing ought to be stopped,' said Margo. 'I found the *most revolting* jar of wriggling things on the dressing-table, of all places.'

'He doesn't mean any harm, poor little chap,' said Mother pacifically; 'he's so interested in all these things.'

'I wouldn't mind being attacked by bumble-bees, if it *led* anywhere,' Larry pointed out. 'But it's just a phase . . . he'll grow out of it by the time he's fourteen.'

'He's been in this phase from the age of two,' said Mother, 'and he's showing no signs of growing out of it.'

'Well, if you insist on stuffing him full of useless information, I suppose George would have a shot at teaching him,' said Larry.

*That's* a brain-wave,' said Mother delightedly. 'Will you go over and see him? I think the sooner he starts the better.'

Sitting under the open window in the twilight, with my arm round Roger's shaggy neck, I had listened with interest, not unmixed with indignation, to the family discussion on my fate. Now it was settled, I wondered vaguely who George was, and why it was so necessary for me to have lessons. But the dusk

40

was thick with flower-scents, and the olive-groves were dark, mysterious, and fascinating. I forgot about the imminent danger of being educated, and went off with Roger to hunt for glow-worms in the sprawling brambles.

I discovered that George was an old friend of Larry's who had come to Corfu to write. There was nothing very unusual about this, for all Larry's acquaintances in those days were either authors, poets, or painters. It was George, moreover, who was really responsible for our presence in Corfu, for he had written such eulogistic letters about the place that Larry had become convinced we could live nowhere else. Now George was to pay the penalty for his rashness. He came over to the villa to discuss my education with Mother, and we were introduced. We regarded each other with suspicion. George was a very tall and extremely thin man who moved with the odd disjointed grace of a puppet. His lean, skull-like face was partially concealed by a finely pointed brown beard and a pair of large tortoise-shell spectacles. He had a deep, melancholy voice, a dry and sarcastic sense of humour. Having made a joke he would smile in his beard with a sort of vulpine pleasure which was quite unaffected by anyone else's reactions.

Gravely George set about the task of teaching me. He was undeterred by the fact that there were no school-books available on the island; he simply ransacked his own library and appeared on the appointed day armed with a most unorthodox selection of tomes. Sombrely and patiently he taught me the rudiments of geography from the maps in the back of an ancient copy of *Pears Cyclopaedia*, English from books that ranged from Wilde to Gibbon. French from a fat and exciting book called *Le Petit Larousse*, and mathematics from memory. From my point of view, however, the most important thing was that we devoted some of our time to natural history, and George meticulously and carefully taught me how to observe and how to note down observations in a diary. At once my enthusiastic but haphazard interest in nature became focused, for I found that by writing things down I could learn and remember much more. The only mornings that I was ever on time for my lessons were those which were given up to natural history.

Every morning at nine George would come stalking through the olive-trees, clad in shorts, sandals, and an enormous straw hat with a frayed brim, clutching a wedge of books under one arm, swinging a walking-stick vigorously.

'Good morning. The disciple awaits the master agog with anticipation, I trust?' he would greet me, with a saturnine smile.

In the little dining-room of the villa the shutters would be closed against the sun, and in the green twilight George would loom over the table, methodically arranging the books. Flies, heat-drugged, would crawl slowly on the walls or fly drunkenly about the room, buzzing sleepily. Outside the cicadas were greeting the new days with shrill enthusiasm.

'Let me see, let me see,' George would murmur, running a long forefinger down our carefully prepared time-table; 'yes, yes, mathematics. If I remember rightly we were involved in the Herculean task of discovering how long it would take six men to build a wall if three of them took a week. I seem to recall that we have spent almost as much time on this problem as the men spent on the wall. Ah, well, let us gird our loins and do battle once again. Perhaps it's the *shape* of the problem that worries you, eh? Let us see if we can make it more exciting.'

He would droop over the exercise-book pensively, pulling at his beard. Then in his large, clear writing he would set the problem out in a fresh way.

'If it took two caterpillars a week to eat eight leaves, how long would four caterpillars take to eat the same number? Now, apply yourself to that.'

While I struggled with the apparently insoluble problem of the caterpillars' appetites, George would be otherwise occupied. He was an expert fencer, and was at that time engaged in learning some of the local peasant dances, for which he had a passion. So, while waiting for me to finish the sum, he would drift about in the gloom of the room, practising fencing stances or complicated dancing-steps, a habit that I found disconcerting, to say the least, and to which I shall always attribute my inability to do mathematics. Place any simple sum before me, even now, and it immediately conjures up a vision of George's lanky body swaying and jerking round the dimly lit dining-room. He would accompany the dancing sequences with a deep and tuneless humming, like a hive of distraught bees.

'Tum-ti-tum-ti-tum . . . tiddle tiddle tumty *dee* . . . left leg over . . . three steps right . . , tum-ti-tum-ti-tum-ti – *dum* . . . back, round, down and up . . . tiddle iddle umpty *dee* . . .' he would drone, as he paced and pirouetted like a dismal crane. Then, suddenly, the humming would stop, a steely look would creep into his eyes, and he would throw himself into an attitude of

42

defence, pointing an imaginary foil at an imaginary enemy. His eyes narrowed, his spectacles a-glitter, he would drive his adversary back across the room, skilfully avoiding the furniture. When his enemy was backed into the corner, George would dodge and twist round him with the agility of a wasp, stabbing, thrusting, guarding. I could almost see the gleam of steel. Then came the final moment, the upward and outward flick that would catch his opponent's weapon and twist it harmlessly to one side, the swift withdrawal, followed by the long, straight lunge that drove the point of his foil right through the adversary's heart. Through all this I would be watching him, fascinated, the exercise-book lying forgotten in front of me. Mathematics was not one of our more successful subjects.

In geography we made better progress, for George was able to give a more zoological tinge to the lesson. We would draw giant maps, wrinkled with mountains, and then fill in the various places of interest, together with drawings of the more exciting fauna to be found there. Thus for me the chief products of Ceylon were tapirs and tea; of India tigers and rice; of Australia kangaroos and sheep, while the blue curves of currents we drew across the oceans carried whales, albatross, penguins, and walrus, as well as hurricanes, trade winds, fair weather and foul. Our maps were works of art. The principal volcanoes belched such flames and sparks one feared they would set the paper continents alight; the mountain ranges of the world were so blue and white with ice and snow that it made one chilly to look at them. Our brown, sun-drenched deserts were lumpy with camel-humps and pyramids, and our tropical forests so tangled and luxuriant that it was only with difficulty that the slouching jaguars, lithe snakes, and morose gorillas managed to get through them, while on their outskirts emaciated natives hacked wearily at the painted trees, forming little clearings apparently for the purpose of writing 'coffee' or perhaps 'cereals' across them in unsteady capitals. Our rivers were wide, and blue as forget-me-nots, freckled with canoes and crocodiles. Our oceans were anything but empty, for where they had not frothed themselves into a fury of storms or drawn themselves up into an awe-inspiring tidal wave that hung over some remote, palm-shaggy island, they were full of life. Good-natured whales allowed unseaworthy galleons, armed with a forest of harpoons, to pursue them relentlessly; bland and innocent-looking octopi tenderly engulfed small

43

boats in their arms; Chinese junks, with jaundiced crews, were followed by shoals of well-dentured sharks, while fur-clad Eskimos pursued obese herds of walrus through ice-fields thickly populated by polar bears and penguins. They were maps that lived, maps that one could study, frown over and add to; maps, in short, that really *meant* something.

Our attempts at history were not, at first, conspicuously successful, until George discovered that by seasoning a series of unpalatable facts with a sprig of zoology and a sprinkle of completely irrelevant detail, he could get me interested. Thus I became conversant with some historical data which, to the best of my knowledge, have never been recorded before. Breathlessly, history lesson by history lesson, I followed Hannibal's progress over the Alps. His reason for attempting such a feat, and what he intended to do on the other side, were details that scarcely worried me. No, my interest in what I considered to be a very badly planned expedition lay in the fact that *I knew the name of each and every elephant.* I also knew that Hannibal had appointed a special man not only to feed and look after the elephants, *but to give them hot-water bottles when the weather got cold.* This interesting fact seems to have escaped most serious historians. Another thing that most history books never seem to mention is that Columbus's first words on setting foot ashore in America were: 'Great heavens, look . . . a jaguar!' With such an introduction, how could one fail to take an interest in the continent's subsequent history? So George, hampered by inadequate books and a reluctant pupil, would strive to make his teaching interesting, so that the lessons did not drag.

Roger, of course, thought that I was simply wasting my mornings. However, he did not desert me, but lay under the table asleep while I wrestled with my work. Occasionally, if I had to fetch a book, he would wake, get up, shake himself, yawn loudly, and wag his tail. Then, when he saw me returning to the table, his ears would droop, and he would walk heavily back to his private corner and flop down with a sigh of resignation. George did not mind Roger being in the room, for he behaved himself well, and did not distract my attention. Occasionally, if he was sleeping very heavily and heard a peasant dog barking, Roger would wake up with a start and utter a raucous roar of rage before realizing where he was. Then he would give an embarrassed look at our disapproving faces, his tail would twitch, and he would glance round the room sheepishly.

For a short time Quasimodo also joined us for lessons, and behaved very well as long as he was allowed to sit in my lap. He would drowse there, cooing to himself, the entire morning. It was I who banished him, in fact, for one day he upset a bottle of green ink in the exact centre of a large and very beautiful map that we had just completed. I realized, of course, that this vandalism was not intentional, but even so I was annoyed. Quasimodo tried for a week to get back into favour by sitting outside the door and cooing seductively through the crack, but each time I weakened I would catch a glimpse of his tail-feathers, a bright and horrible green, and harden my heart again.

Achilles also attended one lesson, but he did not approve of being inside the house. He spent the morning wandering about the room and scratching at the skirting-boards and door. Then he kept getting wedged under bits of furniture and scrabbling frantically until we lifted the object and rescued him. The room being small, it meant that in order to move one bit of furniture we had to move practically everything else. After a third upheaval George said that as he had never worked with Carter Paterson and was unused to such exertions he thought Achilles would be happier in the garden.

So there was only Roger left to keep me company. It was comforting, it's true, to be able to rest my feet on his woolly bulk while I grappled with a problem, but even then it was hard to concentrate, for the sun would pour through the shutters, tiger-striping the table and floor, reminding me of all the things I might be doing.

There around me were the vast, empty olive-groves echoing with cicadas; the moss-grown stone walls that made the vineyards into steps where the painted lizards ran; the thickets of myrtle alive with insects, and the rough headland where the flocks of garish goldfinches fluttered with excited piping from thistle-head to thistle-head.

Realizing this, George wisely instituted the novel system of outdoor lessons. Some mornings he arrived, carrying a large furry towel, and together we would make our way down through the olive-groves and along the road that was like a carpet of white velvet under its layer of dust. Then we branched off on to a goat-track that ran along the top of miniature cliffs, until it led us to a bay, secluded and small, with a crescent-shaped fringe of white sand running round it. A grove of stunted olives grew there, providing a pleasant shade.

From the top of the little cliff the water in the bay looked so still and transparent that it was hard to believe there was any at all. Fishes seemed to drift over the wave-wrinkled sand as though suspended in mid-air; while through six feet of clear water you could see rocks on which anemones lifted frail, coloured arms, and hermit crabs moved, dragging their top-shaped homes.

We would strip beneath the olives and walk out into the warm, bright water, to drift, face down, over the rocks and clumps of seaweed, occasionally diving to bring up something that caught our eye: a shell more brightly coloured than the rest; or a hermit crab of massive proportions, wearing an anemone on his shell, like a bonnet with a pink flower on it. Here and there on the sandy bottom grew rib-shaped beds of black ribbon-weed, and it was among these beds that the sea-slugs lived. Treading water and peering down, we could see below the shining, narrow fronds of green and black weeds growing close and tangled, over which we hung like hawks suspended in air above a strange woodland. In the clearing among the weed-bed lay the sea-slugs, perhaps the ugliest of the sea fauna. Some six inches long, they looked exactly like overgrown sausages made out of thick, brown, carunculated leather; dim, primitive beasts that just lie in one spot, rolling gently with the sea's swing, sucking in sea-water at one end of their bodies and passing it out at the other. The minute vegetable and animal life in the water is filtered off somewhere inside the sausage, and passed to the simple mechanism of the sea-slug's stomach. No one could say that the sea-slugs led interesting lives. Dully they rolled on the sand, sucking in the sea with monotonous regularity. It was hard to believe that these obese creatures could defend themselves in any way, or that they would ever need to, but in fact they had an unusual method of showing their displeasure. Pick them up out of the water, and they would squirt a jet of sea-water out of either end of their bodies, apparently without any muscular effort. It was this water-pistol habit of theirs that led us to invent a game. Each armed with a sea-slug we would make our weapons squirt, noting how and where the water struck the sea. Then we moved over to that spot, and the one who discovered the greatest amount of sea fauna in his area won a point. Occasionally, as in any game, feeling would run high, indignant accusations of cheating would be made and denied. It was then we found our sea-slugs useful for turning on our opponent. Whenever we had made use of the sea-slugs' services we always swam out and returned them to their forest of weed. Next time we came down they would still be there, probably in exactly the same position as we had left them, rolling quietly to and fro.

Having exhausted the possibilities of the slugs, we would hunt for new shells for my collection, or hold long discussions on the other fauna we had found; George would suddenly realize that all this, though most enjoyable, could hardly be described as education in the strictest sense of the word, so we would drift back to the shallows and lie there. The lesson then proceeded, while the shoals of little fish would gather about us and nibble gently at our legs.

'So the French and British Fleets were slowly drawing together for what was to be the decisive sea battle of the war. When the enemy was sighted, Nelson was on the bridge bird-watching through his telescope . . . he had already been warned of the Frenchmen's approach by a friendly gull . . . eh? . . . oh, a greater black-backed gull I think it was . . . well, the ships manoeuvred round each other . . . of course they couldn't move so fast in those days, for they did everything by sail . . . no engines . . . no, not even outboard engines . . . The British sailors were a bit worried because the French seemed so strong, but when they saw that Nelson was so little affected by the whole thing that he was sitting on the bridge labelling his birds'-egg collection, they decided that there was really nothing to be scared about . . .'

The sea was like a warm silky coverlet that moved my body gently to and fro. There were no waves, only this gentle underwater movement, the pulse of the sea, rocking me softly. Around my legs the coloured fish flicked and trembled, and stood on their heads while they mumbled at me with toothless gums. In the drooping clusters of olives a cicada whispered gently to itself.

'. . . and so they carried Nelson down below as quickly as possible, so that none of the crew would know he had been hit . . . He was mortally wounded, and lying below decks with the battle still raging above, he murmured his last words: "Kiss me, Hardy," and then he died . . . What? Oh yes. Well, he had already told Hardy that if anything happened to him he could have his birds' eggs . . . so, though England had lost her finest seaman, the battle had been won, and it had far-reaching effects in Europe . . .'

Across the mouth of the bay a sun-bleached boat would pass,

rowed by a brown fisherman in tattered trousers, standing in the stern and twisting an oar in the water like a fish's tail. He would raise one hand in lazy salute, and across the still, blue water you could hear the plaintive squeak of the oar as it twisted, and the soft clop as it dug into the sea.

# 5

# A Treasure of Spiders

One hot, dreamy afternoon, when everything except the shouting cicadas seemed to be asleep, Roger and I set out to see how far we could climb over the hills before dark. We made our way up through the olive-groves, striped and dappled with white sunlight, where the air was hot and still, and eventually we clambered above the trees and out on to a bare, rocky peak, where we sat down for a rest. The island dozed below us, shimmering like a water-picture in the heat-haze: grey-green olives; black cypresses; multi-coloured rocks of the sea-coast; and the sea smooth and opalescent, kingfisher-blue, jade-green, with here and there a pleat or two in its sleek surface where it curved round a rocky, olive-tangled promontory. Directly below us was a small bay with a crescent-shaped rim of white sand, a bay so shallow, and with a floor of such dazzling sand that the water was a pale blue, almost white. I was sweaty after the ascent, and Roger sat with flopping tongue and froth-flecked whiskers. We decided that we would not climb the hills after all; we would go for a bathe instead. So we hurried down the hillside until we reached the little bay, empty, silent, asleep under the brilliant shower of sunlight. We sat in the warm, shallow waters, drowsily, and I delved in the sand around me. Occasionally I found a smooth pebble, or a piece of bottle which had been rubbed and licked by the sea until it was like an astonishing jewel, green and translucent. These finds I handed to Roger, who sat watching me. He, not certain what I expected him to do but not wishing to offend me, took them delicately in his mouth. Then, when he thought I was not looking, he would drop them back into the water and sigh deeply.

Later, I lay on a rock to dry, while Roger sneezed and clopped his way along the shallows in an attempt to catch one of the blue-finned blennies, with their pouting, vacant faces, which flipped from rock to rock with the speed of swallows. Breathing heavily and staring down into the clear water, Roger followed them, a look of intense concentration on his face. When I was dry, I put on my shorts and shirt and called to Roger. He came reluctantly, with many a backward glance at the blennies which still flicked across the sandy, sun-ringed floor of the bay. Coming as close to me as possible, he shook himself vigorously, showering me with water from his curly coat.

After the swim, my body felt heavy and relaxed, and my skin as though it was covered with a silky crust of salt. Slowly and dreamily we made our way on to the road. Discovering that I was hungry, I wondered which was the nearest cottage where I could get something to eat. I stood kicking up puffs of fine white dust from the road as I considered this problem. If I went to see Leonora, who undoubtedly lived the nearest, she would give me figs and bread, but she would also insist on giving me the latest bulletin on her daughter's state of health. Her daughter was a husky-voiced virago with a cast in one eye, whom I cordially disliked, so I had no interest in her health. I decided not to go to Leonora; it was a pity, for she had the best fig-trees for miles around, but there was a limit to what I could endure for the sake of black figs. If I went to see Taki, the fisherman, he would be having his siesta, and would merely shout, 'Go away, little corntop,' from the depths of his tightly shuttered house. Christaki and his family would probably be about, but in return for food they would expect me to answer a lot of tedious questions: Was England bigger than Corfu? How many people lived there? Were they all lords? What was a train like? Did trees grow in England? and so on, interminably. If it had been morning I could have cut through the fields and vineyards, and before reaching home I would have fed well on contributions from various of my friends on the way: olives, bread, grapes, figs, ending perhaps with a short detour that would take me through Philomena's fields, where I could be sure of ending my snack with a crisp, pink slice of water-melon, cold as ice. But now it was siesta time, and most of the peasants were asleep in their houses behind tightly closed doors and shutters. It was a difficult problem, and while I thought about it the pangs of hunger grew, and I kicked more energetically at the dusty road, until Roger sneezed protestingly and gave me an injured look.

Suddenly I had an idea. Just over the hill lived Yani, the old shepherd, and his wife, in a minute, sparkling white cottage. Yani, I knew, had his siesta in front of his house, in the shade of the grape-vine, and if I made enough noise approaching the house he would wake up. Once awake, it was certain that he would offer me hospitality. There was not a single peasant house you could visit and come empty away. Cheered by this thought, I set off up the stony, meandering pathway created by the pattering hooves of Yani's goats, over the brow of the hill and into the valley, where the red roof of the shepherd's house gleamed among the giant olive-trunks. When I judged I was close enough, I stopped and threw a stone for Roger to retrieve. This was one of Roger's favourite pastimes, but once having started it you had to continue, or else he would stand in front of you and bark hideously until you repeated the performance in sheer desperation. He retrieved the stone, dropped it at my feet and backed away expectantly, ears cocked, eyes gleaming, muscles taut and ready for action. I ignored both him and the stone. He looked faintly surprised; he examined the stone carefully, and then looked at me again. I whistled a short tune and looked up into the sky. Roger gave an experimental yap; then seeing I still took no notice, he followed it up with a volley of deep, rich barks that echoed among the olives. I let him bark for about five minutes. By this time I felt sure Yani must be aware of our arrival. Then I threw the stone for Roger, and as he fled after it joyfully, I made my way round to the front of the house.

The old shepherd, as I expected, was in the tattered shade of the vine that sprawled on its iron trellis-work above my head, but to my intense annoyance he had not woken up. He was sprawling in a plain deal chair, which was tilted back against the wall at a dangerous angle. His arms dangled limply, his legs were spread out, and his magnificent moustache, orange and white with nicotine and age, lifted and trembled with his snores, like some strange seaweed that is raised and lowered by a gentle swell. The thick fingers of his stumpy hands twitched as he slept, and I could see the thick-ribbed yellow nails, like flakes cut from a tallow candle. His brown face, wrinkled and furrowed as the bark of a pine, was expressionless, the eyes tightly shut. I stared at him, trying to will him to wake up, but with no result. It was not etiquette for me to wake him, and I was debating whether it would be worth while waiting until he awoke naturally, or whether it

51

would be better to go and be bored by Leonora, when Roger came in search of me, bustling round the side of the house, ears pricked, tongue drooping. He saw me, wagged his tail in brief greeting, and glanced round with the air of a visitor who knows he is welcome. Suddenly he froze, his moustache bristled, and he started to walk forward slowly, stiff-legged and quivering. He had seen something that I had failed to observe: curled up under Yani's tilted chair sat a large, lanky grey cat, who was watching us with insolent green eyes. Before I could reach out and grab him, Roger had pounced. The cat, in a lithe movement that argued long practice, fled like a skimming stone to where the gnarled grape-vine twisted drunkenly round the trellis, and shot up it with a scutter of sharp claws. Crouched among the bunches of white grapes, she stared down at Roger and spat delicately. Roger, frustrated and angry, threw back his head and barked threats and insults. Yani's eyes flew open, his chair rocked, and his arms flailed violently in an effort to keep his balance. The chair teetered uncertainly, and then settled on to all four legs with a thud.

'Saint Spiridion save me!' he implored loudly. 'God have mercy!'

He glared round, his moustache quivering, to find the cause of the uproar, and saw me sitting demurely on the wall. I greeted him sweetly and politely, as though nothing had happened, and asked if he had slept well. He rose to his feet, grinning, and scratched his stomach vigorously.

'Ah, it's you making enough noise to split my head. Your health, your health. Sit down, little lord,' he said, dusting off his chair and placing it for me; 'it is good to see you. You will eat with me, and have a drink, perhaps? It is a very hot afternoon, very hot – hot enough to melt a bottle.'

He stretched and, yawning loudly, displayed gums as innocent of teeth as a baby's. Then, turning towards the house, he roared:

'Aphrodite ... *Aphrodite* ... wake, woman ... foreigners have come ... the little lord is sitting with me ... Bring food ... d'you hear?'

'I heard, I heard,' came a muffled voice from behind the shutters.

Yani grunted, wiped his moustache, and made his way to the nearest olive-tree and retired discreetly behind it. He reappeared, doing up his trousers and yawning, and came over to sit on the wall near me.

'Today I should have taken my goats to Gastouri. But it was too hot, much too hot. In the hills the rocks will be so hot you could light a cigarette from them. So I went instead and tasted Taki's new white wine. Spiridion! What a wine ... like the blood of a dragon and as smooth as a fish ... What a wine! When I came back the air was full of sleep, so here I am.'

He sighed deeply but impenitently, and fumbled in his pocket for his battered tin of tobacco and thin grey cigarette papers. His brown, calloused hand cupped to catch the little pile of golden leaf, and the fingers of his other hand tugged and pulled at it gently. He rolled the cigarette swiftly, nipped the tobacco that dangled from the ends and replaced it in the tin, and then lit his smoke with the aid of a huge tin lighter from which a wick curled like an angry snake. He puffed reflectively for a moment, pulled a shred of tobacco off his moustache, and reached into his pocket again.

'Here, you are interested in the little ones of God; look at this that I caught this morning, crouching under a rock like the devil,' he said, pulling from his pocket a tiny bottle, firmly corked and filled with golden olive oil; 'a fine one this, a fighter. The only fighter I know who can do damage with his backside.'

The bottle, filled to the brim with oil, looked as though it were made of pale amber, and enshrined in the centre, held suspended by the thickness of the oil, was a small chocolate-brown scorpion, his tail curved like a scimitar over his back. He was quite dead, suffocated by the glutinous grave. Around his corpse was a faint whisp of discoloration, like a mist in the golden oil.

'See that?' said Yani. 'That's the poison. He was full, that one.'

I asked, curiously, why it was necessary to put the scorpion in oil.

Yani chuckled richly, and wiped his moustache.

'You do not know, little lord, though you spend all your time on your stomach catching these things, eh?' he said, greatly amused. 'Well, I will tell you. You never know, it may be of use to you. First catch the scorpion, catch him alive, and catch him as gently as a falling feather. Then you put him, alive – mark you, alive – in a bottle of oil. Let him simmer, let him die in it, let the sweet oil soak up the poison. Then, should you ever be stung by one of his brothers (and Saint Spiridion protect you from that), you must rub the place with the oil. That will cure the sting for you so that it is of no more discomfort than the prick of a thorn.

While I digested this curious information, Aphrodite appeared from the house, her wrinkled face as red as a pomegranate seed, bearing a tin tray on which was a bottle of wine, a jug of water, and a plate with bread, olives, and figs on it. Yani and I drank the wine, watered to a delicate pale pink, and ate the food in silence. In spite of his toothless gums, Yani tore large pieces of the bread off and champed them hungrily, swallowing great lumps that made his wrinkled throat swell. When we had finished, he sat back, wiped his moustache carefully, and took up the conversation again, as if there had been no pause.

'I knew a man once, a shepherd like myself, who had been to a fiesta in a distant village. On the way back, as his stomach was warm with wine, he decided to have a sleep, so he found a spot beneath some myrtles. But while he slept a scorpion crept out from under the leaves and crawled into his ear, and when he awoke it stung him.'

Yani paused at this psychological moment to spit over the wall and roll himself another cigarette.

'Yes,' he sighed at last, 'it was very sad . . . one so young. The tiny scorpion stung him in the ear . . . phut! . . . like that. The poor fellow flung himself about in his agony. He ran screaming through the olives, tearing at his head . . . Ah! it was dreadful. There was no one to hear his cries and help him . . . no one at all. In terrible pain he started to run for the village, but he never reached it. He fell down dead, down there in the valley, not far from the road. We found him the next morning when we were going to the fields. What a sight! What a sight! With that one little bite his head had swollen up as though his brains were pregnant, and he was dead, quite dead.'

Yani sighed deeply and lugubriously, twirling the little bottle of oil in his fingers.

'That is why,' he went on, 'I never go up into the hills and sleep. And, in case I should perhaps share some wine with a friend and forget the danger, I always carry a scorpion bottle with me.

The talk drifted to other and equally absorbing topics, and after an hour or so I rose, dusted the crumbs off my lap, thanked the old man and his wife for their hospitality, accepted a bunch of grapes as a parting present, and set off towards home. Roger walked close to me, his eyes fixed on my pocket, for he had noticed the grapes. At length, finding an olive-grove, dark and cool with the long shadows of evening, we sat down by a mossy bank and shared the fruit. Roger ate his whole, pips and all. I spat out my pips into a circle around me, and imagined with satisfaction the flourishing vineyard that would grow up on the spot. When the grapes were finished I rolled over on to my stomach and, with my chin in my hands, examined the bank behind me.

A tiny green grasshopper with a long, melancholy face sat twitching his hind legs nervously. A fragile snail sat on a moss sprig, meditating and waiting for the evening dew. A plump scarlet mite, the size of a match-head, struggled like a tubby huntsman through the forest of moss. It was a microscopic world, full of fascinating life. As I watched the mite making his slow progress I noticed a curious thing. Here and there on the green plush surface of the moss were scattered faint circular marks, each the size of a shilling. So faint were they that it was only from certain angles they were noticeable at all. They reminded me of a full moon seen behind thick clouds, a faint circle that seemed to shift and change. I wondered idly what could have made them. They were too irregular, too scattered to be the prints of some beast, and what was it that would walk up an almost vertical bank in such a haphazard manner? Besides, they were not like imprints. I prodded the edge of one of these circles with a piece of grass. It remained unmoved. I began to think the mark was caused by some curious way in which the moss grew. I probed again, more vigorously, and suddenly my stomach gave a clutch of tremendous excitement. It was as though my grass-stalk had found a hidden spring, for the whole circle lifted up like a trapdoor. As I stared, I saw to my amazement that it *was* in fact a trapdoor, lined with silk, and with a neatly bevelled edge that fitted snugly into the mouth of the silk-lined shaft it concealed. The edge of the door was fastened to the lip of the tunnel by a small flap of silk that acted as a hinge. I gazed at this magnificent piece of workmanship and wondered what on earth could have made it. Peering down the silken tunnel, I could see nothing; I poked my grass-stalk down, but there was no response. For a long time I sat staring at this fantastic home, trying to decide what sort of beast had made it. I thought that it might be a wasp of some sort, but had never heard of a wasp that fitted its nest with secret doors. I felt that I must get to the bottom of this problem immediately. I would go down and ask George if he knew what this mysterious beast was. Calling Roger, who was busily trying to uproot an olive-tree, I set off at a brisk trot.

I arrived at George's villa out of breath, bursting with suppressed excitement, gave a perfunctory knock at the door, and dashed in. Only then did I realize he had company. Seated in a chair near him was a figure which, at first glance, I decided must be George's brother, for he also wore a beard. He was, however, in contrast to George, immaculately dressed in a grey flannel suit with waistcoat, a spotless white shirt, a tasteful but sombre tie, and large, solid, highly polished boots. I paused on the threshold, embarrassed, while George surveyed me sardonically.

'Good evening,' he greeted me. 'From the joyful speed of your entry I take it that you have not come for a little extra tuition.'

I apologized for the intrusion, and then told George about the curious nests I had found.

'Thank heavens you're here, Theodore,' he said to his bearded companion. 'I shall now be able to hand the problem over to expert hands.'

'Hardly an expert . . .' mumbled the man called Theodore, deprecatingly.

'Gerry, this is Doctor Theodore Stephanides,' said George. 'He is an expert on practically everything you care to mention. And what you don't mention, he does. He, like you, is an eccentric nature-lover. Theodore, this is Gerry Durrell.'

I said how do you do, politely, but to my surprise the bearded man rose to his feet, stepped briskly across the room, and held out a large white hand.

'Very pleased to meet you,' he said, apparently addressing his beard, and gave me a quick, shy glance from twinkling blue eyes.

I shook his hand and said I was very pleased to meet him, too. Then we stood in awkward silence, while George watched us, grinning.

'Well, Theodore,' he said at last, 'and what d'you think produced these strange secret passages?'

Theodore clasped his hands behind his back, lifted himself on to his toes several times, his boots squeaking protestingly, and gravely considered the floor.

'Well . . . er . . .' he said, his words coming slowly and meticulously, 'it sounds to me as though they might be the burrows of the trapdoor spider . . . er . . . it is a species which is quite common here in Corfu . . . that is to say, when I say common, I suppose I have found some thirty or . . . er . . . forty specimens during the time I have been here.'

'Ah,' said George, 'trapdoor spiders, eh?'

'Yes,' said Theodore. 'I feel that it's more than probable that that is what they are. However, I may be mistaken.'

He rose and fell on his toes, squeaking gently, and then he shot me a keen glance.

'Perhaps, if they are not too far away, we could go and verify it,' he suggested tentatively. 'I mean to say, if you have nothing better to do, and it's not too far . . .'

His voice trailed away on a faintly interrogative note. I said that they were only just up the hill, not really far.

'Um,' said Theodore.

'Don't let him drag you about all over the place, Theodore,' said George. 'You don't want to be galloped about the countryside.'

'No, no, not at all,' said Theodore; 'I was just about to leave, and I can easily walk that way back. It is quite a simple matter for me to . . . er . . . cut down through the olive-groves and reach Canoni.'

He picked up a neat grey homburg and placed it squarely on his head. At the door he held out his hand and shook George's briefly.

'Thank you for a delightful tea,' he said, and stumped gravely off along the path by my side.

As we walked along I studied him covertly. He had a straight, well-shaped nose; a humorous mouth lurking in the ash-blond beard; straight, rather bushy eyebrows under which his eyes, keen but with a twinkle in them and laughter-wrinkles at the corners, surveyed the world. He strode along energetically, humming to himself. When we came to a ditch full of stagnant water he stopped for a moment and stared down into it, his beard bristling.

'Um,' he said conversationally, '*daphnia magna*.'

He rasped at his beard with his thumb, and then set off down the path again.

'Unfortunately,' he said to me, 'I was coming out to see some people . . . er . . . *friends* of mine, and so I did not bring my collecting bag with me. It is a pity, for that ditch might have contained something.'

When we branched off the fairly smooth path we had been travelling along and started up the stony goat-track, I expected some sort of protest, but Theodore strode behind me with unabated vigour, still humming. At length we came to the gloomy olive-grove, and I led Theodore to the bank and pointed out the mysterious trapdoor.

He peered down at it, his eyes narrowed.

'Ah ha,' he said, 'yes . . . um . . . yes.'

He produced from his waistcoat pocket a tiny penknife, opened it, inserted the point of the blade delicately under the little door and flipped it back.

'Um, yes,' he repeated; '*cteniza.*'

He peered down the tunnel, blew down it, and then let the trapdoor fall into place again.

'Yes, they are the burrows of the trapdoor spiders,' he said, 'but this one does not appear to be inhabited. Generally, the creature will hold on to the . . . er . . . *trapdoor* . . . with her legs, or rather, her *claws*, and she holds on with such tenacity that you have to be careful or you will damage the door, trying to force it open. Um . . . yes . . . these are the burrows of the females, of course. The male makes a similar burrow, but it is only about half the size.'

I remarked that it was the most curious structure I had seen.

'Ah ha! yes,' said Theodore, 'they are certainly very curious. A thing that always puzzles me is how the female knows when the male is approaching.'

I must have looked blank, for he teetered on his toes, shot me a quick look, and went on:

'The spider, of course, waits inside its burrow until some insect – a fly or a grasshopper, or something similar – chances to walk past. They can judge, it seems, whether the insect is close enough to be caught. If it is, the spider . . . er . . . pops out of its hole and catches the creature. Now when the male comes in search of the female he must walk over the moss to the trapdoor, and I have often wondered why it is that he is not . . . er . . . devoured by the female in mistake. It is possible, of course, that his footsteps sound different. Or he may make some sort of . . . you know . . . some sort of *sound* which the female recognizes.'

We walked down the hill in silence. When we reached the place where the paths forked I said that I must leave him.

'Ah, well, I'll say good-bye,' he said, staring at his boots. 'I have enjoyed meeting you.'

We stood in silence for a moment. Theodore was afflicted with the acute embarrassment that always seemed to overwhelm him when greeting or saying good-bye to someone. He stared hard at his boots for a moment longer, and then he held out his hand and shook mine gravely.

'Good-bye,' he said. 'I . . . er . . . I expect we shall meet again.'

He turned and stumped off down the hill, swinging his stick, staring about him with observant eyes. I watched him out of sight and then walked slowly in the direction of the villa. I was at once confused and amazed by Theodore. First, since he was obviously a scientist of considerable repute (and I could have told this by his beard), he was to me a person of great importance. In fact he was the only person I had met until now who seemed to share my enthusiasm for zoology. Secondly, I was extremely flattered to find that he treated me and talked to me exactly as though I was his own age. I liked him for this, as I was not talked down to by my family, and I took rather a poor view of any outsider trying to do so. But Theodore not only talked to me as though I was grown up, but also as though I was as knowledgeable as he.

The facts he told me about the trapdoor spider haunted me: the idea of the creature crouching in its silken tunnel, holding the door closed with its hooked claws, listening to the movement of the insects on the moss above. What, I wondered, did things sound like to a trapdoor spider? I could imagine that a snail would trail over the door with a noise like sticking-plaster being slowly torn off. A centipede would sound like a troop of cavalry. A fly would patter in brisk spurts, followed by a pause while it washed its hands – a dull rasping sound like a knife-grinder at work. The larger beetles, I decided, would sound like steam-rollers, while the smaller ones, the lady-birds and others, would probably purr over the moss like clockwork motor-cars. Fascinated by this thought, I made my way back home through the darkening fields, to tell the family of my new discovery and of my meeting with Theodore. I hoped to see him again, for there were many things I wanted to ask him, but I felt it would be unlikely that he would have very much time to spare for me. I was mistaken, however, for two days later Leslie came back from an excursion into the town, and handed me a small parcel.

'Met that bearded johnny,' he said laconically; 'you know, that scientist bloke. Said this was for you.'

Incredulously I stared at the parcel. Surely it couldn't be for me? There must be some mistake, for a great scientist would hardly bother to send me parcels, I turned it over, and there, written on it in neat, spidery writing, was my name. I tore off the paper as quickly as I could. Inside was a small box and a letter.

My dear Gerry Durrell,

I wondered, after our conversation the other day, if it might not assist your investigations of the local natural history to have some form of magnifying instrument. I am therefore sending you this pocket microscope, in the hope that it will be of some use to you. It is, of course, not of very high magnification, but you will find it sufficient for *field* work.

With best wishes<br>
Yours sincerely,<br>
Theo. Stephanides

P.S. If you have nothing better to do on Thursday, perhaps you would care to come to tea, and I could then show you some of my microscope slides.

# 6

# The Sweet Spring

During the last days of the dying summer, and throughout the warm, wet winter that followed, tea with Theodore became a weekly affair. Every Thursday I would set out, my pockets bulging with matchboxes and test-tubes full of specimens, to be driven into the town by Spiro. It was an appointment that I would not have missed for anything.

Theodore would welcome me in his study, a room that met with my full approval. It was, in my opinion, just what a room should be. The walls were lined with tall bookshelves filled with volumes on freshwater biology, botany, astronomy, medicine, folk-lore, and similar fascinating and sensible subjects. Interspersed with these were selections of ghost and crime stories. Thus Sherlock Holmes rubbed shoulders with Darwin, and Le Fanu with Fabre, in what I considered to be a thoroughly well-balanced library. At one window of the room stood Theodore's telescope, its nose to the sky like a howling dog, while the sills of every window bore a parade of jars and bottles containing minute freshwater fauna, whirling and twitching among the delicate fronds of green weed. On one side of the room was a massive desk, piled high with scrapbooks, micro-photographs, X-ray plates, diaries, and note-books. On the opposite side of the room was the microscope table, with its powerful lamp on the jointed stem leaning like a lily over the flat boxes that housed Theodore's collection of slides. The microscopes themselves, gleaming like magpies, were housed under a series of beehive-like domes of glass.

'How are you?' Theodore would inquire, as if I were a complete stranger, and give me his characteristic handshake – a sharp downward tug, like a man testing a knot in a rope.

The formalities being over, we could then turn our minds to more important topics.

'I was ... er ... you know ... looking through my slides just before your arrival, and I came across one which may interest you. It is a slide of the mouth-parts of the rat flea ... *ceratophyllus fasciatus*, you know. Now, I'll just adjust the microscope ... There! ... you see? Very curious. I mean to say, you could almost imagine it was a human face, couldn't you? Now I had another ... er ... slide here ... That's funny. Ah! got it. Now this one is of the spinnerets of the garden or cross spider ... er ... *epeira fasciata* ...'

So, absorbed and happy, we would pore over the microscope. Filled with enthusiasm, we would tack from subject to subject, and if Theodore could not answer my ceaseless flow of questions himself, he had books that could. Gaps would appear in the bookcase as volume after volume was extracted to be consulted, and by our side would be an ever-growing pile of volumes.

'Now this one is a cyclops ... *cyclops viridis* ... which I caught out near Govino the other day. It is a female with egg-sacs ... Now, I'll just adjust ... you'll be able to see the eggs quite clearly ... I'll just put her in the live box ... er ... hum ... there are several species of cyclops found here in Corfu ...'

Into the brilliant circle of white light a weird creature would appear, a pear-shaped body, long antennae that twitched indignantly, a tail like sprigs of heather, and on each side of it (slung like sacks of onions on a donkey) the two large sacs bulging with pink beads.

'... called cyclops because, as you can see, it has a single eye situated in the centre of its forehead. That's to say, in the centre of what *would* be its forehead if a cyclops had one. In Ancient Greek mythology, as you know, a cyclops was one of a group of giants ... er ... each of whom had one eye. Their task was to forge iron for Hephaestus.'

Outside, the warm wind would shoulder the shutters, making them creak, and the rain-drops would chase each other down the window-pane like transparent tadpoles.

'Ah ha! It is curious that you should mention that. The peasants in Salonika have a very similar ... er ... superstition ... No, no, merely a superstition. I have a book here that gives a most *interesting* account of vampires in ... um ... Bosnia. It seems that the local people there ...'

Tea would arrive, the cakes squatting on cushions of cream,

toast in a melting shawl of butter, cups a-gleam, and a faint wisp of steam rising from the teapot spout.

'. . . but, on the other hand, it is impossible to say that there is *no* life on Mars. It is, in my opinion, quite possible that some form of life will be found . . . er . . . *discovered* there, should we ever succeed in *getting* there. But there is no reason to suppose that any form of life found there would be identical . . .'

Sitting there, neat and correct in his tweed suit, Theodore would chew his toast slowly and methodically, his beard bristling, his eyes kindling with enthusiasm at each new subject that swam into our conversation. To me his knowledge seemed inexhaustible. He was a rich vein of information, and I mined him assiduously. No matter what the subject, Theodore could contribute something interesting to it. At last I would hear Spiro honking his horn in the street below, and I would rise reluctantly to go.

'Good-bye,' Theodore would say, tugging my hand. 'It's been a pleasure having you . . . er . . . no, no, not at all. See you next Thursday. When the weather gets better . . . er . . . less damp . . . in the *spring*, you know . . . perhaps we might go for some walks together . . . see what we can obtain. There are some most interesting ditches in the Val de Ropa . . . um, yes . . . Well, good-bye . . . Not at all.'

Driving back along the dark, rain-washed roads, Spiro humming richly as he squatted behind the wheel, I would dream of the spring to come, and of all the wonderful creatures that Theodore and I would capture.

Eventually the warm wind and the rain of winter seemed to polish the sky, so that when January arrived it shone a clear, tender blue . . . the same blue as that of the tiny flames that devoured the olive-logs in the charcoal pits. The nights were still and cool, with a moon so fragile it barely freckled the sea with silver points. The dawns were pale and translucent until the sun rose, mist-wrapped, like a gigantic silkworm cocoon, and washed the island with a delicate bloom of gold dust.

With March came the spring, and the island was flower-filled, scented, and a-flutter with new leaves. The cypress-trees that had tossed and hissed during the winds of winter now stood straight and sleek against the sky, covered with a misty coat of greenish-white cones. Waxy yellow crocuses appeared in great clusters, bubbling out among the tree-roots and tumbling down the banks. Under the myrtles, the grape-hyacinths lifted buds like magenta sugar-drops, and the gloom of the oak-thickets was filled with the dim smoke of a thousand blue day-irises. Anemones, delicate and easily wind-bruised, lifted ivory flowers the petals of which seemed to have been dipped in wine. Vetch, marigold, asphodel, and a hundred others flooded the fields and woods. Even the ancient olives, bent and hollowed by a thousand springs, decked themselves in clusters of minute creamy flowers, modest and yet decorative, as became their great age. It was no half-hearted spring, this: the whole island vibrated with it as though a great, ringing chord had been struck. Everyone and everything heard it and responded. It was apparent in the gleam of flower-petals, the flash of bird wings and the sparkle in the dark, liquid eyes of the peasant girls. In the water-filled ditches the frogs that looked newly enamelled snored a rapturous chorus in the lush weeds. In the village coffee-shops the wine seemed redder and, somehow, more potent. Blunt, work-calloused fingers plucked at guitar strings with strange gentleness, and rich voices rose in lilting, haunting song.

Spring affected the family in a variety of ways. Larry bought himself a guitar and a large barrel of strong red wine. He interspersed his bouts of work by playing haphazardly on the instrument and singing Elizabethan love-songs in a meek tenor voice, with frequent pauses for refreshment. This would soon induce a mood of melancholy, and the love-songs would become more doleful, while between each Larry would pause to inform whichever member of the family happened to be present that spring, for him, did not mean the beginning of a new year, but the death of the old one. The grave, he would proclaim, making the guitar rumble ominously, yawned a little wider with each season.

One evening the rest of us had gone out and left Mother and Larry alone together. Larry had spent the evening singing more and more dismally, until he had succeeded in working them both into a fit of acute depression. They attempted to alleviate this state with the aid of wine, but unfortunately this had the reverse effect, for they were not used to the heavy wines of Greece. When we returned we were somewhat startled to be greeted by Mother, standing at the door of the villa with a hurricane lantern. She informed us with lady-like precision and dignity that she wished to be buried under the rose-bushes. The novelty of this lay in the fact that she had chosen such an accessible place for the disposal of her remains. Mother spent a lot of her spare time choosing places to be buried in, but they were generally situated in the most remote areas, and one had visions of the funeral *cortège* dropping exhausted by the wayside long before it had reached the grave.

When left undisturbed by Larry, however, spring for Mother meant an endless array of fresh vegetables with which to experiment, and a riot of new flowers to delight her in the garden. There streamed from the kitchen a tremendous number of new dishes, soups, stews, savouries, and curries, each richer, more fragrant, and more exotic than the last. Larry began to suffer from dyspepsia. Scorning the simple remedy of eating less, he procured an immense tin of bicarbonate of soda, and would solemnly take a dose after every meal.

'Why do you *eat* so much if it upsets you, dear?' Mother asked.

'It would be an insult to your cooking to eat less,' Larry replied unctuously.

'You're getting terribly fat,' said Margo; 'it's very bad for you.'

'Nonsense!' said Larry in alarm. 'I'm not getting fat, Mother, am I?'

'You look as though you've put on a little weight,' Mother admitted, surveying him critically.

'It's your fault,' Larry said unreasonably. 'You will keep tempting me with these aromatic delicacies. You're driving me to ulcers, I shall have to go on a diet. What's a good diet, Margo?'

'Well,' said Margo, launching herself with enthusiasm into her favourite topic, 'you could try the orange-juice and salad one; that's awfully good. There's the milk and raw vegetable one . . . that's good too, but it takes a little time. Or there's the boiled fish and brown bread one. I don't know what that's like, I haven't tried it yet.'

'Dear God!' exclaimed Larry, genuinely shocked, 'are those diets?'

'Yes, and they're all very good ones,' said Margo earnestly. 'I've been trying the orange-juice one and it's done wonders for my acne.'

'No,' said Larry firmly. 'I'm not going to do it if it means that I have to champ my way like a damned ungulate through bushels of raw fruit and vegetables. You will all have to resign yourselves to the fact that I shall be taken from you at an early age, suffering from fatty degeneration of the heart.'

At the next meal he took the precaution of having a large dose of bicarbonate beforehand, and then protested bitterly that the food tasted queer.

Margo was always badly affected by the spring. Her personal appearance, always of absorbing interest to her, now became almost an obsession. Piles of freshly laundered clothes filled her bedroom, while the washing-line sagged under the weight of clothes newly washed. Singing shrilly and untunefully she would drift about the villa, carrying piles of flimsy underwear or bottles of scent. She would seize every opportunity to dive into the bathroom, in a swirl of white towels, and once in there she was as hard to dislodge as a limpet from a rock. The family in turn would bellow and batter on the door, getting no more satisfaction than an assurance that she was nearly finished, an assurance which we had learnt by bitter experience not to have any faith in. Eventually she would emerge, glowing and immaculate, and drift from the house, humming, to sun-bathe in the olive-groves or go down to the sea and swim. It was during one of these excursions to the sea that she met an over-good-looking young Turk. With unusual modesty she did not inform anyone of her frequent bathing assignations with this paragon, feeling, as she told us later, that we would not be interested. It was, of course, Spiro who discovered it. He watched over Margo's welfare with the earnest concern of a St Bernard, and there was precious little she could do without Spiro knowing about it. He cornered Mother in the kitchen one morning, glanced surreptitiously round to make sure they were not overheard, sighed deeply, and broke the news to her.

'I'm very sorrys to haves to tells you this, Mrs Durrells,' he rumbled, 'buts I thinks you oughts to knows.'

Mother had by now become quite used to Spiro's conspiratorial air when he came to deliver some item of information about the family and it no longer worried her.

'What's the matter now, Spiro?' she asked.

'It's Missy Margo,' said Spiro sorrowfully.

'What about her?'

Spiro glanced round uneasily.

'Dos you knows shes meetings a *mans*?' he inquired in a vibrant whisper.

'A man? Oh ... er ... yes, I did know,' said Mother, lying valiantly.

Spiro hitched up his trousers over his belly and leant forward.

'But dids you knows he's a *Turk*?' he questioned in tones of blood-curdling ferocity.

'A Turk?' said Mother vaguely. 'No, I didn't know he was a Turk. What's wrong with that?'

Spiro looked horrified.

'Gollys, Mrs Durrells, whats wrongs with it? He's a *Turk*. I wouldn't trust a sonofabitch Turk with any girls. He'll cuts her throats, thats what he'll do. Honest to Gods, Mrs Durrells, its not safe, Missy Margo swimmings with hims.'

'All right, Spiro,' said Mother soothingly, 'I'll speak to Margo about it.'

'I just thoughts you oughts to knows, thats all. Buts donts you worrys . . . if he dids anythings to Missy Margo I'd fix the bastard,' Spiro assured her earnestly.

Acting on the information received, Mother mentioned the matter to Margo, in a slightly less bloodcurdling manner than Spiro's, and suggested that the young Turk be brought up to tea. Delighted, Margo went off to fetch him, while Mother hastily made a cake and some scones, and warned the rest of us to be on our best behaviour. The Turk, when he arrived, turned out to be a tall young man, with meticulously waved hair, a flashy smile that managed to convey the minimum of humour with the maximum of condescension. He had all the sleek, smug self-possession of a cat in season. He pressed Mother's hand to his lips as though he was conferring an honour on her, and scattered the largesse of his smile for the rest of us. Mother, feeling the hackles of the family rising, threw herself desperately into the breach.

'Lovely having you . . . wanted so often . . . never seems time, you know . . . days simply *fly* past . . . Margo's told us so much about you . . . do have a scone . . .' she said breathlessly, smiling with dazzling charm and handing him a piece of cake.

'So kind,' murmured the Turk, leaving us in some doubt as to whether he was referring to us or himself. There was a pause.

'He's on holiday here,' announced Margo suddenly, as though it was something quite unique.

'Really?' said Larry waspishly. 'On holiday? Amazing!'

'I had a holiday once,' said Leslie indistinctly through a mouthful of cake; 'remember it clearly.'

Mother rattled the tea-things nervously, and glared at them.

'Sugar?' she inquired fruitily. 'Sugar in your tea?'

'Thank you, yes.'

There was another short silence, during which we all sat and watched Mother pouring out the tea and searching her mind desperately for a topic of conversation. At length the Turk turned to Larry.

'You write, I believe?' he said with complete lack of interest.

Larry's eyes glittered. Mother, seeing the danger signs, rushed in quickly before he could reply.

'Yes, yes,' she smiled, 'he writes away, day after day. Always tapping at the typewriter.'

'I always feel that I could write superbly if I tried,' remarked the Turk.

'Really?' said Mother. 'Yes, well, it's a gift, I suppose, like so many things.'

'He swims well,' remarked Margo, 'and he goes out terribly far.'

'I have no fear,' said the Turk modestly. 'I am a superb swimmer, so I have no fear. When I ride the horse, I have no fear, for I ride superbly. I can sail the boat magnificently in the typhoon without fear.'

He sipped his tea delicately, regarding our awestruck faces with approval.

'You see,' he went on, in case we had missed the point, 'you see, I am not a fearful man.'

The result of the tea-party was that the next day Margo received a note from the Turk asking her if she would accompany him to the cinema that evening.

'Do you think I ought to go?' she asked Mother.

'If you want to, dear,' Mother answered, adding firmly, 'but tell him I'm coming too.'

'That should be a jolly evening for you,' remarked Larry.

'Oh, Mother, you can't,' protested Margo; 'he'll think it so queer.'

'Nonsense, dear,' said Mother vaguely. 'Turks are quite used to chaperones and things . . . look at their harems.'

So that evening Mother and Margo, dressed becomingly, made their way down the hill to meet the Turk. The only cinema was an open-air one in the town, and we calculated that the show should be over by ten at the latest. Larry, Leslie, and I waited eagerly for their return. At half past one in the morning Margo and Mother, in the last stages of exhaustion, crept into the villa and sank into chairs.

'Oh, so you've come back?' said Larry: 'we thought you'd flown with him. We imagined you galloping about

Constantinople on camels, your yashmaks rippling seductively in the breeze.'

'We've had the most awful evening,' said Mother, easing her shoes off, 'really awful.'

'What happened?' asked Leslie.

'Well, to begin with he stank of the most frightful perfume,' said Margo, 'and that put me off straight away.'

'We went in the cheapest seats, so close to the screen that I got a headache,' said Mother, 'and simply crammed together like sardines. It was *so* oppressive I couldn't breathe. And then, to crown it all, I got a flea. It was nothing to laugh at, Larry; really I didn't know what to do. The blessed thing got inside my corsets and I could feel it running about. I couldn't very well scratch, it would have looked so peculiar. I had to keep pressing myself against the seat. I think he noticed, though . . . he kept giving me funny looks from the corner of his eye. Then in the interval he went out and came back with some of that horrible, sickly Turkish Delight, and before long we were all covered with white sugar, and I had a dreadful thirst. In the second interval he went out and came back with flowers, I ask you, dear, flowers in the middle of the cinema. That's Margo's bouquet, on the table.'

Mother pointed to a massive bunch of spring flowers, tied up in a tangle of coloured ribbons. She delved into her bag and produced a minute bunch of violets that looked as though they had been trodden on by an exceptionally hefty horse.

'This,' she said, 'was for me.'

'But the worst part was coming home,' said Margo.

'A dreadful journey!' Mother agreed. 'When we came out of the cinema I thought we were going to get a car, but no, he hustled us into a cab, and a very smelly one at that. Really I think he must be mental to try and come all that way in a cab. Anyway, it took us hours and *hours*, because the poor horse was tired, and I was sitting there trying to be polite, dying to scratch myself, and longing for a drink. All the fool could do was to sit there grinning at Margo and singing Turkish love-songs. I could have cheerfully hit him. I thought we were *never* going to get back. We couldn't even get rid of him at the bottom of the hill. He insisted on coming up with us, armed with a huge stick, because he said the forests were full of serpents at this time of the year. I was *so* glad to see the back of him. I'm afraid you'll just *have* to choose your boy friends more carefully in future, Margo. I can't go through that sort of thing again. I was terrified he'd come right up to the door and we'd have to ask him in. I thought we'd *never* get away.'

'You obviously didn't make yourself fearful enough,' said Larry.

For Leslie the coming of spring meant the soft pipe of wings as the turtle-doves and wood-pigeons arrived, and the sudden flash and scuttle of a hare among the myrtles. So, after visiting numerous gun-shops and after much technical argument, he returned to the villa one day proudly carrying a double-barrelled shotgun. His first action was to take it to his room, strip it down and clean it, while I stood and watched, fascinated by the gleaming barrels and stock, sniffing rapturously at the rich heavy scent of the gun-oil.

'Isn't she a beauty?' he crooned, more to himself than to me, his vivid blue eyes shining. 'Isn't she a honey?'

Tenderly he ran his hands over the silken shape of the weapon. Then he whipped it suddenly to his shoulder and followed an imaginary flock of birds across the ceiling of the room.

'Pow! ... pow!' he intoned, jerking the gun against his shoulder. 'A left and a right, and down they come.'

He gave the gun a final rub with the oily rag and set it carefully in the corner of the room by his bed.

'We'll have a try for some turtle-doves tomorrow, shall we?' he continued, splitting open a packet and spilling the scarlet shells on to the bed. 'They start coming over about six. That little hill across the valley is a good place.'

So at dawn he and I hurried through the hunched and misty olive-groves, up the valley where the myrtles were wet and squeaky with dew, and on to the top of the little hill. We stood waist-deep among the vines, waiting for the light to strengthen and for the birds to start flighting. Suddenly the pale morning sky was flecked with dark specks, moving as swiftly as arrows, and we could hear the quick wheep of wings. Leslie waited, standing stockily with legs apart, gun-stock resting on his hip, his eyes, intense and gleaming, following the birds. Nearer and nearer they flew, until it seemed that they must fly past us and be lost in the silvery, trembling olive-tops behind. At the very last moment the gun leapt smoothly to his shoulder, the beetle-shiny barrels lifted their mouths to the sky, the gun jerked as the report echoed briefly, like the crack of a great branch in a still forest. The turtle dove, one minute so swift and intent in its flight, now fell languidly to earth, followed by a swirl of soft, cinnamon-coloured feathers. When five doves hung from his belt, limp, bloodstained, with demurely closed eyes, he lit a cigarette, pulled his hat-brim down over his eyes, and cuddled the gun under his arm.

'Come on,' he said; 'we've got enough. Let's give the poor devils a rest.'

We returned through the sun-striped olive-groves where the chaffinches were pinking like a hundred tiny coins among the leaves. Yani, the shepherd, was driving his herd of goats out to graze. His brown face, with its great sweep of nicotine-stained moustache, wrinkled into a smile; a gnarled hand appeared from the heavy folds of his sheepskin cloak and was raised in salute.

'*Chairete*,' he called in his deep voice, the beautiful Greek greeting, '*chairete, kyrioi* . . . be happy.'

The goats poured among the olives, uttering stammering cries to each other, the leader's bell clonking rhythmically. The chaffinches tinkled excitedly. A robin puffed out his chest like a tangerine among the myrtles and gave a trickle of song. The island was drenched with dew, radiant with early morning sun, full of stirring life. Be happy. How could one be anything else in such a season?

# Conversation

As soon as we had settled down and started to enjoy the island, Larry, with characteristic generosity, wrote to all his friends and asked them to come out and stay. The fact that the villa was only just big enough to house the family apparently had not occurred to him.

'I've asked a few people out for a week or so,' he said casually to Mother one morning.

'That will be nice dear,' said Mother unthinkingly.

'I thought it would do us good to have some intelligent and stimulating company around. We don't want to stagnate.'

'I hope they're not too *highbrow* dear,' said Mother.

'Good Lord, Mother, of course *not*; just extremely charming, ordinary people. I don't know why you've got this phobia about people being highbrow.'

'I don't like the highbrow ones,' said Mother plaintively. 'I'm not highbrow, and I can't talk about poetry and things. But they always seem to imagine, just because I'm your mother, that I should be able to discuss literature at great length with them. And they always come and ask me silly questions just when I'm in the middle of cooking.'

'I don't ask you to discuss art with them,' said Larry testily, 'but I think you might try and conceal your revolting taste in literature. Here I fill the house with good books and I find your bedside table simply groaning under the weight of cookery books, gardening books, and the most lurid-looking mystery stories. I can't think where you get hold of these things.'

72

'They're very good detective stories,' said Mother defensively. 'I borrowed them from Theodore.'

Larry gave a short, exasperated sigh and picked up his book again.

'You'd better let the Pension Suisse know when they're coming,' Mother remarked.

'What for?' asked Larry, surprised.

'So they can reserve the rooms,' said Mother, equally surprised.

'But I've invited them to stay here,' Larry pointed out.

'Larry! You haven't! Really, you are most *thoughtless*. How can they possibly stay here?'

'I really don't see what you're making a fuss about,' said Larry coldly.

'But where are they going to *sleep*?' said Mother, distraught. 'There's hardly enough room for us, as it is.'

'Nonsense, Mother, there's plenty of room if the place is organized properly. If Margo and Les sleep out on the veranda, that gives you two rooms; you and Gerry could move into the drawing-room, and that would leave those rooms free.'

'Don't be silly, dear. We can't all camp out all over the place like gypsies. Besides, it's still chilly at night, and I don't think Margo and Les ought to sleep outside. There simply isn't room to entertain in this villa. You'll just have to write to these people and put them off.'

'I can't put them off,' said Larry, 'they're on their way.'

'Really, Larry, you are the most annoying creature. Why on earth didn't you tell me before? You wait until they're nearly here, and then you tell me.'

'I didn't know you were going to treat the arrival of a few friends as if it was a major catastrophe,' Larry explained.

'But, dear, it's so silly to invite people when you know there's no room in the villa.'

'I do wish you'd stop fussing,' said Larry irritably; 'there's quite a simple solution to the whole business.'

'What?' asked Mother suspiciously.

'Well, since the villa isn't big enough, let's move to one that is.'

'Don't be ridiculous. Whoever heard of moving into a larger house because you've invited some friends to stay?'

'What's the matter with the idea? It seems a perfectly sensible solution to me; after all, if you say there's no room here, the obvious thing to do is to move.'

'The obvious thing to do is not to invite people,' said Mother severely.

'I don't think it's good for us to live like hermits,' said Larry. 'I only really invited them for you. They're a charming crowd. I thought you'd like to have them. Liven things up a bit for you.'

'I'm quite lively enough, thank you,' said Mother with dignity.

'Well, I don't know what we're going to do.'

'I really don't see why they can't stay in the Pension Suisse, dear.'

'You can't ask people out to stay with you and then make them live in a third-rate hotel.'

'How many have you invited?' asked Mother.

'Oh, just a few . . . two or three . . . They won't all be coming at once. I expect they'll turn up in batches.'

'I think at least you might be able to tell me how many you've invited,' said Mother.

'Well, I can't remember now. Some of them didn't reply, but that doesn't mean anything . . . they're probably on their way and thought it was hardly worth letting us know. Anyway, if you budget for seven or eight people I should think that would cover it.'

'You mean, including ourselves?'

'No, no, I mean seven or eight people as well as the family.'

'But it's absurd, Larry; we can't possibly fit thirteen people into this villa, with all the good will in the world.'

'Well, let's *move*, then. I've offered you a perfectly sensible solution. I don't know what you're arguing about.'

'But don't be ridiculous, dear. Even if we did move into a villa large enough to house thirteen people, what are we going to do with the extra space when they've gone?'

'Invite some more people,' said Larry, astonished that Mother should not have thought of this simple answer for herself.

Mother glared at him, her spectacles askew.

'Really Larry, you do make me cross,' she said at last.

'I think it's rather unfair that you should blame me because your organization breaks down with the arrival of a few guests,' said Larry austerely.

'A few guests!' squeaked Mother. 'I'm glad you think eight people are a few guests.'

'I think you're adopting a most unreasonable attitude.'

'I suppose there's nothing unreasonable in inviting people and not letting me know?'

Larry gave her an injured look, and picked up his book.

'Well, I've done all I can,' he said: 'I can't do any more.'

There was a long silence, during which Larry placidly read his book and Mother piled bunches of roses into vases and placed them haphazardly round the room, muttering to herself.

'I wish you wouldn't just *lie* there,' she said at last. 'After all, they're your friends. It's up to you to do something.'

Larry, with a long-suffering air, put down his book.

'I really don't know what you expect me to do,' he said. 'Every suggestion I've made you've disagreed with.'

'If you made sensible suggestions I wouldn't disagree.'

'I don't see anything ludicrous in anything I suggested.'

'But, Larry dear, do be reasonable. We can't just rush to a new villa because some people are coming. I doubt whether we'd find one in time, anyway. And there's Gerry's lessons.'

'All that could easily be sorted out it you put your mind to it.'

'We are *not* moving to another villa,' said Mother firmly; 'I've made up my mind about that.'

She straightened her spectacles, gave Larry a defiant glare, and strutted off towards the kitchen, registering determination in every inch.

# PART II

Be not forgetful to entertain strangers:
for thereby some have entertained angels unawares.
*Hebrews xiii:2*

# 7

# The Daffodil-Yellow Villa

The new villa was enormous, a tall, square Venetian mansion, with faded daffodil-yellow walls, green shutters, and a fox-red roof. It stood on a hill overlooking the sea, surrounded by unkempt olive-groves and silent orchards of lemon- and orange-trees. The whole place had an atmosphere of ancient melancholy about it: the house with its cracked and peeling walls, its tremendous echoing rooms, its verandas piled high with drifts of last year's leaves and so overgrown with creepers and vines that the lower rooms were in a perpetual green twilight; the little walled and sunken garden that ran along one side of the house, its wrought-iron gates scabby with rust, had roses, anemones, and geraniums sprawling across the weed-grown paths, and the shaggy, untended tangerine-trees were so thick with flowers that the scent was almost overpowering; beyond the garden the orchards were still and silent, except for the hum of bees and an occasional splutter of birds among the leaves. The house and land were gently, sadly decaying, lying forgotten on the hillside overlooking the shining sea and the dark, eroded hills of Albania. It was as though villa and landscape were half asleep, lying there drugged in the spring sunshine, giving themselves up to the moss, the ferns, and the crowds of tiny toadstools.

It was Spiro, of course, who had found the place, and who organized our move with the minimum of fuss and the maximum of efficiency. Within three days of seeing the villa for the first time the long wooden carts were trailing in a dusty procession along the roads, piled high with our possessions, and on the fourth day we were installed.

At the edge of the estate was a small cottage inhabited by the gardener and his wife, an elderly, rather decrepit pair who seemed to have decayed with the estate. His job was to fill the water-tanks, pick the fruit, crush the olives, and get severely stung once a year extracting honey from the seventeen bee-hives that simmered beneath the lemon-trees. In a moment of misguided enthusiasm Mother engaged the gardener's wife to work for us in the villa. Her name was Lugaretzia, and she was a thin, lugubrious individual, whose hair was forever coming adrift from the ramparts of pins and combs with which she kept it attached to her skull. She was extremely sensitive, as Mother soon discovered, and the slightest criticism of her work, however tactfully phrased, would make her brown eyes swim with tears in an embarrassing display of grief. It was such a heart-rending sight to watch that Mother very soon gave up criticizing her altogether.

There was only one thing in life that could bring a smile to Lugaretzia's gloomy countenance, a glint to her spaniel eyes, and that was a discussion of her ailments. Where most people are hypochondriacs as a hobby, Lugaretzia had turned it into a full-time occupation. When we took up residence it was her stomach that was worrying her. Bulletins on the state of her stomach would start at seven in the morning when she brought up the tea. She would move from room to room with the trays, giving each one of us a blow-by-blow account of her nightly bout with her inside. She was a master of the art of graphic description; groaning, gasping, doubling up in agony, stamping about the rooms, she would give us such a realistic picture of her suffering that we would find our own stomachs aching in sympathy.

'Can't you *do* something about that woman?' Larry asked Mother one morning, after Lugaretzia's stomach had been through a particularly bad night.

'What do you expect me to do?' she asked. 'I gave her some of your bicarbonate of soda.'

'That probably accounts for her bad night.'

'I'm sure she doesn't *eat* properly,' said Margo. 'What she probably wants is a good diet.'

'Nothing short of a bayonet would do her stomach any good,' said Larry caustically, 'and I know ... during the last week I have become distressingly familiar with every tiny convolution of her larger intestine.'

'I know she's a bit trying,' said Mother, 'but, after all, the poor woman is obviously suffering.'

'Nonsense,' said Leslie; 'she enjoys every minute of it. Like Larry does when he's ill.'

'Well, anyway,' said Mother hurriedly, 'we'll just have to put up with her; there's no one else we can get locally. I'll get Theodore to look her over next time he comes out.'

'If all she told me this morning was true,' said Larry, 'you'll have to provide him with a pick and a miner's lamp.'

'Larry, don't be disgusting,' said Mother severely.

Shortly afterwards, to our relief, Lugaretzia's stomach got better, but almost immediately her feet gave out, and she would hobble pitifully round the house, groaning loudly and frequently. Larry said that Mother hadn't hired a maid, but a ghoul, and suggested buying her a ball and chain. He pointed out that this would at least let us know when she was coming, and allow us time to escape, for Lugaretzia had developed the habit of creeping up behind one and groaning loudly and unexpectedly in one's ear. Larry started having breakfast in his bedroom after the morning when Lugaretzia took off her shoes in the dining-room in order to show us exactly which toes were hurting.

But, apart from Lugaretzia's ailments, there were other snags in the house. The furniture (which we had rented with the villa) was a fantastic collection of Victorian relics that had been locked in the rooms for the past twenty years. They crouched everywhere, ugly, ungainly, unpractical, creaking hideously to each other, and shedding bits of themselves with loud cracks like musket-shots, accompanied by clouds of dust if you walked past them too heavily. The first evening the leg came off the dining-room table, cascading the food on to the floor. Some days later Larry sat down on an immense and solid-looking chair, only to have the back disappear in a cloud of acrid dust. When Mother went to open a wardrobe the size of a cottage and the entire door came away in her hand, she decided that something must be done.

'We simply can't have people to stay in a house where everything comes to bits if you look at it,' she said. 'There's nothing for it, we'll have to buy some new furniture. Really, these guests are going to be the most expensive we've ever had.'

The next morning Spiro drove Mother, Margo and myself into the town to buy furniture. We noticed that the town was more crowded, more boisterous, than usual, but it never occurred to us that anything special was happening until we had finished bargaining with the dealer and made our way out of his shop into the narrow, twisted streets. We were jostled and pushed as we struggled to get back to the place where we had left the car. The crowd grew thicker and thicker, and the people were so tightly wedged together that we were carried forward against our will.

'I think there must be something going on,' said Margo observantly. 'Maybe it's a fiesta or something interesting.'

'I don't care *what* it is, as long as we get back to the car,' said Mother.

But we were swept along, in the opposite direction to the car, and eventually pushed out to join a vast crowd assembled in the main square of the town. I asked an elderly peasant woman near me what was happening, and she turned to me, her face lit up with pride.

'It is Saint Spiridion, *kyria*,' she explained. 'Today we may enter the church and kiss his feet.'

Saint Spiridion was the patron saint of the island. His mummified body was enshrined in a silver coffin in the church, and once a year he was carried in a procession round the town. He was very powerful, and could grant requests, cure illness, and do a number of other wonderful things for you if he happened to be in the right mood when asked. The islanders worshipped him, and every second male on the island was called Spiro in his honour. Today was a special day; apparently they would open the coffin and allow the faithful to kiss the slippered feet of the mummy, and make any request they cared to. The composition of the crowd showed how well loved the saint was by the Corfiots: there were elderly peasant women in their best black clothes, and their husbands, hunched as olive-trees, with sweeping white moustaches; there were fishermen, bronzed and muscular, with the dark stains of octopus ink on their shirts; there were the sick too, the mentally defective, the consumptive, the crippled, old people who could hardly walk, and babies wrapped and bound like cocoons, their pale, waxy little faces crumpled up as they coughed and coughed. There were even a few tall, wild-looking Albanian shepherds, moustached and with shaven heads, wearing great sheepskin cloaks. This dark multi-coloured wedge of humanity moved slowly towards the dark door of the church, and we were swept along with it, wedged like pebbles in a larva-flow. By now Margo had been pushed well ahead of me, while Mother was equally far behind. I was caught firmly between five fat peasant women, who pressed on me like cushions and exuded sweat and garlic, while Mother was hopelessly entangled between two of the enormous Albanian shepherds. Steadily, firmly, we were pushed up the steps and into the church.

Inside, it was dark as a well, lit only by a bed of candles that bloomed like yellow crocuses along one wall. A bearded, tall-hatted priest clad in black robes flapped like a crow in the gloom, making the crowd form into a single line that filed down the church, past the great silver coffin, and out through another door into the street. The coffin was standing upright, looking like a silver chrysalis, and at its lower end a portion had been removed so that the saint's feet, clad in the richly-embroidered slippers, peeped out. As each person reached the coffin he bent, kissed the feet, and murmured a prayer, while at the top of the sarcophagus the saint's black and withered face peered out of a glass panel with an expression of acute distaste. It became evident that, whether we wanted to or not, we were going to kiss Saint Spiridion's feet. I looked back and saw Mother making frantic efforts to get to my side, but the Albanian bodyguard would not give an inch, and she struggled ineffectually. Presently she caught my eye and started to grimace and point at the coffin, shaking her head vigorously. I was greatly puzzled by this, and so were the two Albanians, who were watching her with undisguised suspicion. I think they came to the conclusion that Mother was about to have a fit, and with some justification, for she was scarlet in the face, and her grimaces were getting wilder and wilder. At last, in desperation, she threw caution to the winds and hissed at me over the heads of the crowd:

'Tell Margo . . . *not* to kiss . . . kiss the air . . . kiss the air.'

I turned to deliver Mother's message to Margo, but it was too late; there she was, crouched over the slippered feet, kissing them with an enthusiasm that enchanted and greatly surprised the crowd. When it came to my turn I obeyed Mother's instructions, kissing loudly and with a considerable show of reverence a point some six inches above the mummy's left foot. Then I was pushed along and disgorged through the church door and out into the street, where the crowd was breaking up into little groups, laughing and chattering. Margo was waiting on the steps, looking extremely self-satisfied. The next moment Mother appeared, shot from the door by the brawny shoulders of her shepherds. She staggered wildly down the steps and joined us.

81

'Those *shepherds*,' she exclaimed faintly. 'So ill-mannered . . . the smell nearly killed me . . . a mixture of incense and garlic . . . How do they manage to smell like that?'

'Oh, well,' said Margo cheerfully. 'It'll have been worth it if Saint Spiridion answers my request.'

A most *insanitary* procedure,' said Mother, 'more likely to spread disease than cure it. I dread to think what we would have caught if we'd *really* kissed his feet.'

'But I kissed his feet,' said Margo, surprised.

'Margo! You didn't!'

'Well, everyone else was doing it.'

'And after I expressly told you *not* to.'

'You never told me not to . . .'

I interrupted and explained that I had been too late with Mother's warning.

'After all those people have been slobbering over those slippers you have to go and kiss them.'

'I was only doing what the others did.'

'I can't think what on earth possessed you to *do* such a thing.'

'Well, I thought he might cure my acne.'

'Acne!' said Mother scornfully. 'You'll be lucky if you don't catch something to go with the acne.'

The next day Margo went down with a severe attack of influenza, and Saint Spiridion's prestige with Mother reached rock bottom. Spiro was sent racing into the town for a doctor, and he returned bringing a little dumpy man with patent-leather hair, a faint wisp of moustache, and boot-button eyes behind great horn-rimmed spectacles.

This was Doctor Androuchelli. He was a charming man, with a bedside manner that was quite unique.

'Po-po-po,' he said, strutting into the bedroom and regarding Margo with scorn, 'po-po-*po*! Remarkably unintelligent you have been, no? Kissing the Saint's feet! Po-po-po-po-po! Nearly you might have caught some bugs unpleasant. You are lucky; she is influenza. Now you will do as I tell you, or I will rinse my hands of you. And please do not increase my work with such stupidity. If you kiss another saint's feet in the future I will not come to cure you . . . Po-po-po . . . such a thing to do.'

So while Margo languished in bed for three weeks, with Androuchelli po-po-ing over her every two or three days, the rest of us settled into the villa. Larry took possession of one enormous attic and engaged two carpenters to make bookshelves; Leslie converted the large covered veranda behind the house into a shooting-gallery, and hung an enormous red flag up outside whenever he was practising; Mother pottered absent-mindedly round the vast, subterranean, stone-flagged kitchen, preparing gallons of beef-tea and trying to listen to Lugaretzia's monologues and worry about Margo at the same time. For Roger and myself, of course, there were fifteen acres of garden to explore, a vast new paradise sloping down to the shallow, tepid sea. Being temporarily without a tutor (for George had left the island) I could spend the whole day out, only returning to the villa for hurried meals.

In this varied terrain so close at hand I found many creatures which I now regarded as old friends: the rose-beetles, the blue carpenter-bees, the lady-birds, and the trapdoor spiders. But I also discovered many new beasts to occupy me. In the crumbling walls of the sunken garden lived dozens of little black scorpions, shining and polished as if they had been made out of bakelite; in the fig- and lemon-trees just below the garden were quantities of emerald-green tree-frogs, like delicious satiny sweets among the leaves; up on the hillside lived snakes of various sorts, brilliant lizards and tortoises. In the fruit orchards there were many kinds of birds: goldfinches, greenfinches, redstarts, wagtails, orioles, and an occasional hoopoe, salmon-pink, black, and white, probing the soft ground with long curved beaks, erecting their crests in astonishment when they saw me, and flying off.

Under the eaves of the villa itself the swallows had taken up residence. They had arrived a short time before we had, and their knobbly mud houses were only just completed, still dark brown and damp like rich plum cake. As these were drying to a lighter biscuit brown, the parent birds were busy lining them, foraging round the garden for rootlets, lambs' wool, or feathers. Two of the swallows' nests were lower than the others, and it was on these that I concentrated my attention. Over a period of days I leant a long ladder against the wall, midway between the two nests, and then slowly, day by day, I climbed higher and higher, until I could sit on the top rung and look into the nests, now some four feet away from me. The parent birds seemed in no way disturbed by my presence, and continued their stern work of preparing for a family, while I crouched on top of the ladder, and Roger lay at the bottom.

I grew to know these swallow families very well, and watched their daily work with considerable interest. What I took to be the two females were very similar in behaviour, earnest, rather preoccupied, over-anxious, and fussy. The two males, on the other hand, displayed totally different characters. One of them, during the work of lining the nest, brought excellent material, but he refused to treat it as a job of work. He would come swooping home, carrying a wisp of sheep's wool in his mouth, and would waste several minutes skating low over the flowers in the garden, drawing figures of eight, or else weaving in and out of the columns that held up the grape-vine. His wife would cling to the nest and chitter at him exasperatedly, but he refused to take life seriously. The other female also had trouble with her mate, but it was trouble of a different sort. He was, if anything, over-enthusiastic. He seemed determined to leave no stone unturned in his efforts to provide his young with the finest nest-lining in the colony. But, unfortunately, he was no mathematician, and, try as he would, he could not remember the size of his nest. He would come flying back, twittering in an excited if somewhat muffled manner, carrying a chicken or turkey feather as big as himself, and with such a thick quill it was impossible to bend it. It would generally take his wife several minutes to convince him that, no matter how they struggled and juggled, the feather would not fit into the nest. Acutely disappointed he would eventually drop the feather so that it whirlpooled down to join the ever-increasing pile on the ground beneath, and then fly off in search of something more suitable. In a little while he would be back, struggling under a load of sheep's wool so matted and hard with earth and dung that he would have difficulty in getting up to the eaves, let alone into the nest.

When at last the nests were lined, the freckled eggs laid and hatched, the two husbands' characters seemed to change. The one who had brought so much futile nest-lining now swooped and hawked about the hillsides in a carefree manner and would come drifting back carelessly carrying a mouthful of insect life of just the right size and softness to appeal to his fuzzy trembling brood. The other male now became terribly harassed and apparently a prey to the dreadful thought that his babies might starve. So he would wear himself to a shadow in the pursuit of food, and return carrying the most unsuitable items, such as large spiky beetles, all legs and wing-case, and immense, dry, and completely indigestible dragon-flies. He would cling to the edge of the nest and make valiant but vain attempts to get these gigantic offerings rammed down the ever-open gullet of his young. I dread to think what would have happened if he had succeeded in wedging one of these spiky captures down their throats. Luckily, however, he never succeeded, and eventually, looking more harassed than ever, he would drop the insect on to the ground and fly off hurriedly in search of something else. I was very grateful to this swallow, for he provided me with three species of butterfly, six dragon-flies, and two ant-lions which were new to my collection.

The females, once the young were hatched, behaved in much the same way as they had always done: they flew a little faster, there was an air of brisk efficiency about them, but that was all. It intrigued me to see for the first time the hygienic arrangements of a bird's nest. I had often wondered, when hand-rearing a young bird, why it hoisted its bottom skywards with much waggling when it wanted to excrete. Now I discovered the reason. The excreta of the baby swallows was produced in globules which were coated with mucus that formed what was almost a gelatine packet round the dropping. The young would stand on their heads, waggle their bottoms in a brief but enthusiastic rumba, and deposit their little offerings on the rim of the nest. When the females arrived they could cram the food they had collected down the gaping throats, and then delicately pick up the dropping in their beaks and fly off to deposit it somewhere over the olive-groves. It was an admirable arrangement, and I would watch the whole performance fascinated, from the bottom-waggle – which always made me giggle – to the final swoop of the parent over the tree-top, and the dropping of the little black-and-white bomb earthwards.

Owing to the male swallow's habit of collecting strange and unsuitable insects for his young, I always used to examine the area below the nest twice a day, in the hope of finding new specimens to add to my collection. It was here that, one morning, I found the most extraordinary-looking beetle crawling about. I did not think that even that mentally defective swallow could have brought back such a large creature, or even that he could have caught it, but it was certainly there, underneath the colony. It was a large, clumsy, blue-black beetle, with a large round head, long jointed antennae, and a bulbous body. The weird thing about it was its wing-cases; it looked as though it had sent them to the laundry and they had shrunk, for they were very small and appeared to have been constructed for a beetle half the size. I toyed with the idea that it may have found itself without a pair of clean wing-cases to put on that morning and had to borrow its younger brother's pair, but I eventually decided that this idea, however enchanting, could not be described as scientific. I noticed, after I had picked it up, that my fingers smelled faintly acrid and oily, though it had not appeared to have exuded any liquid that I could see. I gave it to Roger to smell, to see if he agreed with me, and he sneezed violently and backed away, so I concluded that it must be the beetle and not my hand. I preserved it carefully, so that Theodore could identify it when he came.

Now that the warm days of spring had arrived, Theodore would come out to the villa every Thursday for tea, arriving in a horse-drawn cab from the town, his immaculate suit, stiff collar, and homburg hat making a strange contrast to the nets, bags, and boxes full of test-tubes with which he was surrounded. Before tea we would examine any new specimens I had acquired and identify them. After tea we would wander about the grounds in search of creatures, or else make what Theodore would call an excursion to some neighbouring pond or ditch in search of new microscopic life for Theodore's collection. He identified my strange beetle, with its ill-fitting electra, without much trouble, and proceeded to tell me some extraordinary things about it.

'Ah ha! Yes,' he said, closely scrutinizing the beast, 'it's an oil-beetle ... *meloe proscaraboeus* ... Yes ... they are certainly very curious-looking beetles. What d'you say? Ah, yes, the wing-cases ... Well, you see they are flightless. There are several species of coleoptera that have lost the power of flight, for one reason or another. It is the life-history of this beetle that is very curious. This, of course, is a female. The male is considerably smaller – I should say approximately half the size. It appears that the female lays a number of small yellow eggs in the oil. When these hatch out into larvae they climb up any flowers nearby and wait inside the blooms. There is a certain type of solitary bee which they must wait for, and when it enters the flower, the larvae ... hitch-hike ... er ... get a good grip with their claws on the bee's fur. If they are lucky, the bee is a female who is collecting honey to put in the cells with her egg. Then as soon as the bee has completed the filling of the cell and lays her egg, the larva jumps off on to the egg, and the bee closes the cell. Then the larva eats the egg and develops inside the cell. The thing that always strikes me as curious is that there is only *one* species of bee that the larvae prey on. I should have thought that a great many of the larvae catch hold of the wrong species of bee, and so eventually *die*. Then, of course, even if it's the *right* kind of bee, there is no . . . um . . . guarantee that it's a female about to lay eggs.'

He paused for a moment, raised himself on his toes several times, and thoughtfully contemplated the floor. Then he looked up, his eyes twinkling.

'I mean to say,' he continued, 'it's rather like backing a horse in a race . . . um . . . with the odds heavily against you.'

He waggled the glass-topped box gently so that the beetle slid from one end to the other, waving its antennae in surprise. Then he put it carefully back on the shelf among my other specimens.

'Talking of horses,' said Theodore happily, placing his hands on his hips and rocking gently, 'did I ever tell you about the time when I led the triumphant entry into Smyrna on a white charger? Well, it was in the First World War, you know, and the commander of my battalion was determined that we should march into Smyrna in a . . . er . . . triumphal column, led, if possible, by a man on a white horse. Unfortunately, they gave me the doubtful privilege of leading the troops. Of course, I had learnt to ride, you know, but I would not consider myself . . . um . . . an expert horseman. Well, everything went very well, and the horse behaved with great decorum, until we got into the outskirts of the town. It is custom in parts of Greece, as you know, to throw scent, perfume, rose-water, or something of the sort over the . . . er . . . conquering heroes. As I was riding along at the head of the column, an old woman darted out of a side street and started to hurl eau-de-Cologne about. The horse did not mind *that*, but most unfortunately a small quantity of the scent must have splashed into his *eye*. Well, he was quite used to parades and so forth, and cheering crowds and things, but he was not used to having his eye squirted full of eau-de-Cologne. He became . . . er . . . most upset about it and was acting more like a circus horse than a charger. I only managed to stay on because my feet had become wedged in the stirrups. The column had to break ranks to try to calm him down, but he was so upset that eventually the commander decided it would be unwise to let him take part in the rest of the triumphal entry. So while the column marched through the main streets with bands playing and people cheering and so forth, I was forced to slink through the back streets on my white horse, both of us, to add insult to injury, by now smelling very strongly of eau-de-Cologne. Um . . . I have never really *enjoyed* horse-riding since then.'

# 8

# The Tortoise Hills

Behind the village there was a series of small hills that raised
shaggy crests above the surrounding olive-groves. They were
hills covered with great beds of green myrtle, tall heather,
and a patchy feathering of cypress-trees. This was probably
the most fascinating area of the whole garden, for it was
overflowing with life. In the sandy paths the ant-lion larvae
dug their little cone-shaped pits, and lay in wait to spatter any
unwary ant that stepped over the edge with a bombardment
of sand that would send it tumbling down to the bottom of
the trap, to be seized in the ant-lion larva's terrible, pincer-like
jaws. In the red sand-banks the hunting wasps were digging
their tunnels, and hawking low in pursuit of spiders; they
would stab with their sting, paralysing them and carrying
them off to serve as food for their larvae. Among the
heather-blooms the great fat, furry caterpillars of emperor
moths fed slowly, looking like animated fur collars. Among
the myrtles in the warm, scented twilight of their leaves, the
mantids prowled, heads turning this way and that as they
watched for prey. Among the cypress branches the chaffinches
had their neat nests, full of gawping, goggle-eyed babies; and
on the lower branches the goldcrests weaved their tiny fragile
cups of moss and hair, or foraged for insects, hanging upside
down on the ends of the branches, giving almost inaudible
squeaks of joy at the discovery of a tiny spider or a gnat, their
golden crests gleaming like little forage caps as they flipped
daintily through the gloom of the tree.

It was not long after we arrived at the villa that I discovered
these hills really belonged to the tortoises. One hot afternoon
Roger and I were concealed behind a bush, waiting patiently

for a large swallow-tail butterfly to return to its favourite sunning patch, so that we might capture it. It was the first really hot day we had had that year, and everything seemed to be lying drugged and asleep, soaking up the sun. The swallow-tail was in no hurry; he was down by the olive-groves doing a ballet dance by himself, twisting, diving, pirouetting in the sun. As we watched him, I saw, from the corner of my eye, a faint movement at one side of the bush we were sheltering behind. I glanced quickly to see what it was, but the brown earth was sun-drenched and empty of life. I was just about to turn my attention to the butterfly again when I saw something that I could hardly believe: the patch of earth I had been looking at suddenly heaved upwards, as though pushed by a hand from beneath; the soil cracked and a tiny seedling waved about wildly before its pale roots gave way and it fell on its side.

What I wondered, could be the cause of this sudden eruption? An earthquake? Surely not so small and confined. A mole? Not in such dry and waterless terrain. As I was speculating, the earth gave another heave, clods of it cracked off and rolled away, and I was looking at a brown and yellow shell. More earth was swept out of the way as the shell bucked upwards, and then, slowly and cautiously, a wrinkled, scaly head appeared out of the hole, a long, skinny neck followed it. The bleary eyes blinked once or twice as the tortoise surveyed me; then, deciding I must be harmless, he hoisted himself with infinite care and effort out of his earth cell, walked two or three steps, and sank down in the sunshine, drowsing gently. After the long winter under the damp and chilly soil, that first sun-bath must have been like a drink of wine to the reptile. His legs were spread out from his shell, his neck extended as far as it could, his head resting on the ground; with eyes closed, the creature seemed to be absorbing sunshine through every bit of his body and shell. He remained lying there for about ten minutes, and then he rose, slowly and deliberately, and rolled off down the path to where a patch of dandelion and clover spread in the shade of a cypress. Here his legs seemed to give way and he collapsed on to the bottom of his shell with a thump. Then his head appeared from his shell, bent slowly down towards the rich green pile of the clover patch, his mouth opened wide, there was a moment's suspense, and then his mouth closed round the succulent leaves, his head jerked back to tear them off and he sat there munching happily, his mouth stained with the first food of the year.

This must have been the first tortoise of spring, and as if his appearance from the subterranean dormitory was a signal, the hills suddenly became covered with tortoises. I have never seen so many congregated in so small an area: big ones the size of a soup plate and little ones the size of a cup, chocolate-coloured great-grandfathers and pale, horn-coloured youngsters, all lumbering heavily along the sandy paths, in and out of the heather and myrtles, occasionally descending to the olive-groves where the vegetation was more succulent. Sitting in one spot for an hour or so you could count as many as ten tortoises pass you, and on one afternoon, as an experiment, I collected thirty-five specimens in two hours, just walking about the hillside and picking them up as they wandered about with an air of preoccupied determination, their club feet thumping on the ground.

No sooner had the shelled owners of the hills appeared from their winter quarters and had their first meal, than the males became romantically inclined. Stalking along on tip-toe with stumbling rapidity, their necks stretched out to the fullest extent, they would set out in search of a mate, pausing now and then to give a strange, yawping cry, the passionate love-song of a male tortoise. The females, ambling heavily through the heather and pausing now and then for a snack, would answer in an off-hand manner. Two or three males, travelling at what – for a tortoise – was a gallop, would generally converge on the same female. They would arrive, out of breath and inflamed with passion, and glare at each other, their throats gulping convulsively. Then they would prepare to do battle.

These battles were exciting and interesting to watch, resembling all-in wrestling more than boxing, for the combatants did not possess either speed or the physical grace to indulge in fancy footwork. The general idea was for one to charge his rival as rapidly as possible, and just before impact to duck his head into his shell. The best blow was considered to be the broadside, for this gave the opportunity – by wedging yourself against your rival's shell and pushing hard – of overturning him and leaving him flapping helplessly on his back. If they couldn't manage to get in a broadside, any other part of the rival's anatomy did just as well. Charging each other, straining and pushing, their shells clattering together, occasionally taking a slow-motion bite at each other's necks or retreating into their shells with a hiss, the males would do battle. Meanwhile the object of their frenzy would amble slowly onwards, pausing now and then for a bite to eat, apparently unconcerned by the scraping and cracking of shells behind her. On more than one occasion these battles became so furious that a male in a fit of misplaced enthusiasm would deliver a broadside to his lady-love by mistake. She would merely fold herself into her shell with an outraged sniff, and wait patiently until the battle had passed her by. These fights seemed to me the most ill-organized and unnecessary affairs, for it was not always the strongest tortoise that won; with good terrain in his favour a small specimen could easily overturn one twice his size. Nor, indeed, was it invariably one of the warriors that got the lady, for on several occasions I saw a female wander away from a pair of fighting males to be accosted by a complete stranger (who had not even chipped his shell on her behalf) and go off with him quite happily.

Roger and I would squat by the hour in the heather, watching the tortoise knights in their ill-fitting armour jousting for the ladies, and the contests never failed to entertain us. Sometimes we would lay bets with each other as to which one was going to win, and by the end of the summer Roger had backed so many losers that he owed me a considerable amount of money. Sometimes, when the battle was very fierce, Roger would get carried away by the spirit of the thing and want to join in, and I would have to restrain him.

When the lady had eventually made her choice, we would follow the happy couple on their honeymoon among the myrtles, and even watch (discreetly hidden behind the bushes) the final acts in the romantic drama. The wedding night – or rather day – of a tortoise is not exactly inspiring. To begin with, the female performs in a disgracefully coy manner, and becomes heavily skittish in evading her bridegroom's attentions. She irritates him in this way until he is forced to adopt cave-man tactics, and subdues her maidenly antics with a few short, sharp broadsides. The actual sexual act was the most awkward and fumbling thing I had ever seen. The incredibly heavy-handed and inexpert way the male would attempt to hoist himself on to the female's shell, slipping and slithering, clawing desperately for a foothold on the shiny shields, overbalancing and almost overturning, was extremely painful to watch; the urge to go and assist the poor creature was almost overwhelming, and I had the greatest difficulty in restraining myself from interference. Once a male was infinitely more bungling than usual, and fell down three times during the mounting, and generally behaved in such an imbecile manner I was beginning to wonder if he were going to take all summer about it ... At last, more by luck than skill, he hoisted himself up, and I was just heaving a sigh of relief when the female, obviously bored by the male's inadequacy, moved a few steps towards a dandelion leaf. Her husband clawed wildly at her moving shell, but could get no foothold; he slipped off, teetered for a minute, and then rolled ignominiously over on to his back. This final blow seemed to be too much for him, because, instead of trying to right himself, he simply folded himself up in his shell and lay there mournfully. The female, meanwhile, ate the dandelion leaf. At last, since his passion seemed to have died, I rolled the male over, and after a minute or so he wandered off, peering about him in a dazed fashion, and ignoring his erstwhile bride, who regarded him unemotionally, her mouth full of food. As a punishment for her callous behaviour I carried her up to the most barren and desiccated part of the hillside and left her there, so that she would have an extremely long walk to the nearest clover patch.

I came to know many of the tortoises by sight, so closely and enthusiastically did I watch their daily lives. Some I could recognize by their shape and colour, others by some physical defect – a chip from the edge of their shells, the loss of a toe-nail, and so on. There was one large, honey-and-tar coloured female who was unmistakable, for she had only one eye. I got on such intimate terms with her that I christened her Madame Cyclops. She came to know me quite well, and, realizing that I meant her no harm, she would not disappear into her shell at my approach, but stretch up her neck to see if I had brought her a tit-bit in the shape of a lettuce leaf or some tiny snails, of which she was inordinately fond. She would roll about her business quite happily, while Roger and I followed her, and occasionally, as a special treat, we would carry her down to the olive-groves for a picnic lunch on the clover. To my infinite regret I was not present at her wedding, but I was lucky enough to witness the outcome of the honeymoon.

I found her one day busily engaged in digging a hole in the soft soil at the base of a bank. She had dug to a fair depth when I arrived, and seemed quite glad to have a rest and a little refreshment in the shape of some clover flowers. Then she set to work once more, scraping the earth out with her fore-feet and barging it to one side with her shell. Not being quite certain what she was trying to achieve, I did not attempt to help her, but merely lay on my stomach in the heather and watched. After some time, when she had excavated quite a pile of earth, she carefully scrutinized the hole from all angles and was apparently satisfied. She turned round, lowered her hind end over the hole, and sat there with a rapt look on her face while she absent-mindedly laid nine white eggs. I was most surprised and delighted, and congratulated her heartily on this achievement, while she gulped at me in a meditative sort of way. She then proceeded to scrape the soil back over the eggs and pat it down firmly by the simple method of standing over it and flopping down on her tummy several times. This task accomplished, she had a rest and accepted the remains of the clover blooms.

I found myself in an awkward position, for I dearly wanted one of the eggs to add to my collection; I did not like to take it while she was there, for fear that she might feel insulted and perhaps dig up the remaining eggs and eat them, or do something equally horrible. So I had to sit and wait patiently while she finished her snack, had a short doze, and then ambled off among the bushes. I followed her for some distance to make sure she did not turn back, and then hurried to the nest and carefully unearthed one of the eggs. It was about the size of a pigeon's, oval in shape and with a rough, chalky shell. I patted the earth back over the nest so that she would never know it had been disturbed, and carried my trophy triumphantly back to the villa. I blew the sticky yolk out of it with great care, and enshrined the shell among my natural history collection in a small glass-topped box of its own. The label, which was a nice blend of scientific and sentimental, read: *Egg of Greek Tortoise (Testudo graeca). Laid by Madame Cyclops.*

Throughout the spring and early summer, while I was studying the courtship of the tortoises, the villa was filled with an apparently endless stream of Larry's friends. No sooner had we seen one lot off, and sighed with relief, than another steamer would arrive, and the line of taxis and horse-carriages would hoot and clatter their way up the drive, and the house would be filled once more. Sometimes the fresh load of guests would turn up before we had got rid of the previous group, and the chaos was indescribable; the house and garden would be dotted with poets, authors, artists, and playwrights arguing, painting, drinking, typing, and composing. Far from being the ordinary, charming people that Larry had promised, they all turned out to be the most extraordinary eccentrics who were so highbrow that they had difficulty in understanding one another.

One of the first to arrive was Zatopec, an Armenian poet, a short, stocky individual with a swooping eagle nose, a shoulder-length mane of silvery hair and hands bulbous and twisted by arthritis. He arrived wearing an immense, swirling black cloak and a broad-brimmed black hat, riding in a carriage piled high with wine. His voice shook the house like a sirocco as he swept into it, his cloak rippling, his arms full of bottles. He scarcely stopped talking the whole time he stayed. He talked from morning till night, drinking prodigious quantities of wine, snatching forty winks wherever he happened to be and rarely going to bed at all. In spite of his advanced years he had lost none of his enthusiasm for the opposite sex, and, while he treated Mother and Margo with a sort of creaking, antique courtesy, no peasant girl for miles was free from his attentions. He would hobble through the olive-groves after them, roaring with laughter, shouting endearments, his cloak flapping behind him, his pocket bulging with a bottle of wine. Even Lugaretzia was not safe, and had her bottom pinched while she was sweeping under the sofa. This proved something of a blessing, as it made her forget her ailments for a few days, and blush and giggle kittenishly whenever Zatopec appeared. Eventually Zatopec departed as he had arrived, lying back regally in a cab, his cloak wrapped round him, shouting endearments to us as it clopped off down the drive, promising to return soon from Bosnia and bring some more wine for us.

The next invasion consisted of three artists, Jonquil, Durant, and Michael. Jonquil looked, and sounded, like a cockney owl with a fringe; Durant was lank and mournful and so nervous that he would almost jump out of his skin if you spoke to him suddenly; by contrast, Michael was a short, fat, somnambulistic little man who looked like a well-boiled prawn with a mop of dark curly hair. These three had only one thing in common, and that was a desire to get some work done. Jonquil, on striding into the house for the first time, made this quite clear to a startled Mother.

'I didn't come for no bleeding 'oliday,' she said severely; 'I came to get some work done, so I'm not interested in picnics and such, see?'

'Oh ... er ... no, no, of course not,' said Mother guiltily, as though she had been planning vast banquets among the myrtle bushes for Jonquil's benefit.

'Jus' so long as you know,' said Jonquil. 'I didn't want to upset nothing, see? I jus' want to get some work done.'

So she promptly retired to the garden, clad in a bathing costume, and slept peacefully in the sun throughout her stay.

Durant, he informed us, wanted to work too, but first he had to get his nerve back. He was shattered, he told us, quite shattered by his recent experience. Apparently, while in Italy he had suddenly been seized with the desire to paint a masterpiece. After much thought he decided that an almond orchard in full bloom should give a certain scope to his brush. He spent considerable time and money driving about the countryside in search of the right orchard. At long last he found the perfect one, the setting was magnificent, and the blooms were full and thick. Feverishly he set to work, and by the end of the first day he had got the basis down on canvas. Tired, but satisfied, he packed up his things and returned to the village. After a good night's sleep he awoke refreshed and invigorated, and rushed back to the orchard to complete his picture. On arrival there he was struck dumb with horror and amazement, for every tree was gaunt and bare, while the ground was thickly carpeted with pink and white petals. Apparently during the night a spring storm had playfully stripped all the orchards in the vicinity of their blossom, including Durant's special one.

'I vas stricken,' he told us, his voice quivering, his eyes filled with tears. 'I swore I vould never paint again . . . never! But slowly I am recovering my nerves . . . I am feeling less shattered . . . Some time I vill start to paint again.'

On inquiry, it turned out that this unfortunate experience had taken place two years previously, and Durant had still not recovered from it.

Michael got off to a bad start. He was captivated by the colouring of the island, and told us enthusiastically that he would begin work on an immense canvas that would capture the very essence of Corfu. He could hardly wait to start. It was most unfortunate that he happened to be a prey to asthma. It was equally unfortunate that Lugaretzia had placed on a chair in his room a blanket which I used for horse-riding, there being no saddles available. In the middle of the night we were awakened by a noise that sounded like a troop of bloodhounds being slowly strangled. Assembling sleepily in Michael's room we found him wheezing and gasping, the sweat running down his face. While Margo rushed to make some tea, Larry to get some brandy and Leslie opened the windows, Mother put Michael back to bed, and, since he was now clammy with sweat, tenderly covered him with the horse-blanket. To our surprise, in spite of all remedies, he got worse. While he could still speak, we questioned him interestedly about his complaint and its cause.

'Psychological, purely psychological,' said Larry. 'What does the wheezing sound remind you of?'

Michael shook his head mutely.

'I think he ought to sniff something up . . . something like ammonia or something,' said Margo. 'It's wonderful if you're going to faint.'

'Well, he's not going to faint,' said Leslie tersely, 'but he probably would if he sniffed ammonia.'

'Yes, dear, it is a bit strong,' said Mother. 'I wonder what could have brought it on . . . Are you allergic to something, Michael?'

Between gasps Michael informed us that he was only allergic to three things: the pollen of the lilac flowers, cats, and horses. We all peered out of the window, but there was not a lilac-tree for miles. We searched the room, but there was no cat hidden anywhere. I indignantly denied Larry's accusation that I had smuggled a horse into the house. It was only when Michael seemed on the verge of death that we noticed the horse-rug, which Mother had tucked carefully under his chin. This incident had such a bad effect on the poor man that he was quite unable to put a brush to canvas during his stay; he and Durant lay side by side in deckchairs, recovering their nerve together.

While we were still coping with these three, another guest arrived in the shape of Melanie, Countess de Torro. She was tall, thin, with a face like an ancient horse, crow-black eyebrows, and an enormous cushion of scarlet hair on her head. She had hardly been in the house five minutes before she complained of the heat, and to Mother's consternation and my delight, she caught hold of her scarlet hair and removed it, revealing a head as bald as a mushroom top. Seeing Mother's startled gaze, the Countess explained in her harsh, croaking voice. 'I've just recovered from erysipelas,' she said; 'lost all my hair . . . couldn't find eyebrows and wig to match in Milan . . . might get something in Athens.'

It was unfortunate that, owing to a slight impediment due to ill-fitting false teeth, the Countess was inclined to mumble, so Mother was under the impression that the disease she had just recovered from was of a much more unlady-like character. At the first available opportunity she got Larry into a corner.

'Disgusting!' she said in a vibrant whisper. 'Did you *hear* what she's had? And you call her a friend.'

'Friend?' said Larry in surprise. 'Why, I hardly know her . . . can't stand the woman; but she's an interesting character and I wanted to study her at close hand.'

'I like that,' said Mother indignantly. 'So you invite that *creature* here and we all catch some revolting disease while you take notes. No, I'm sorry, Larry, but she'll have to go.'

'Don't be silly, Mother,' said Larry irritably; 'you can't catch it . . . not unless you intend to share a bed with her.'

'Don't be *revolting*,' said Mother, glaring. 'I won't stand that obscene person in this house.'

They argued in whispers for the rest of the day, but Mother was adamant. Eventually Larry suggested asking Theodore out and getting his opinion on the matter, and to this Mother agreed. So a note was despatched, asking Theodore to come out and spend the day. His reply accepting the invitation was brought by a carriage in which reclined the cloak-swathed form of Zatopec, who, it turned out, had drunk a farewell of prodigious size to Corfu, got on the wrong boat, and ended up in Athens. As by then he had missed his appointment in Bosnia, he had philosophically boarded the next vessel back to Corfu, bringing with him several crates of wine. Theodore turned up the next day, wearing, as a concession to summer, a panama instead of his usual homburg. Before Mother had a chance to warn him about our hairless guest, Larry had introduced them.

'A doctor?' said Melanie, Countess de Torro, her eyes gleaming. 'How interesting. Perhaps you can advise me . . . I've just had erysipelas.'

'Ah ha! Really?' said Theodore, eyeing her keenly. 'Which . . . er . . . treatment did you have?'

They embarked on a long and technical discussion with enthusiasm, and it was only the most determined efforts on Mother's part that got them away from what she still considered to be an indelicate subject.

'Really, Theodore's as bad as that woman,' she said to Larry. 'I do *try* and be broad-minded, but there is a limit, and I don't think things like that should be discussed at tea.'

Later Mother got Theodore alone, and the subject of the Countess's disease was explained. Mother was then stricken with a guilty conscience at having misjudged the woman, and was immensely affable to her for the rest of the day, even telling her to take her wig off if she felt the heat.

The dinner that night was colourful and extraordinary, and I was so fascinated by the assembly of characters and the various conversations that I did not know which one to listen to with undivided attention. The lamps smoked gently and cast a warm, honey-coloured light over the table, making the china and glass glitter, and setting fire to the red wine as it splashed into the glasses.

'But, dear boy, you have missed the meaning of it . . . yes, yes, you have!' Zatopec's voice booming out, his nose curving over his wine glass. 'You cannot discuss poetry as if it were house painting . . .'

'. . . so I says to 'im, "I'm not doing a bleeding drawing for less than a tenner a time, so that's dirt cheap," I says . . .'

'. . . and the next morning I vas paralysed . . . shocked beyond everything . . . thousands of blossoms, bruised and torn . . . I say I vill never paint again . . . my nerves had been shattered . . . the whole orchard gone . . . phuit! like that . . . and there vas I . . .'

'. . . and then, of course, I had the sulphur baths.'

'Ah, yes . . . um . . . though, mind you, I think the bath treatment is . . . er . . . a little . . . er . . . you know . . . a little *overrated*. I believe that ninety-two per cent of sufferers . . .'

The plates of food, piled like volcanoes, steaming gently; the early fruit in a polished pile in the centre dish; Lugaretzia hobbling round the table, groaning gently to herself; Theodore's beard twinkling in the lamplight; Leslie carefully manufacturing bread pellets to shoot at a moth that hovered round the lamps; Mother, ladling out the food, smiling vaguely at everyone and keeping a watchful eye on Lugaretzia; under the table Roger's cold nose pressed hard against my knee in mute appeal.

Margo and the still-wheezing Michael discussing art: '. . . but then I think that Lawrence does that sort of thing so much *better*. He has a certain rich bloom as it were . . . don't you agree? I mean, take Lady Chatterley, eh?'

'Oh, yes, quite. And then, of course, he did wonderful things in the desert, didn't he? . . . and writing that wonderful book . . . the . . . er . . . *The Seven Pillows of Wisdom*, or whatever it was called . . .'

Larry and the Countess discussing art: '. . . but you must have the straightforward simplicity, the clarity of a child's eyes . . . Take the finest *fundamental* verse . . . take Humpty Dumpty . . . Now, there's poetry for you . . . the simplicity and freedom from clichés and out-dated shibboleths . . .'

'. . . but then it's useless prating about the simple approach to poetry, if you're going to produce jingles which are about as straightforward and uncomplicated as a camel's stomach . . .'

Mother and Durant: '. . . and you can imagine the effect it had on me . . . I vas shattered.'

'Yes, you must have been. Such a shame, after all that trouble. Will you have a little more rice?'

Jonquil and Theodore: '. . . and the Latvian peasants . . . well, I've never seen anything like it . . .'

'Yes, here in Corfu and . . . er . . . I believe . . . in some parts of Albania, the peasants have a very . . . er . . . similar custom . . .'

Outside, the moon's face was peering through a filigree of vine-leaves, and the owls were giving their strange, chiming cries. Coffee and wine were served on the balcony, between the vine-shaggy pillars. Larry strummed on the guitar and sang an Elizabethan marching song. This reminded Theodore of one of his fantastic but true Corfu anecdotes, which he related to us with impish glee.

'As you know, here in Corfu nothing is ever done the correct way. Everyone starts out with the . . . er . . . *best intentions*, but something always seems to go wrong. When the Greek King visited the island some years ago the . . . er . . . climax of his tour was to be a . . . er . . . sort of stage show . . . a play. The climax of the drama was the Battle of Thermopylae, and, as the curtain fell, the Greek army was supposed to drive . . . um . . . the Persian army triumphantly into the . . . what d'you call them? Ah, yes, the *wings*. Well, it appears that the people playing the part of the Persians were a bit disgruntled at the thought of having to retreat in front of the King, and the fact that they had to play the part of Persians also . . . you know . . . rankled. It only required a little incident to set things off. Unfortunately, during the battle scene the leader of the Greek army . . . um . . . misjudged the distance and caught the leader of the Persian army quite a heavy blow with his wooden sword. This, of course, was an accident. I mean to say, the poor fellow didn't *mean* to do it. But nevertheless it was sufficient to . . . er . . . inflame the Persian army to such an extent that instead of . . . er . . . retreating, they *advanced*. The centre of the stage became a milling mob of helmeted soldiers locked in mortal combat. Two of them were thrown into the orchestra pit before someone had the sense to lower the curtain. The King remarked later that he had been greatly impressed by the . . . um . . . *realism* shown in the battle scene.'

The burst of laughter sent the pale geckos scuttling up the wall in alarm.

'Theodore!' Larry laughed mockingly. 'I'm sure you made that up.'

'No, no!' Theodore would protest; 'it's quite true . . . I saw it myself.'

'It sounds the most unlikely story.'

'Here in Corfu,' said Theodore, his eyes twinkling with pride, '*anything* can happen.'

The sea striped with moonlight gleamed through the olives. Down by the well the tree-frogs croaked excitedly to each other. Two owls were having a contest in the tree below the veranda. In the grape-vine above our heads the geckos crept along the gnarled branches, eagerly watching the drifts of insects that were drawn, like a tide, by the lamplight.

# 9

# The World in a Wall

The crumbling wall that surrounded the sunken garden
alongside the house was a rich hunting ground for me. It
was an ancient brick wall that had been plastered over, but
now this outer skin was green with moss, bulging and sagging
with the damp of many winters. The whole surface was an
intricate map of cracks some several inches wide, others as
fine as hairs. Here and there large pieces had dropped off
and revealed the rows of rose-pink bricks lying beneath like
ribs. There was a whole landscape on this wall if you peered
closely enough to see it; the roofs of a hundred tiny toadstools,
red, yellow, and brown, showed in patches like villages on
the damper portions; mountains of bottle-green moss grew in
tuffets so symmetrical that they might have been planted and
trimmed; forests of small ferns sprouted from cracks in the
shady places, drooping languidly like little green fountains.
The top of the wall was a desert land, too dry for anything
except a few rust-red mosses to live in it, too hot for anything
except sun-bathing by the dragon-flies. At the base of the wall
grew a mass of plants, cyclamen, crocus, asphodel, thrusting
their leaves among the piles of broken and chipped roof-tiles
that lay there. This whole strip was guarded by a labyrinth
of blackberry hung, in season, with fruit that was plump and
juicy and black as ebony.

The inhabitants of the wall were a mixed lot, and they
were divided into day and night workers, the hunters and the
hunted. At night the hunters were the toads that lived among
the brambles, and the geckos, pale, translucent with bulging
eyes, that lived in the cracks higher up the wall. Their prey
was the population of stupid, absent-minded crane-flies that

zoomed and barged their way among the leaves; moths of all sizes and shapes, moths striped, tessellated, checked, spotted, and blotched, that fluttered in soft clouds along the withered plaster; the beetles, rotund and neatly clad as business men, hurrying with portly efficiency about their night's work. When the last glow-worm had dragged his frosty emerald lantern to bed over the hills of moss, and the sun rose, the wall was taken over by the next set of inhabitants. Here it was more difficult to differentiate between the prey and the predators, for everything seemed to feed indiscriminately off everything else. Thus the hunting wasps searched out caterpillars and spiders; the spiders hunted for flies; the dragon-flies, big, brittle, and hunting-pink, fed off the spiders and the flies; and the swift, lithe, and multi-coloured wall lizards fed off everything.

But the shyest and most self-effacing of the wall community were the most dangerous; you hardly ever saw one unless you looked for it, and yet there must have been several hundred living in the cracks of the wall. Slide a knife-blade carefully under a piece of the loose plaster and lever it gently away from the brick, and there, crouching beneath it, would be a little black scorpion an inch long, looking as though he were made out of polished chocolate. They were weird-looking things, with their flattened, oval bodies, their neat, crooked legs, the enormous crab-like claws, bulbous and neatly jointed as armour, and the tail like a string of brown beads ending in a sting like a rose-thorn. The scorpion would lie there quite quietly as you examined him, only raising his tail in an almost apologetic gesture of warning if you breathed too hard on him. If you kept him in the sun too long he would simply turn his back on you and walk away, and then slide slowly but firmly under another section of plaster.

I grew very fond of these scorpions. I found them to be pleasant, unassuming creatures with, on the whole, the most charming habits. Provided you did nothing silly or clumsy (like putting your hand on one) the scorpions treated you with respect, their one desire being to get away and hide as quickly as possible. They must have found me rather a trial, for I was always ripping sections of the plaster away so that I could watch them, or capturing them and making them walk about in jam-jars so that I could see the way their feet moved. By means of my sudden and unexpected assaults on the wall I discovered quite a bit about the scorpions. I found that they would eat bluebottles (though how they caught them was a mystery I never solved), grasshoppers, moths, and lacewing-flies. Several times I found them eating each other, a habit I found most distressing in a creature otherwise so impeccable.

By crouching under the wall at night with a torch, I managed to catch some brief glimpses of the scorpions' wonderful courtship dances. I saw them standing, claws clasped, their bodies raised to the skies, their tails lovingly entwined; I saw them waltzing slowly in circles among the moss cushions, claw in claw. But my view of these performances was all too short, for almost as soon as I switched on the torch the partners would stop, pause for a moment, and then, seeing that I was not going to extinguish the light, they would turn round and walk firmly away, claw in claw, side by side. They were definitely beasts that believed in keeping themselves to themselves. If I could have kept a colony in captivity I would probably have been able to see the whole of the courtship, but the family had forbidden scorpions in the house, despite my arguments in favour of them.

Then one day I found a fat female scorpion in the wall, wearing what at first glance appeared to be a pale fawn fur coat. Closer inspection proved that this strange garment was made up of a mass of tiny babies clinging to the mother's back. I was enraptured by this family, and I made up my mind to smuggle them into the house and up to my bedroom so that I might keep them and watch them grow up. With infinite care I manoeuvred the mother and family into a matchbox, and then hurried to the villa. It was rather unfortunate that just as I entered the door lunch should be served; however, I placed the matchbox carefully on the mantelpiece in the drawing-room, so that the scorpions should get plenty of air, and made my way to the dining-room and joined the family for the meal. Dawdling over my food, feeding Roger surreptitiously under the table and listening to the family arguing, I completely forgot about my exciting new captures. At last Larry, having finished, fetched the cigarettes from the drawing-room, and lying back in his chair he put one in his mouth and picked up the matchbox he had brought. Oblivious of my impending doom I watched him interestedly as, still talking glibly, he opened the matchbox.

Now I maintain to this day that the female scorpion meant no harm. She was agitated and a trifle annoyed at being shut up in a matchbox for so long, and so she seized the first opportunity to escape. She hoisted herself out of the box with great rapidity, her babies clinging on desperately, and scuttled on to the back of Larry's hand. There, not quite certain what to do next, she paused, her sting curved up at the ready. Larry, feeling the movement of her claws, glanced down to see what it was, and from that moment things got increasingly confused.

He uttered a roar of fright that made Lugaretzia drop a plate and brought Roger out from beneath the table, barking wildly. With a flick of his hand he sent the unfortunate scorpion flying down the table, and she landed midway between Margo and Leslie, scattering babies like confetti as she thumped on the cloth. Thoroughly enraged at this treatment, the creature sped towards Leslie, her sting quivering with emotion. Leslie leapt to his feet, overturning his chair, and flicked out desperately with his napkin, sending the scorpion rolling across the cloth towards Margo, who promptly let out a scream that any railway engine would have been proud to produce. Mother, completely bewildered by this sudden and rapid change from peace to chaos, put on her glasses and peered down the table to see what was causing the pandemonium, and at that moment Margo, in a vain attempt to stop the scorpion's advance, hurled a glass of water at it. The shower missed the animal completely, but successfully drenched Mother, who, not being able to stand cold water, promptly lost her breath and sat gasping at the end of the table, unable even to protest. The scorpion had now gone to ground under Leslie's plate, while her babies swarmed wildly all over the table. Roger, mystified by the panic, but determined to do his share, ran round and round the room, barking hysterically.

'It's that bloody boy again . . .' bellowed Larry.

'Look out! Look out! They're coming!' screamed Margo.

'All we need is a book,' roared Leslie; 'don't panic, hit 'em with a book.'

'What on earth's the *matter* with you all?' Mother kept imploring, mopping her glasses.

'It's that bloody boy . . . he'll kill the lot of us . . . Look at the table . . . knee-deep in scorpions.'

'Quick . . . quick . . . do something . . . Look out, look out!'

'Stop screeching and get a book, for God's sake . . . You're worse than the dog . . . Shut *up*, Roger . . .'

'By the Grace of God I wasn't bitten . . .'

'Look out . . . there's another one . . . Quick . . . quick . . .'

'Oh, shut up and get me a book or something . . .'

'But *how* did the scorpions get on the table, dear?'

'That bloody boy ... Every matchbox in the house is a deathtrap ...'

'Look out, it's coming towards me ... Quick, quick, do something ...'

'Hit it with your knife ... *your knife* ... Go on, hit it ...'

Since no one had bothered to explain things to him, Roger was under the mistaken impression that the family were being attacked, and that it was his duty to defend them. As Lugaretzia was the only stranger in the room, he came to the logical conclusion that she must be the responsible party, so he bit her in the ankle. This did not help matters very much.

By the time a certain amount of order had been restored, all the baby scorpions had hidden themselves under various plates and bits of cutlery. Eventually, after impassioned pleas on my part, backed up by Mother, Leslie's suggestion that the whole lot be slaughtered was quashed. While the family, still simmering with rage and fright, retired to the drawing-room, I spent half an hour rounding up the babies, picking them up in a teaspoon, and returning them to their mother's back. Then I carried them outside on a saucer and, with the utmost reluctance, released them on the garden wall. Roger and I went and spent the afternoon on the hillside, for I felt it would be prudent to allow the family to have a siesta before seeing them again.

The results of this incident were numerous. Larry developed a phobia about matchboxes and opened them with the utmost caution, a handkerchief wrapped round his hand. Lugaretzia limped round the house, her ankle enveloped in yards of bandage, for weeks after the bite had healed, and came round every morning, with the tea, to show us how the scabs were getting on. But, from my point of view, the worst repercussion of the whole affair was that Mother decided I was running wild again, and that it was high time I received a little more education. While the problem of finding a full-time tutor was being solved, she was determined that my French, at least, should be kept in trim. So arrangements were made, and every morning Spiro would drive me into the town for my French lesson with the Belgian consul.

The consul's house was situated in the maze of narrow, smelly alley-ways that made up the Jewish quarter of the town. It was a fascinating area, the cobbled streets crammed with stalls that were piled high with gaily-coloured bales of cloth, mountains of shining sweetmeats, ornaments of beaten silver, fruit, and vegetables. The streets were so narrow that you had to stand back against the wall to allow the donkeys to stagger past with their loads of merchandise. It was a rich and colourful part of the town, full of noise and bustle, the screech of bargaining women, the cluck of hens, the barking of dogs, and the wailing cry of the men carrying great trays of fresh hot loaves on their heads. Right in the very centre, in the top flat of a tall, rickety building that leant tiredly over a tiny square, lived the Belgian consul.

He was a sweet little man, whose most striking attribute was a magnificent three-pointed beard and carefully waxed moustache. He took his job rather seriously, and was always dressed as though he were on the verge of rushing off to some important official function, in black cut-away coat, striped trousers, fawn spats over brightly polished shoes, an immense cravat like a silk waterfall, held in place by a plain gold pin, and a tall and gleaming top hat that completed the ensemble. One could see him at any hour of the day, clad like this, picking his way down the dirty, narrow alleys, stepping daintily among the puddles, drawing himself back against the wall with a magnificently courteous gesture to allow a donkey to pass, and tapping it coyly on the rump with his malacca cane. The people of the town did not find his garb at all unusual. They thought that he was an Englishman, and as all Englishmen were lords it was not only right but necessary that they should wear the correct uniform.

The first morning I arrived, he welcomed me into a living-room whose walls were decorated with a mass of heavily-framed photographs of himself in various Napoleonic attitudes. The Victorian chairs, covered with red brocade, were patched with antimacassars by the score; the table on which we worked was draped in a wine-red cloth of velvet, with a fringe of bright green tassels round the edge. It was an intriguingly ugly room. In order to test the extent of my knowledge of French, the consul sat me down at the table, produced a fat and battered edition of *Le Petit Larousse*, and placed it in front of me, open at page one.

'You will please to read zis,' he said, his gold teeth glittering amicably in his beard.

He twisted the points of his moustache, pursed his lips, clasped his hands behind his back, and paced slowly across to the window, while I started down the list of words beginning with A. I had hardly stumbled through the first three when the consul stiffened and uttered a suppressed exclamation.

I thought at first he was shocked by my accent, but it was apparently nothing to do with me. He rushed across the room, muttering to himself, tore open a cupboard, and pulled out a powerful-looking air rifle, while I watched him with increasing mystification and interest, not unmixed with a certain alarm for my own safety. He loaded the weapon, dropping pellets all over the carpet in his frantic haste. Then he crouched and crept back to the window, where, half concealed by the curtain, he peered out eagerly. Then he raised the gun, took careful aim at something, and fired. When he turned round, slowly and sadly shaking his head, and laid the gun aside, I was surprised to see tears in his eyes. He drew a yard or so of silk handkerchief out of his breast pocket and blew his nose violently.

'Ah, ah, ah,' he intoned, shaking his head dolefully, 'ze poor lizzle fellow. Buz we musz work . . . please continuez wiz your reading, *mon ami*.'

For the rest of the morning I toyed with the exciting idea that the consul had committed a murder before my very eyes, or, at least, that he was carrying out a blood feud with some neighbouring householder. But when, after the fourth morning, the consul was still firing periodically out of his window, I decided that my explanation could not be the right one, unless it was an exceptionally large family he was feuding with, and a family, moreover, who were apparently incapable of firing back. It was a week before I found out the reason for the consul's incessant fusillade, and the reason was cats. In the Jewish quarter, as in other parts of the town, the cats were allowed to breed unchecked. There were literally hundreds of them. They belonged to no one and were uncared for, so that most of them were in a frightful state, covered with sores, their fur coming out in great bald patches, their legs bent with rickets, and all of them so thin that it was a wonder they were alive at all. The consul was a great cat-lover, and he possessed three large and well-fed Persians to prove it. But the sight of all these starving, sore-ridden felines stalking about on the roof-tops opposite his window was too much for his sensitive nature.

'I cannot feed zem all,' he explained to me, 'so I like to make zem happiness by zooting zem. Zey are bezzer so, buz iz makes me feel so zad.'

He was, in fact, performing a very necessary and humane service, as anyone who had seen the cats would agree. So my lessons in French were being continuously interrupted while

107

the consul leapt to the window to send yet another cat to a happier hunting ground. After the report of the gun there would be a moment's silence, in respect for the dead, and then the consul would blow his nose violently, sigh tragically, and we would plunge once more into the tangled labyrinth of French verbs.

For some inexplicable reason the consul was under the impression that Mother could speak French, and he would never lose an opportunity of engaging her in conversation. If she had the good fortune, while shopping in the town, to notice his top hat bobbing through the crowd towards her, she would hastily retreat into the nearest shop and buy a number of things she had no use for, until the danger was past. Occasionally, however, the consul would appear suddenly out of an alley-way and take her by surprise. He would advance, smiling broadly and twirling his cane, sweep off his top hat and bow almost double before her, while clasping her reluctantly offered hand and pressing it passionately into his beard. Then they would stand in the middle of the street, occasionally being forced apart by a passing donkey, while the consul swamped Mother under a flood of French, gesturing elegantly with his hat and stick, apparently unaware of the blank expression on Mother's face. Now and then he would punctuate his speech with a questioning *'n'est-ce pas, madame?'* and this was Mother's cue. Summoning up all her courage, she would display her complete mastery over the French tongue.

*'Oui, oui!'* she would exclaim, smiling nervously, and then add, in case it had sounded rather unenthusiastic, 'OUI, OUI.'

This procedure satisfied the consul, and I'm sure he never realized that this was the only French word that Mother knew. But these conversations were a nerve-racking ordeal for her, and we had only to hiss 'Look out, Mother, the consul's coming,' to set her tearing off down the street at a lady-like walk that was dangerously near to a gallop.

In some ways these French lessons were good for me; I did not learn any French, it's true, but by the end of the morning I was so bored that my afternoon sorties into the surrounding country were made with double the normal enthusiasm. And then, of course, there was always Thursday to look forward to. Theodore would come out to the villa as soon after lunch as was decent, and stay until the moon was high over the Albanian mountains. Thursday was happily chosen, from his point of view, because it was on this day that the seaplane from Athens arrived and landed in the bay not far from the house. Theodore had a passion for watching seaplanes land. Unfortunately the only part of the house from which you could get a good view of the bay was the attic, and then it meant leaning perilously out of the window and craning your neck. The plane would invariably arrive in the middle of tea; a dim, drowsy hum could be heard, so faint one could not be sure it was not a bee. Theodore, in the middle of an anecdote or an explanation, would suddenly stop talking, his eyes would take on a fanatical gleam, his beard would bristle, and he would cock his head on one side.

'Is that . . . er . . . you know . . . is that the sound of a *plane*?' he would inquire.

Everyone would stop talking and listen; slowly the sound would grow louder and louder. Theodore would carefully place his half-eaten scone on his plate.

'Ah ha!' he would say, wiping his fingers carefully. 'Yes, that certainly *sounds* like a plane . . . er . . . um . . . yes.'

The sound would grow louder and louder, while Theodore shifted uneasily in his seat. At length Mother would put him out of his misery.

'Would you like to go up and watch it land?' she would ask.

'Well . . . er . . . if you're sure . . .' Theodore would mumble, vacating his seat with alacrity. 'I . . . er . . . find the sight very attractive . . . if you're sure you don't mind.'

The sound of the plane's engines would now be directly overhead; there was not a moment to lose.

'I have always been . . . er . . . you know . . . attracted . . .'

'Hurry up, Theo, or you'll miss it,' we would chorus.

The entire family then vacated the table, and, gathering Theodore *en route*, we sped up the four flights of stairs, Roger racing ahead, barking joyfully. We burst into the attic, out of breath, laughing, our feet thumping like gunfire on the uncarpeted floor, threw open the windows, and leaned out, peering over the olive-tops to where the bay lay like a round blue eye among the trees, its surface as smooth as honey. The plane, like a cumbersome overweight goose, flew over the olive-groves, sinking lower and lower. Suddenly it would be over the water, racing its reflection over the blue surface. Slowly the plane dropped lower and lower. Theodore, eyes narrowed, beard bristling, watched it with bated breath. Lower and lower, and then suddenly it touched the surface briefly, left a widening petal of foam, flew on, and then settled on the surface and surged across the bay, leaving a spreading fan of white foam behind it. As it came slowly to rest, Theodore would rasp the side of his beard with his thumb, and ease himself back into the attic.

'Um . . . yes,' he would say, dusting his hands, 'it is certainly a . . . very . . . er . . . *enjoyable* sight.'

The show was over. He would have to wait another week for the next plane. We would shut the attic windows and troop noisily downstairs to resume our interrupted tea. The next week exactly the same thing would happen all over again.

It was on Thursday, that Theodore and I went out together, sometimes confining ourselves to the garden, sometimes venturing further afield. Loaded down with collecting boxes and nets, we wended our way through the olives, Roger galloping ahead of us, nose to the ground. Everything that we came across was grist to our mill: flowers, insects, rocks, or birds. Theodore had an apparently inexhaustible fund of knowledge about everything, but he imparted this knowledge with a sort of meticulous diffidence that made you feel he was not so much teaching you something new, as reminding you of something which you were already aware of, but which had, for some reason or other, slipped your mind. His conversation was sprinkled with hilarious anecdotes, incredibly bad puns, and even worse jokes, which he would tell with great relish, his eyes twinkling, his nose wrinkled as he laughed silently in his beard, as much at himself as at his own humour.

Every water-filled ditch or pool was, to us, a teeming and unexplored jungle, with the minute cyclops and water-fleas, green and coral pink, suspended like birds among the under-water branches, while on the muddy bottom the tigers of the pool would prowl: the leeches and the dragon-fly larvae. Every hollow tree had to be closely scrutinized in case it should contain a tiny pool of water in which mosquito-larvae were living, every mossy wigged rock had to be overturned to find out what lay beneath it, and every rotten log had to be dissected. Standing straight and immaculate at the edge of a pool, Theodore would carefully sweep his little net through the water, lift it out, and peer keenly into the tiny glass bottle that dangled at the end, into which all the minute water life had been sifted.

'Ah ha!' he might say, his voice ringing with excitement, his beard bristling. 'I believe it's *ceriodaphnia laticaudata*.'

He would whip a magnifying glass from his waistcoat pocket and peer more closely.

'Ah, um . . . yes . . . very curious . . . it is *laticaudata*. Could

110

you just . . . er . . . hand me a clean test-tube . . . um . . . thank
you . . .'

He would suck the minute creature out of the bottle with a
fountain-pen filler, enshrine it carefully in the tube, and then
examine the rest of the catch.

'There doesn't seem to be anything else that's particularly
exciting . . . Ah, yes, I didn't notice . . . there is rather a
curious caddis larva . . . there, d'you see it? . . . um . . . it
appears to have made its case of the shells of certain molluscs
. . . It's certainly very pretty.'

At the bottom of the little bottle was an elongated case, half
an inch long, constructed out of what appeared to be silk, and
thick with tiny flat snail-shells like buttons. From one end
of this delightful home the owner peered, an unattractive
maggot-like beast with a head like an ant's. Slowly it crawled
across the glass, dragging its beautiful house with it.

'I tried an interesting experiment once,' Theodore said. 'I
caught a number of these . . . er . . . larvae, and removed their
shells. Naturally it doesn't *hurt* them. Then I put them in some
jars which contained perfectly clear water and nothing in the
way of . . . er . . . materials with which to build new cases.
Then I gave each set of larvae different-coloured materials
to build with: some I gave very tiny blue and green beads,
and some I gave chips of brick, white sand, even some . . .
er . . . fragments of coloured glass. They all built new cases
out of these different things, and I must say the result was
very curious and . . . er . . . colourful. They are certainly very
clever *architects*.'

He emptied the contents of the bottle back into the pool, put
his net over his shoulder, and we walked on our way.

'Talking of *building*,' Theodore continued, his eyes sparkling, 'did I tell you what happened to . . . a . . . er . . . a
friend of mine? Um, yes. Well, he had a small house in the
country, and, as his family . . . um . . . increased, he decided
that it was not big enough. He decided to add another floor
to the house. He was, I think, a little *over-confident* of his
own architectural . . . um . . . prowess, and he insisted on
designing the new floor himself. Um, ha, yes. Well, everything
went well and in next to no time the new floor was ready,
complete with bedrooms, bathrooms, and so forth. My friend
had a party to celebrate the completion of the work, we all
drank toasts to the . . . um . . . new piece of building, and with
great ceremony the scaffolding was taken down . . . um . . .
removed. No one noticed anything . . . um . . . anything *amiss*,

111

until a late arrival at the celebration wanted to look round the new rooms. It was then discovered that there was no staircase. It appears that my friend had forgotten to put a staircase in his plans, you know, and during the actual . . . er . . . the actual *building* operations he and the workmen had got so used to climbing to the top floor by means of the scaffolding that no one apparently noticed the . . . er . . . the *defect*.'

So we would walk on through the hot afternoon, pausing by the pools and ditches and streams, wading through the heavily scented myrtle-bushes, over the hillside crisp with heather, along white, dusty roads where we were occasionally passed by a drooping, plodding donkey carrying a sleepy peasant on its back.

Towards evening, our jars, bottles, and tubes full of strange and exciting forms of life, we would turn for home. The sky would be fading to a pale gold as we marched through the olive-groves, already dim with shadow, and the air would be cooler and more richly scented. Roger would trot ahead of us, his tongue flapping out, occasionally glancing over his shoulder to make sure we were following him. Theodore and I, hot and dusty and tired, our bulging collecting bags making our shoulders ache pleasantly, would stride along singing a song that Theodore had taught me. It had a rousing tune that gave a new life to tired feet and Theodore's baritone voice and my shrill treble would ring out gaily through the gloomy trees:

'There was an old man who lived in Jerusalem,
   Glory Halleluiah, Hi-ero-jerum.
He wore a top hat and he looked very sprucelum,
   Glory Halleluiah, Hi-ero-jerum.
Skinermer rinki doodle dum, skinermer rinki doodle dum,
   Glory Halleluiah, Hi-ero-jerum . . .'

# 10

# The Pageant of Fireflies

Spring merged slowly into the long, hot, sun-sharp days of summer sung in by cicadas, shrill and excited, making the island vibrate with their cries. In the fields the maize was starting to fill out, the silken tassels turning from brown to butter-blond; when you tore off the wrapping of leaves and bit into the rows of pearly seeds the juice would spurt into your mouth like milk. On the vines the grapes hung in tiny clusters, freckled and warm. The olives seemed weighed down under the weight of their fruit, smooth drops of green jade among which the choirs of cicadas zithered. In the orange-groves, among the dark and shiny leaves, the fruit was starting to glow redly, like a blush spreading up the green, pitted skins.

Up on the hills, among the dark cypress and the heather, shoals of butterflies danced and twisted like wind-blown confetti, pausing now and then on a leaf to lay a salvo of eggs. The grasshoppers and locusts whirred like clockwork under my feet, and flew drunkenly across the heather, their wings shining in the sun. Among the myrtles the mantids moved, lightly, carefully, swaying slightly, the quintessence of evil. They were lank and green, with chinless faces and monstrous globular eyes, frosty gold, with an expression of intense predatory madness in them. The crooked arms, with their fringes of sharp teeth, would be raised in mock supplication to the insect world, so humble, so fervent, trembling slightly when a butterfly flew too close.

Towards evening, when it grew cooler, the cicadas stopped singing; their place being taken by the green tree-frogs, glued damply to the lemon-tree leaves down by the well. With bulging eyes staring as though hypnotized, their backs as shiny as the

113

leaves they sat amongst, they swelled out their vocal sacs and croaked harshly and with such violence that they seemed in danger of splitting their damp bodies with the effort. When the sun sank there was a brief apple-green twilight which faded and became mauve, and the air cooled and took on the scents of evening. The toads appeared, putty-coloured with strange, map-like blotches of bottle-green on their skins. They hopped furtively among the long grass clumps in the olive-groves, where the crane-flies' unsteady flight seemed to cover the ground with a drifting curtain of gauze. They sat there blinking and then would suddenly snap at a passing crane-fly; sitting back, looking a trifle embarrassed, they stuffed the trailing ends of wing and leg into their great mouths with the aid of their thumbs. Above them, on the crumbling walls of the sunken garden, the little black scorpions walked solemnly, hand in hand, among the plump mounds of green moss and the groves of tiny toadstools.

The sea was smooth, warm, and as dark as black velvet, not a ripple disturbing the surface. The distant coastline of Albania was dimly outlined by a faint reddish glow in the sky. Gradually, minute by minute, this glow deepened and grew brighter, spreading across the sky. Then suddenly the moon, enormous, wine-red, edged herself over the fretted battlement of mountains, and threw a straight, blood-red path across the dark sea. The owls appeared now, drifting from tree to tree as silently as flakes of soot, hooting in astonishment as the moon rose higher and higher, turning to pink, then gold, and finally riding in a nest of stars, like a silver bubble.

With the summer came Peter to tutor me, a tall, handsome young man, fresh from Oxford, with decided ideas on education which I found rather trying to begin with. But gradually the atmosphere of the island worked its way insidiously under his skin, and he relaxed and became quite human. At first the lessons were painful to an extreme: interminable wrestling with fractions and percentages, geological strata and warm currents, nouns, verbs, and adverbs. But, as the sunshine worked its magic on Peter, the fractions and percentages no longer seemed to him an overwhelming important part of life and they were gradually pushed more and more into the background; he discovered that the intricacies of geological strata and the effects of warm currents could be explained much more easily while swimming along the coast, while the simplest way of teaching me English was to allow me to write something each day which he would correct. He had suggested a diary, but I was against this, pointing out that I already kept one on nature, in which was recorded everything of interest that happened each day. If I were to keep another diary, what was I to put in it? Peter could find no answer to this argument. I suggested that I might try something a little more ambitious and interesting than a diary. Diffidently, I suggested I wrote a book, and Peter, somewhat startled, but not being able to think of any reason why I should *not* write a book, agreed. So every morning I spent a happy hour or so adding another chapter to my epic, a stirring tale which involved a voyage round the world with the family, during which we captured every conceivable kind of fauna in the most unlikely traps. I modelled my style on the *Boy's Own Paper*, and so each chapter ended on a thrilling note, with Mother being attacked by a jaguar, or Larry struggling in the coils of an enormous python. Sometimes these climaxes were so complicated and fraught with danger that I had great difficulty in extracting the family intact on the following day. While I was at work on my masterpiece, breathing heavily, tongue protruding, breaking off for discussions with Roger on the finer points of the plot, Peter and Margo would take a stroll in the sunken garden to look at the flowers. To my surprise, they had both suddenly become very botanically minded. In this way the mornings passed very pleasantly for all concerned. Occasionally, in the early days, Peter suffered from sudden spasms of conscience, my epic would be relegated to a drawer, and we would pore over mathematical problems. But as the summer days grew longer, and Margo's interest in gardening became more sustained, these irritating periods became less frequent.

After the unfortunate affair of the scorpion, the family had given me a large room on the first floor in which to house my beasts, in the vague hope that this would confine them to one particular portion of the house. This room – which I called my study, and which the rest of the family called the Bug House – smelt pleasantly of ether and methylated spirits. It was here that I kept my natural history books, my diary, microscope, dissecting instruments, nets, collecting bags, and other important items. Large cardboard boxes housed my birds'-egg, beetle, butterfly, and dragon-fly collections, while on the shelves above were a fine range of bottles full of methylated spirits in which were preserved such interesting items as a four-legged chicken (a present from Lugaretzia's husband), various lizards and snakes, frog-spawn in different stages of growth, a baby octopus, three half-grown brown rats (a contribution from Roger), and a minute tortoise, newly hatched, that had been unable to survive the winter. The walls were sparsely, but tastefully, decorated with a slab slate containing the fossilized remains of a fish, a photograph of myself shaking hands with a chimpanzee, and a stuffed bat. I had prepared the bat myself, without assistance, and I was extremely proud of the result. Considering how limited my knowledge of taxidermy was, it looked, I thought, extremely *like* a bat, especially if you stood at the other side of the room. With wings outstretched it glowered down from the wall from its slab of cork. When summer came, however, the bat appeared to feel the heat: it sagged a little, its coat no longer glossy, and a new and mysterious smell started to make itself felt above the ether and methylated spirits. Poor Roger was wrongly accused at first, and it was only later, when the smell had penetrated even Larry's bedroom, that a thorough investigation traced the odour to my bat. I was surprised and not a little annoyed. Under pressure I was forced to get rid of it. Peter explained that I had not cured it properly, and said that if I could obtain another specimen he would show me the correct procedure. I thanked him profusely, but tactfully suggested that we keep the whole thing a secret; I explained that I felt the family now looked with a suspicious eye on the art of taxidermy, and it would require a lot of tedious persuasion to get them into an agreeable frame of mind.

My efforts to secure another bat were unsuccessful. Armed with a long bamboo I waited for hours in the moon-splashed corridors between the olive-trees, but the bats flickered past like quicksilver and vanished before I could use my weapon. But, while waiting in vain for a chance to hit a bat, I saw a number of other night creatures which I would not otherwise have seen. I watched a young fox hopefully digging for beetles in the hillside, scrabbling slim paws at the earth, and scrunching the insects up hungrily as he unearthed them. Once, five jackals appeared out of the myrtle-bushes, paused in surprise at seeing me, and then melted among the trees, like shadows. The night-jars on silent, silky wings would slide as smoothly as great black swallows along the rows of olives, sweeping across the grass in pursuit of the drunken whirling crane-flies. One night a pair of squirrel dormice appeared in the tree above me, and chased each other in wild exuberance up and down the grove, leaping from branch to branch like acrobats, skittering up and down the tree-trunks, their bushy

116

tails like puffs of grey smoke in the moonlight. I was so fascinated by these creatures that I was determined to try to catch one. The best time to search for them was, of course, during the day, when they would be asleep. So, I hunted laboriously through the olive-groves for their hideout, but it was a hopeless quest, for every gnarled and twisted trunk was hollow, and each contained half a dozen holes. However, my patience did not go entirely unrewarded, for one day I thrust my arm into a hole, and my fingers closed round something small and soft, something that wiggled as I pulled it out. At first glance my capture appeared to be an outsize bundle of dandelion seeds, furnished with a pair of enormous golden eyes; closer inspection proved it to be a young Scops owl, still clad in his baby down. We regarded each other for a moment, and then the bird, apparently indignant at my ill-mannered laughter at his appearance, dug his tiny claws deeply into my thumb, and I lost my grip on the branch, so that we fell out of the tree together.

I carried the indignant owlet back home in my pocket, and introduced him to the family with a certain trepidation. To my surprise, he was greeted with unqualified approval, and no objection was raised to my keeping him. He took up residence in a basket kept in my study and, after much argument, he was christened Ulysses. From the first he showed that he was a bird of great strength of character, and not to be trifled with. Although he would have fitted comfortably into a tea-cup, he showed no fear and would unhesitatingly attack anything and everyone, regardless of size. As we all had to share the room, I felt it would be a good idea if he and Roger got on intimate terms, so, as soon as the owl had settled down, I performed the introductions by placing Ulysses on the floor, and telling Roger to approach and make friends. Roger had become very philosophical about having to make friends with the various creatures that I adopted, and he took the appearance of an owl in his stride. Wagging his tail briskly, in an ingratiating manner, he approached Ulysses, who squatted on the floor with anything but a friendly expression on his face. He watched Roger's approach in an unwinking stare of ferocity. Roger's advance became less confident. Ulysses continued to glare as though trying to hypnotize the dog. Roger stopped, his ears drooped, his tail wagging only feebly, and he glanced at me for inspiration. I ordered him sternly to continue his overtures of friendship. Roger looked nervously at the owl, and then with great nonchalance walked round him, in an effort to approach him from the back. Ulysses, however, let his head revolve too, and kept his eyes still fixed on the dog. Roger, never having met a creature that could look behind itself without turning round, seemed a trifle non plussed. After a moment's thought he decided to try the skittish, let's-all-have-a-jolly-game approach. He lay down on his stomach, put his head between his paws, and crept slowly towards the bird, whining gently and wagging his tail with abandon. Ulysses continued to look as though he were stuffed. Roger, still progressing on his stomach, managed to get quite close, but then he made a fatal mistake. He pushed his woolly face forward and sniffed loudly and interestedly at the bird. Now Ulysses would stand a lot, but he was not going to be sniffed at by a mountainous dog covered with black curls. He decided that he would have to show this ungainly and wingless beast exactly where he got off. He lowered his eyelids, clicked his beak, hopped up into the air, and landed squarely on the dog's muzzle, burying his razor-sharp claws in the black nose. Roger, with a stricken yelp, shook the bird off and retired beneath the table; no amount of coaxing would get him to come out until Ulysses was safely back in his basket.

When Ulysses grew older he lost his baby down and developed the fine ash-grey, rust-red, and black plumage of his kind, with the pale breast handsomely marked with Maltese crosses in black. He also developed long ear-tufts, which he would raise in indignation when you attempted to take liberties with him. As he was now far too old to be kept in a basket, and strongly opposed to the idea of a cage, I was forced to give him the run of the study. He performed his flying lessons between the table and door-handle, and, as soon as he had mastered the art, chose the pelmet above the window as his home, and would spend the day sleeping up there, eyes closed, looking exactly like an olive-stump. If you spoke to him he would open his eyes a fraction, raise his ear-tufts, and elongate his whole body, so that he looked like some weird, emaciated Chinese idol. If he was feeling particularly affectionate he would click his beak at you, or, as a great concession, fly down and give you a hurried peck on the ear.

As the sun sank and the geckos started to scuttle about the shadowy walls of the house, Ulysses would wake up. He would yawn delicately, stretch his wings, clean his tail, and then shiver violently so that all his feathers stood out like the petals of a wind-blown chrysanthemum. With great

118

nonchalance he would regurgitate a pellet of undigested food on to the newspaper spread out below for this, and other, purposes. Having prepared himself for the night's work, he would utter an experimental 'tywhoo?' to make sure his voice was in trim, and then launch himself on soft wings, to drift round the room as silently as a flake of ash and land on my shoulder. For a short time he would sit there, nibbling my ear, and then he would give himself another shake, put sentiment to one side, and become business-like. He would fly on to the window-sill and give another questioning 'tywhoo?', staring at me with his honey-coloured eyes. This was the signal that he wanted the shutters opened. As soon as I threw them back he would float out through the window, to be silhouetted for a moment against the moon before diving into the dark olives. A moment later a loud challenging 'tywhoo! tywhoo!' would ring out, the warning that Ulysses was about to start his hunting.

The length of time Ulysses spent on his hunts varied; sometimes he would swoop back into the room after only an hour, and on other occasions he would be out all night. But, wherever he went, he never failed to come back to the house between nine and ten for his supper. If there was no light in my study, he would fly down and peer through the drawing-room window to see if I was there. If I was not there, he would fly up the side of the house again to land on my bedroom window-sill and tap briskly on the shutters, until I opened them and served him with his saucer of mince, or chopped chicken's heart, or whatever delicacy was on the menu that day. When the last gory morsel had been swallowed he would give a soft, hiccoughing chirrup, sit meditating for a moment, and then fly off over the moon-bright tree-tops.

Since he had proved himself an able fighter, Ulysses became fairly friendly towards Roger, and if we were going down for a late evening swim I could sometimes prevail upon him to honour us with his company. He would ride on Roger's back, clinging tight to the black wool; if, as occasionally happened, Roger forgot his passenger and went too fast, or skittishly jumped over a stone, Ulysses's eye would blaze, his wings flap in a frantic effort to keep his balance, and he would click his beak loudly and indignantly until I reprimanded Roger for his carelessness. On the shore Ulysses would perch on my shorts and shirt, while Roger and I gambolled in the warm, shallow water. Ulysses would watch our antics with round and faintly disapproving eyes, sitting up as straight as a guardsman. Now and then he would leave his post to skim out over us, click his beak, and return to shore, but whether he did this in alarm for our safety or in order to join in our game, I could never decide. Sometimes, if we took too long over the swim, he would get bored, and fly up the hill to the garden, crying 'Tywhoo!' in farewell.

In the summer, when the moon was full, the family took to bathing at night, for during the day the sun was so fierce that the sea became too hot to be refreshing. As soon as the moon had risen we would make our way down through the trees to the creaking wooden jetty, and clamber into the *Sea Cow*. With Larry and Peter on one oar, Margo and Leslie on the other, and Roger and myself in the bows to act as look-outs, we would drift down the coast for half a mile or so to where there was a small bay with a lip of white sand and a few carefully arranged boulders, smooth, and still sun-warm, ideal for sitting on. We would anchor the *Sea Cow* in deep water and then dive over the side to gambol and plunge, and set the moonlight shaking across the waters of the bay. When tired, we swam languidly to the shore and lay on the warm rocks, gazing up into the star-freckled sky. Generally after half an hour or so I would get bored with the conversation, and slip back into the water and swim slowly out across the bay, to lie on my back, cushioned by the warm sea, gazing up at the moon. One night, while I was thus occupied, I discovered that our bay was used by other creatures as well.

Lying spread-eagled in the silky water, gazing into the sky, only moving my hands and feet slightly to keep afloat, I was looking at the Milky Way stretched like a chiffon scarf across the sky and wondering how many stars it contained. I could hear the voices of the others, laughing and talking on the beach, echoing over the water, and by lifting my head I could see their position on the shore by the pulsing lights of their cigarettes. Drifting there, relaxed, and dreamy, I was suddenly startled to hear, quite close to me, a clop and gurgle of water, followed by a long, deep sigh, and a series of gentle ripples rocked me up and down. Hastily I righted myself and trod water, looking to see how far from the beach I had drifted. To my alarm I found that not only was I some considerable distance from the shore, but from the *Sea Cow* as well, and I was not at all sure what sort of creature it was swimming around in the dark waters beneath me. I could hear the others laughing on the shore at some joke or other, and I saw someone flip a cigarette-end high into the sky like a red star that curved over and extinguished itself at the rim of the sea. I was feeling more and more uncomfortable, and I was just about to call for assistance when, some twenty feet away from me, the sea seemed to part with a gentle swish and gurgle, a gleaming back appeared, gave a deep, satisfied sigh, and sank below the surface again. I had hardly time to recognize it as a porpoise before I found I was right in the midst of them. They rose all around me, sighing luxuriously, their black backs shining as they humped in the moonlight. There must have been about eight of them, and one rose so close that I could have swum forward three strokes and touched his ebony head. Heaving and sighing heavily, they played across the bay, and I swam with them, watching fascinated as they rose to the surface, crumpling the water, breathed deeply, and then dived beneath the surface again, leaving only an expanding hoop of foam to mark the spot. Presently, as if obeying a signal, they turned and headed out of the bay towards the distant coast of Albania, and I trod water and watched them go, swimming up the white chain of moonlight, backs a-gleam as they rose and plunged with heavy ecstasy in the water as warm as fresh milk. Behind them they left a trail of great bubbles that rocked and shone briefly like miniature moons before vanishing under the ripples.

After this we often met the porpoises when we went moonlight bathing, and one evening they put on an illuminated show for our benefit, aided by one of the most attractive insects that inhabited the island. We had discovered that in the hot months of the year the sea became full of phosphorescence. When there was moonlight this was not so noticeable – a faint greenish flicker round the bows of the boat, a brief flash as someone dived into the water. We found that the best time for the phosphorescence was when there was no moon at all. Another illuminated inhabitant of the summer months was the firefly. These slender brown beetles would fly as soon as it got dark, floating through the olive-groves by the score, their tails flashing on and off, giving a light that was greenish-white, not golden-green, as the sea was. Again, however, the fireflies were at their best when there was no bright moonlight to detract from their lights. Strangely enough, we would never have seen the porpoises, the fireflies, and the phosphorescence acting together if it had not been for Mother's bathing-costume.

For some time Mother had greatly envied us our swimming, both in the daytime, and at night, but, as she pointed out when we suggested she join us, she was far too old for that sort of thing. Eventually, however, under constant pressure from us, Mother paid a visit into town and returned to the villa coyly bearing a mysterious parcel. Opening this she astonished us all by holding up an extraordinary shapeless garment of black cloth, covered from top to bottom with hundreds of frills and pleats and tucks.

'Well, what d'you think of it?' Mother asked.

We stared at the odd garment and wondered what it was for.

'What is it?' asked Larry at length.

'It's a bathing-costume, of course,' said Mother. 'What on earth did you think it was?'

'It looks to me like a badly-skinned whale,' said Larry, peering at it closely.

'You can't *possibly* wear that, Mother,' said Margo, horrified, 'why, it looks as though it was made in nineteen-twenty.'

'What are all those frills and things for?' asked Larry with interest.

'Decoration, of course,' said Mother indignantly.

'What a jolly idea! Don't forget to shake the fish out of them when you come out of the water.'

'Well, *I* like it, anyway,' Mother said firmly, wrapping the monstrosity up again, 'and I'm going to wear it.'

'You'll have to be careful you don't get waterlogged, with all that cloth around you,' said Leslie seriously.

'Mother, it's *awful*; you can't wear it,' said Margo. 'Why on earth didn't you get something more up to date.'

'When you get to my age, dear, you can't go around in a two-piece bathing suit . . . you don't have the figure for it.'

'I'd love to know what sort of figure that was designed for,' remarked Larry.

'You really are *hopeless*, Mother,' said Margo despairingly.

'But I *like* it . . . and I'm not asking you to wear it,' Mother pointed out belligerently.

'That's right, you do what you want to do,' agreed Larry; 'don't be put off. It'll probably suit you very well if you can grow another three or four legs to go with it.

Mother snorted indignantly and swept upstairs to try on her costume. Presently she called us to come and see the effect, and we all trooped up to the bedroom. Roger was the first to enter, and on being greeted by this strange apparition clad in its voluminous black costume rippling with frills, he retreated hurriedly through the door, backwards, barking ferociously. It was some time before we could persuade him that it really was

Mother, and even then he kept giving her vaguely uncertain looks from the corner of his eye. However, in spite of all opposition, Mother stuck to her tent-like bathing-suit; and in the end we gave up.

In order to celebrate her first entry into the sea we decided to have a moonlight picnic down at the bay, and sent an invitation to Theodore, who was the only stranger that Mother would tolerate on such a great occasion. The day for the great immersion arrived, food and wine were prepared, the boat was cleaned out and filled with cushions, and everything was ready when Theodore turned up. On hearing that we had planned a moonlight picnic and swim he reminded us that on that particular night there was no moon. Everyone blamed everyone else for not having checked on the moon's progress, and the argument went on until dusk. Eventually we decided that we would go on the picnic in spite of everything, since all the arrangements were made, so we staggered down to the boat, loaded down with food, wine, towels, and cigarettes, and set off down the coast. Theodore and I sat in the bows as look-outs, and the rest took it in turn to row while Mother steered. To begin with, her eyes not having become accustomed to the dark, Mother skilfully steered us in a tight circle, so that after ten minutes' strenuous rowing the jetty suddenly loomed up and we ran into it with a splintering crash. Unnerved by this, Mother went to the opposite extreme and steered out to sea, and we would eventually have made a landfall somewhere on the Albanian coastline if Leslie had not noticed in time. After this Margo took over the steering, and she did it quite well, except that she would, in a crisis, get flurried and forget that to turn right one put the tiller over to the left. The result was that we had to spend ten minutes straining and tugging at the boat which Margo had, in her excitement, steered on to, instead of away from, a rock. Taken all round it was an inauspicious start to Mother's first bathe.

Eventually we reached the bay, spread out the rugs on the sand, arranged the food, placed the battalion of wine bottles in a row in the shallows to keep cool, and the great moment had arrived. Amid much cheering Mother removed her housecoat and stood revealed in all her glory, clad in the bathing-costume which made her look, as Larry pointed out, like a sort of marine Albert Memorial. Roger behaved very well until he saw Mother wade into the shallow water in a slow and dignified manner. He then got terribly excited. He seemed to be under the impression that the bathing-costume was some sort of sea monster that had enveloped Mother and was now about to carry her out to sea. Barking wildly he flung himself to the rescue, grabbed one of the frills dangling so plentifully round the edge of the costume, and tugged with all his strength in order to pull Mother back to safety. Mother, who had just remarked that she thought the water a little cold, suddenly found herself being pulled backwards. With a squeak of dismay she lost her footing and sat down heavily in two feet of water, while Roger tugged so hard that a large section of frill gave way. Elated by the fact that the enemy appeared to be disintegrating, Roger, growling encouragement to Mother, set to work to remove the rest of the offending monster from her person. We writhed on the sand, helpless with laughter, while Mother sat gasping in the shallows, making desperate attempts to regain her feet, beat Roger off, and retain at least a portion of her costume. Unfortunately, owing to the extreme thickness of the material from which the costume was constructed, the air was trapped inside; the effect of the water made it inflate like a balloon, and trying to keep this airship of frills and tucks under control added to Mother's difficulties. In the end it was Theodore who shooed Roger away and helped Mother to her feet. Eventually, after we had partaken of a glass of wine to celebrate what Larry referred to as Perseus's rescue of Andromeda, we went in to swim, and Mother sat discreetly in the shallows, while Roger crouched nearby, growling ominously at the costume as it bulged and fluttered round Mother's waist.

The phosphorescence was particularly good that night. By plunging your hand into the water and dragging it along you could draw a wide golden-green ribbon of cold fire across the sea, and when you dived as you hit the surface it seemed as though you had plunged into a frosty furnace of glinting light. When we were tired we waded out of the sea, the water running off our bodies so that we seemed to be on fire, and lay on the sand to eat. Then, as the wine was opened at the end of the meal, as if by arrangement, a few fireflies appeared in the olives behind us – a sort of overture to the show.

First of all there were just two or three green specks, sliding smoothly through the trees, winking regularly. But gradually more and more appeared, until parts of the olive-grove were lit with a weird green glow. Never had we seen so many fireflies congregated in one spot; they flicked through the trees in swarms, they crawled on the grass, the bushes and the olive-trunks, they drifted in swarms over our heads and

124

landed on the rugs, like green embers. Glittering streams of them flew out over the bay, swirling over the water, and then, right on cue, the porpoises appeared, swimming in line into the bay, rocking rhythmically through the water, their backs as if painted with phosphorus. In the centre of the bay they swam round, diving and rolling, occasionally leaping high in the air and falling back into a conflagration of light. With the fireflies above and the illuminated porpoises below it was a fantastic sight. We could even see the luminous trails beneath the surface where the porpoises swam in fiery patterns across the sandy bottom, and when they leapt high in the air the drops of emerald glowing water flicked from them, and you could not tell if it was phosphorescence or fireflies you were looking at. For an hour or so we watched this pageant, and then slowly the fireflies drifted back inland and farther down the coast. Then the porpoises lined up and sped out to sea, leaving a flaming path behind them that flickered and glowed, and then died slowly, like a glowing branch laid across the bay.

# 11

# The Enchanted Archipelago

As the summer grew hotter and hotter we decided that it required too much effort to row the *Sea Cow* down the coast to our bathing bay, so we invested in an outboard engine. The acquisition of this machine opened up a vast area of coastland for us, for we could now venture much farther afield, making trips along the jagged coastline to remote and deserted beaches golden as corn, or lying like fallen moons among the contorted rocks. It was thus that I became aware of the fact that, stretching along the coast for miles, was a scattered archipelago of small islands, some fairly extensive, some that were really outsize rocks with a wig of greenery perched precariously on top. For some reason, which I could not discover, the sea faunae were greatly attracted by this archipelago, and round the edges of the islands, in rockpools and sandy bays the size of a large table, there was a bewildering assortment of life. I managed to inveigle the family into several trips to these islets, but as these had few good bathing spots the family soon got bored with having to sit on sun-baked rocks while I fished interminably in the pools and unearthed at intervals strange, and to them, revolting sea-creatures. Also, the islands were strung out close to the coast, some of them being separated from the mainland only by a channel twenty feet wide, and there were plenty of reefs and rocks. So guiding the *Sea Cow* through these hazards, and making sure the propeller did not strike or break, made any excursion to the islands a difficult navigational problem. Our trips there became less and less frequent, in spite of all arguments on my part, and I was tortured by the thought of all the wonderful animal life waiting in the limpid pools to be caught; but I was unable to do anything about it, simply because I had no boat. I suggested that I might be allowed to take the *Sea Cow* out myself, say once a week, but the family were, for a variety of reasons, against this. But then, just when I had almost given up hope, I was struck with a brilliant idea: my birthday was due fairly soon, and if I dealt with the family skilfully I felt sure I could not only get a boat, but a lot of other equipment as well. I therefore suggested to the family that, instead of letting them choose my birthday presents, I might tell them the things I wanted most. In this way they could be sure of not disappointing me. The family, rather taken aback, agreed, and then, somewhat suspiciously, asked me what I wanted. Innocently, I said that I hadn't thought about it much, but that I would work out a list for each person, and they could then choose one or more items on it.

My list took a lot of time and thought to work out, and a considerable amount of applied psychology. Mother, for instance, I knew, would buy me everything on her list, so I put down some of the most necessary and expensive equipment: five wooden cases, glass-topped, cork-lined, to house my insect collection; two dozen test-tubes; five pints of methylated spirits, five pints of formalin, and a microscope. Margo's list was a little more difficult, for the items had to be chosen so that they would encourage her to go to her favourite shops. So from her I asked for ten yards of butter muslin, ten yards of white calico, six large packets of pins, two bundles of cotton wool, two pints of ether, a pair of forceps, and two fountain-pen fillers. It was, I realized resignedly, quite useless to ask Larry for anything like formalin or pins, but if my list showed some sort of literary leaning I stood a good chance. Accordingly I made out a formidable sheet covered with the titles, authors' names, publishers, and price of all the natural history books I felt in need of, and put an asterisk against those that would be most gratefully received. Since I had only one request left, I decided to tackle Leslie verbally instead of handing him a list, but I knew I should have to choose my moment with care. I had to wait some days for what I considered to be a propitious moment.

I had just helped him to the successful conclusion of some ballistic experiments he was making, which involved tying an ancient muzzle-loader to a tree and firing it by means of a long string attached to the trigger. At the fourth attempt we achieved what apparently Leslie considered to be a success: the barrel burst and bits of metal whined in all directions.

Leslie was delighted and made copious notes on the back of an envelope. Together we set about picking up the remains of the gun. While we were thus engaged I casually asked him what he would like to give me for my birthday.

'Hadn't thought abut it,' he replied absently, examining with evident satisfaction a contorted piece of metal. 'I don't mind . . . anything you like . . . you choose.'

I said I wanted a boat. Leslie, realizing how he had been trapped, said indignantly that a boat was far too large a present for a birthday, and anyway he couldn't afford it. I said, equally indignantly, that he had *told* me to choose what I liked. Leslie said yes, he had, but he hadn't meant a boat, as they were terribly expensive. I said that when one said *anything* one meant anything, which included boats, and anyway I didn't expect him to buy me one. I had thought, since he knew so much about boats, he would be able to build me one. However, if he thought me too difficult . . .

'Of course it's not difficult,' said Leslie, unguardedly, and then added hastily, 'Well . . . not terribly difficult. But it's the *time*. It would take ages and ages to do. Look, wouldn't it be better if I took you out in the *Sea Cow* twice a week?'

But I was adamant; I wanted a boat and I was quite prepared to wait for it.

'Oh, all right, all right,' Leslie said exasperatedly, 'I'll build you a boat. But I'm not having you hanging around while I do it, understand? You're to keep well away. You're not to see it until it's finished.'

Delightedly I agreed to these conditions, and so for the next two weeks Spiro kept turning up with car-loads of planks, and the sounds of sawing, hammering, and blasphemy floated round from the back veranda. The house was littered with wood shavings, and everywhere he walked Leslie left a trail of sawdust. I found it fairly easy to restrain my impatience and curiosity, for I had, at that time, something else to occupy me. Some repairs had just been completed to the back of the house, and three large bags of beautiful pink cement had been left over. These I had appropriated, and I set to work to build a series of small ponds in which I could keep not only my freshwater fauna, but also all the wonderful sea creatures I hoped to catch in my new boat. Digging ponds, in midsummer, was harder work than I had anticipated, but eventually I had some reasonably square holes dug, and a couple of days splashing around in a sticky porridge of lovely coral-pink cement soon revived me. Leslie's trails of sawdust and shaving through the house were now interwoven with a striking pattern of pink footprints.

The day before my birthday the entire family made an expedition into the town. The reasons were three-fold. Firstly, they wanted to purchase my presents. Secondly, the larder had to be stocked up. We had agreed that we would not invite a lot of people to the party; we said we didn't like crowds, and so ten guests, carefully selected, were the most we were prepared to put up with. It would be a small but distinguished gathering of people we liked best. Having unanimously decided on this, each member of the family then proceeded to invite ten people. Unfortunately they didn't all invite the same ten, with the exception of Theodore, who received five separate invitations. The result was that Mother, on the eve of the party, suddenly discovered we were going to have not ten guests but forty-five. The third reason for going to town was to make sure that Lugaretzia attended the dentist. Recently her teeth had been her chief woe, and Doctor Androuchelli, having peered into her mouth, had uttered a series of popping noises indicative of horror, and said that she must have all her teeth out, since it was obvious that they were the cause of all her ailments. After a week's arguing, accompanied by floods of tears, we managed to get Lugaretzia to consent, but she had refused to go without moral support. So, bearing her, white and weeping, in our midst, we swept into town.

We returned in the evening, exhausted and irritable, the car piled high with food, and Lugaretzia lying across our laps like a corpse, moaning frightfully. It was perfectly obvious that she would be in no condition to assist with the cooking and other work on the morrow. Spiro, when asked to suggest a solution, gave his usual answer.

'Nevers you minds,' he scowled; 'leaves everything to me.'

The following morning was full of incident. Lugaretzia had recovered sufficiently to undertake light duties, and she followed us all round the house, displaying with pride the gory cavities in her gums, and describing in detail the agonies she had suffered with each individual tooth. My presents having been duly inspected and the family thanked, I then went round to the back veranda with Leslie, and there lay a mysterious shape covered with a tarpaulin. Leslie drew this aside with the air of a conjurer, and there lay my boat. I gazed at it rapturously; it was surely the most perfect boat that anyone had ever had. Gleaming in her coat of new paint she lay there, my steed to the enchanted archipelago.

The boat was some seven feet long, and almost circular in shape. Leslie explained hurriedly – in case I thought the shape was due to defective craftsmanship – that the reason for this was that the planks had been too short for the frame, an explanation I found perfectly satisfactory. After all, it was the sort of irritating thing that could have happened to anyone. I said stoutly that I thought it was a lovely shape for a boat, and indeed I thought it was. She was not sleek, slim, and rather predatory looking, like most boats, but rotund, placid, and somehow comforting in her circular solidarity. She reminded me of an earnest dungbeetle, an insect for which I had great affection. Leslie, pleased at my evident delight, said deprecatingly that he had been forced to make her flat-bottomed, since, for a variety of technical reasons, this was the safest. I said that I liked flat-bottomed boats the best, because it was possible to put jars of specimens on the floor without so much risk of them upsetting. Leslie asked me if I liked the colour scheme, as he had not been too sure about it. Now, in my opinion, the colour scheme was the best thing about it, the final touch that completed the unique craft. Inside she was painted green and white, while her bulging sides were tastefully covered in white, black, and brilliant orange stripes, a combination of colours that struck me as being both artistic and friendly. Leslie then showed me the long, smooth cypress pole he had cut for a mast, but explained that it could not be fitted into position until the boat was launched. Enthusiastically I suggested launching her at once. Leslie, who was a stickler for procedure, said you couldn't launch a ship without naming her, and had I thought of a name yet? This was a difficult problem, and the whole family were called out to help me solve it. They stood clustered round the boat, which looked like a gigantic flower in their midst, and racked their brains.

'Why not call it the *Jolly Roger*?' suggested Margo.

I rejected this scornfully; I explained that I wanted a sort of *fat* name that would go with the boat's appearance and personality.

'*Arbuckle*,' suggested Mother vaguely.

That was no use, either; the boat simply didn't look like an Arbuckle.

'Call it the *Ark*,' said Leslie, but I shook my head.

There was another silence while we all stared at the boat. Suddenly I had it, the perfect name: *Bootle*, that's what I'd call her.

'Very nice, dear,' approved Mother.

'I was just about to suggest the *Bumtrinket*,' said Larry.

'Larry, dear!' Mother reproved. 'Don't teach the boy things like that.'

I turned Larry's suggestion over in my mind; it was certainly an unusual name, but then so was *Bootle*. They both seemed to conjure up the shape and personality of the boat. After much thought I decided what to do. A pot of black paint was produced and laboriously, in rather trickly capitals, I traced her name along the side: THE BOOTLE-BUMTRINKET. There it was; not only an *unusual* name, but an aristocratically hyphenated one as well. In order to ease Mother's mind I had to promise that I would only refer to the boat as the *Bootle* in conversation with strangers. The matter of the name being settled, we set about the task of launching her. It took the combined efforts of Margo, Peter, Leslie, and Larry to carry the boat down the hill to the jetty, while Mother and I followed behind with the mast and a small bottle of wine with which to do the launching properly. At the end of the jetty the boat-bearers stopped, swaying with exhaustion, and Mother and I struggled with the cork of the wine-bottle.

'What are you *doing*?' asked Larry irritably. 'For heaven's sake hurry up; I'm not used to being a slipway.'

At last we got the cork from the bottle, and I announced in a clear voice that I christened this ship the *Bootle-Bumtrinket*. Then I slapped her rotund backside with the bottle, with the unhappy result that half a pint of white wine splashed over Larry's head.

'Look out, look out,' he remonstrated. 'Which one of us are you supposed to be launching?'

At last they cast the *Bootle-Bumtrinket* off the jetty with a mighty heave, and she landed on her flat bottom with a report like a cannon, showering sea-water in all directions, and then bobbed steadily and confidently on the ripples. She had the faintest suggestion of a list to starboard, but I generously attributed this to the wine and not to Leslie's workmanship.

'Now!' said Leslie, organizing things. 'Let's get the mast in ... Margo, you hold her nose ... that's it ... Now, Peter, if you'll get into the stern, Larry and I will hand you the mast ... all you have to do is stick it in that socket.'

So, while Margo lay on her tummy holding the nose of the boat, Peter leapt nimbly into the stern and settled himself, with legs apart, to receive the mast which Larry and Leslie were holding.

'This mast looks a bit long to me, Les,' said Larry, eyeing it critically.

'Nonsense! It'll be fine when it's in,' retorted Leslie. 'Now . . . are you ready, Peter?'

Peter nodded, braced himself, clasped the mast firmly in both hands, and plunged it into the socket. Then he stood back, dusted his hands, and the *Bootle-Bumtrinket*, with a speed remarkable for a craft of her circumference, turned turtle. Peter, clad in his one decent suit which he had put on in honour of my birthday, disappeared with scarcely a splash. All that remained on the surface of the water was his hat, the mast, and the *Bootle-Bumtrinket*'s bright orange bottom.

'He'll drown! He'll drown!' screamed Margo, who always tended to look on the dark side in a crisis.

'Nonsense! It's not deep enough,' said Leslie.

'I told you that mast was too long,' said Larry unctuously.

'It *isn't* too long,' Leslie snapped irritably; 'that fool didn't set it right.'

'Don't you dare call him a fool,' said Margo.

'You can't fit a twenty-foot mast on to a thing like a wash-tub and expect it to keep upright,' said Larry.

'If you're so damn clever why didn't *you* make the boat?'

'I wasn't asked to . . . Besides, you're supposed to be the expert, though I doubt if they'd employ you on Clydeside.'

'Very funny. It's easy enough to criticize . . . just because that fool . . .'

'Don't call him a fool . . . How dare you?'

'Now, now, don't argue about it, dears,' said Mother peaceably.

'Well, Larry's so damn patronizing . . .'

'Thank God! He's come up,' said Margo in fervent tones as the bedraggled and spluttering Peter rose to the surface.

We hauled him out, and Margo hurried him up to the house to get his suit dry before the party. The rest of us followed, still arguing. Leslie, incensed at Larry's criticism, changed into trunks and, armed with a massive manual on yacht construction and a tape measure, went down to salvage the boat. For the rest of the morning he kept sawing bits off the mast until she eventually floated upright, but by then the mast was only about three feet high. Leslie was very puzzled, but he promised to fit a new mast as soon as he'd worked out the correct specification. So the *Bootle-Bumtrinket*, tied to the end of the jetty, floated there in all her glory, looking like a very vivid, overweight Manx cat.

132

Spiro arrived soon after lunch, bringing with him a tall, elderly man who had the air of an ambassador. This, Spiro explained, was the King of Greece's ex-butler, who had been prevailed upon to come out of retirement and help with the party. Spiro then turned everyone out of the kitchen and he and the butler closeted themselves in there together. When I went round and peered through the window, I saw the butler in his waistcoat, polishing glasses, while Spiro, scowling thoughtfully and humming to himself, was attacking a vast pile of vegetables. Occasionally he would waddle over and blow vigorously at the seven charcoal fires along the wall, making them glow like rubies.

The first guest to arrive was Theodore, sitting spick and span in a carriage, his best suit on, his boots polished, and, as a concession to the occasion, without any collecting gear. He clasped in one hand a walking-stick, and in the other a neatly tied parcel. 'Ah ha! Many . . . er . . . happy returns of the day,' he said, shaking my hand. 'I have brought you a . . . er . . . small . . . er . . . memento . . . a small gift, that is to say, *present* to er . . . commemorate the occasion . . . um.'

On opening the parcel I was delighted to find that it contained a fat volume entitled *Life in Ponds and Streams*.

'I think you will find it a useful . . . um . . . addition to your library,' said Theodore, rocking on his toes. 'It contains some very interesting information on . . . er . . . *general* freshwater life.'

Gradually the guests arrived, and the front of the villa was a surging mass of carriages and taxis. The great drawing-room and dining-room were full of people, talking and arguing and laughing, and the butler (who to Mother's dismay had donned a tail coat) moved swiftly through the throng like an elderly penguin, serving drinks and food with such a regal air that a lot of guests were not at all sure if he was a real butler, or merely some eccentric relative we had staying with us. Down in the kitchen Spiro drank prodigious quantities of wine as he moved among the pots and pans, his scowling face glowing redly in the light from the fires, his deep voice roaring out in song. The air was full of the scent of garlic and herbs, and Lugaretzia was kept hobbling to and fro from kitchen to drawing-room at considerable speed. Occasionally she would succeed in backing some unfortunate guest into a corner and, holding a plate of food under his nose, would proceed to give him the details of her ordeal at the dentist, giving the most life-like and most repulsive imitation of what a molar sounded like when it was torn from its socket, and opening her mouth wide to show her victims the ghastly havoc that had been wrought inside.

More and more guests arrived, and with them came presents. Most of these were, from my point of view, useless, as they could not be adapted for natural history work. The best of the presents were, in my opinion, two puppies brought by a peasant family I knew who lived not far away. One puppy was liver and white, with large ginger eyebrows, and the other was coal black with large ginger eyebrows. As they were presents, the family had, of course, to accept them. Roger viewed them with suspicion and interest, so in order that they should all get acquainted I locked them in the dining-room with a large plate of party delicacies between them. The results were not quite what I had anticipated, for when the flood of guests grew so large that we had to slide back the doors and let some of them into the dining-room, we found Roger seated gloomily on the floor, the two puppies gambolling round him, while the room was decorated in a fashion that left us in no doubt that the new additions had both eaten and drunk to their hearts' content. Larry's suggestion that they be called Widdle and Puke was greeted with disgust by Mother, but the names stuck and Widdle and Puke they remained.

Still the guests came, overflowing the drawing-room into the dining-room, and out of the french windows on to the veranda. Some of them had come thinking that they would be bored, and after an hour or so they enjoyed themselves so much that they called their carriages, went home, and reappeared with the rest of their families. The wine flowed, the air was blue with cigarette smoke, and the geckos were too frightened to come out of the cracks in the ceiling because of the noise and laughter. In one corner of the room Theodore, having daringly removed his coat, was dancing the *Kalamatiano* with Leslie and several other of the more exhilarated guests, their feet crashing and shuddering on the floor as they leapt and stamped. The butler, having perhaps taken a little more wine than was good for him, was so carried away by the sight of the national dance that he put his tray down and joined in, leaping and stamping as vigorously as anyone in spite of his age, his coat tails flapping behind him. Mother, smiling in a rather forced and distraught manner, was wedged between the English padre, who was looking with increasing disapproval at the revelry, and the Belgian consul, who was chattering away in her ear and twirling his moustache. Spiro

134

appeared from the kitchen to find out where the butler had got to, and promptly joined in the *Kalamatiano*. Balloons drifted across the room, bouncing against the dancers' legs, exploding suddenly with loud bangs; Larry, out on the veranda, was endeavouring to teach a group of Greeks some of the finer English limericks. Puke and Widdle had gone to sleep in someone's hat. Doctor Androuchelli arrived and apologized to Mother for being late.

'It was my wife, madame; she has just been delivered of a baby,' he said with pride.

'Oh, congratulations, doctor,' said Mother; 'we must drink to them.'

Spiro, exhausted by the dance, was sitting on the sofa nearby, fanning himself.

'Whats?' he roared at Androuchelli, scowling ferociously. 'You gets another babys?'

'Yes, Spiro, a boy,' said Androuchelli, beaming.

'How manys you gets now?' asked Spiro.

'Six, only six,' said the doctor in surprise. 'Why?'

'You oughts to be ashames of yourself,' said Spiro in disgust. 'Six . . . Gollys! Carrying on like cats and dogses.'

'But I like children,' protested Androuchelli.

'When I gots married I asks my wifes how many she wants,' said Spiro in a loud voice, 'and she says twos, so I gives her twos and then I gets her sewed ups. Six childrens . . . Honest to Gods, you makes me wants to throws . . . cats and dogses.'

At this point the English padre decided that he would, most reluctantly, have to leave, as he had a long day ahead of him tomorrow. Mother and I saw him out, and when we returned Androuchelli and Spiro had joined the dancers.

The sea was dawn-calm, and the eastern horizon flushed with pink when we stood yawning at the front door and the last carriage clopped its way down the drive. As I lay in bed with Roger across my feet, a puppy on each side of me, and Ulysses sitting fluffed out on the pelmet, I gazed through the window at the sky, watching the pink spread across the olive-tops, extinguishing the stars one by one, and thought that, taken all round, it had been an extremely good birthday party.

Very early next morning I packed my collecting gear and some food, and with Roger, Widdle, and Puke as company set off on a voyage in the *Bootle-Bumtrinket*. The sea was calm, the sun was shining out of a gentian-blue sky, and there was just the faintest breeze; it was a perfect day.

The *Bootle-Bumtrinket* wallowed up the coast in a slow and dignified manner, while Roger sat in the bows as look-out, and Widdle and Puke ran from one side of the boat to the other, fighting, trying to lean over the side and drink the sea, and generally behaving in a pathetically land-lubberish fashion.

The joy of having a boat of your own! The feeling of pleasant power as you pulled on the oars and felt the boat surge forward with a quick rustle of water, like someone cutting silk; the sun gently warming your back and making the sea surface flicker with a hundred different colours; the thrill of wending your way through the complex maze of weed-shaggy reefs that glowed just beneath the surface of the sea. It was even with pleasure that I contemplated the blisters that were rising on my palms, making my hands feel stiff and awkward.

Though I spent many days voyaging in the *Bootle-Bumtrinket*, and had many adventures, there was nothing to compare with that very first voyage. The sea seemed bluer, more limpid and transparent, the islands seemed more remote, sun-drenched, and enchanting than ever before, and it seemed as though the life of the sea had congregated in the little bays and channels to greet me and my new boat. A hundred feet or so from an islet I shipped the oars and scrambled up to the bows, where I lay side by side with Roger, peering down through a fathom of crystal water at the sea bottom, while the *Bootle-Bumtrinket* floated towards the shore with the placid buoyancy of a celluloid duck. As the boat's turtle-shaped shadow edged across the sea-bed, the multi-coloured, ever-moving tapestry of sea life was unfolded.

In the patches of silver sand the clams were stuck upright in small clusters, their mouths gaping. Sometimes, perched between the shell's horny lips, there would be a tiny, pale ivory pea-crab, the frail, soft-shelled, degenerate creature that lived a parasitic life in the safety of the great shell's corrugated walls. It was interesting to set off the clam colony's burglar alarm. I drifted over a group of them until they lay below, gaping up at me, and then gently edged the handle of the butterfly net down and tapped on the shell. Immediately the shell snapped shut, the movement causing a small puff of white sand to swirl up like a tornado. As the currents of this shell's alarm slid through the water the rest of the colony felt them. In a moment clams were slamming their front doors shut left and right, and the water was full of little whirls of sand, drifting and swirling about the shells, falling back to the sea-bed like silver dust.

Interspersed with the clams were the serpulas, beautiful feathery petals, forever moving round and round, perched on the end of a long, thick, greyish tube. The moving petals, orange-gold and blue, looked curiously out of place on the end of these stubby stalks, like an orchid on a mushroom stem. Again the serpulas had a burglar-alarm system but it was much more sensitive than the clams'; the net handle would get within six inches of the whirlpool of shimmering petals, and they would suddenly all point skywards, bunch together, and dive head-first down the stalk, so that all that was left was a series of what looked like bits of miniature hosepipe stuck in the sand.

On the reefs that were only a few inches below the water, and that were uncovered at low tide, you found the thickest congregation of life. In the holes were the pouting blennies, which stared at you with their thick lips, giving their faces an expression of negroid insolence as they fluttered their fins at you. In the shady clefts among the weeds the sea urchins would be gathered in clusters, like shiny brown horse-chestnut seed-cases, their spines moving gently like compass needles, towards possible danger. Around them the anemones clung to the rocks, plump and lustrous, their arms waving in an abandoned and somehow Eastern-looking dance in an effort to catch the shrimps that flipped past, transparent as glass. Routing in the dark underwater caverns, I unearthed a baby octopus, who settled on the rocks like a Medusa head, blushed to a muddy brown, and regarded me with rather sad eyes from beneath the bald dome of its head. A further movement on my part and it spat out a small storm-cloud of black ink that hung and rolled in the clear water, while the octopus skimmed off behind it, shooting through the water with its arms trailing behind it, looking like a streamer-decorated balloon. There were crabs too, fat, green, shiny ones on the tops of the reef, waving their claws in what appeared to be a friendly manner, and down below, on the weedy bed of the sea, the spider-crabs with their strange spiky-edged shells, their long, thin legs, each wearing a coat of weeds, sponges, or occasionally an anemone which they had carefully planted on their backs. Everywhere on the reefs, the weed patches, the sandy bottom, moved hundreds of top shells, neatly striped and speckled in blue, silver, grey, and red, with the scarlet and rather indignant face of a hermit crab peering out from underneath. They were like small ungainly caravans moving about, bumping into each other, barging through the weeds, or rumbling swiftly across the sand among the towering clam-shells and sea-fans.

The sun sank lower, and the water in the bays and below the tottering castles of rock was washed with the slate grey of evening shadow. Slowly, the oars creaking softly to themselves, I rowed the *Bootle-Bumtrinket* homewards. Widdle and Puke lay asleep, exhausted by the sun and sea air, their paws twitching, their ginger eyebrows moving as they chased dream crabs across endless reefs. Roger sat surrounded by glass jars and tubes in which tiny fish hung suspended, anemones waved their arms and spider-crabs touched the sides of their glass prisons with delicate claws. He sat staring down into the jars, ears pricked, occasionally looking up at me and wagging his tail briefly, before becoming absorbed once again in his studies. Roger was a keen student of marine life. The sun gleamed like a coin behind the olive-trees, and the sea was striped with gold and silver when the *Bootle-Bumtrinket* brought her round behind bumping gently against the jetty. Hungry, thirsty, tired, with my head buzzing full of the colours and shapes I had seen, I carried my precious specimens slowly up the hill to the villa, while the three dogs, yawning and stretching, followed behind.

# 12

# The Woodcock Winter

As the summer drew to a close I found myself, to my delight, once more without a tutor. Mother had discovered that, as she so delicately put it, Margo and Peter were becoming '*too* fond of one another'. As the family was unanimous in its disapproval of Peter as a prospective relation by marriage, something obviously had to be done. Leslie's only contribution to the problem was to suggest shooting Peter, a plan that was, for some reason, greeted derisively. I thought it was a splendid idea, but I was in the minority. Larry's suggestion that the happy couple should be sent to live in Athens for a month, in order, as he explained, to get it out of their systems, was quashed by Mother on the grounds of immorality. Eventually Mother dispensed with Peter's services, he left hurriedly and furtively and we had to cope with a tragic, tearful, and wildly indignant Margo, who, dressed in her most flowing and gloomy clothing for the event, played her part magnificently. Mother soothed and uttered gentle platitudes, Larry gave Margo lectures on free love, and Leslie, for reasons best known to himself, decided to play the part of the outraged brother and kept appearing at intervals, brandishing a revolver and threatening to shoot Peter down like a dog if he set foot in the house again. In the midst of all this Margo, tears trickling effectively down her face, made tragic gestures and told us her life was blighted. Spiro, who loved a good dramatic situation as well as anyone, spent his time weeping in sympathy with Margo, and posting various friends of his along the docks to make sure that Peter did not attempt to get back on to the island. We all enjoyed ourselves very much. Just as the thing seemed to be dying a natural death, and Margo was able to eat a whole meal without bursting into tears, she got a note from Peter saying he would return for her. Margo, rather panic-stricken by the idea, showed the note to Mother, and once more the family leapt with enthusiasm into the farce. Spiro doubled his guard on the docks, Leslie oiled his guns and practised on a large cardboard figure pinned to the front of the house. Larry went about alternately urging Margo to disguise herself as a peasant and fly to Peter's arms, or to stop behaving like Camille. Margo, insulted, locked herself in the attic and refused to see anyone except me, as I was the only member of the family who had not taken sides. She lay there, weeping copiously, and reading a volume of Tennyson; occasionally she would break off to consume a large meal – which I carried up on a tray – with undiminished appetite.

Margo stayed closeted in the attic for a week. She was eventually brought down from there by a situation which made a fitting climax to the whole affair. Leslie had discovered that several small items had been vanishing from the *Sea Cow*, and he suspected the fishermen who rowed past the jetty at night. He decided that he would give the thieves something to think about, so he attached to his bedroom window three long-barrelled shotguns aiming down the hill at the jetty. By an ingenious arrangement of strings he could fire one barrel after the other without even getting out of bed. The range was, of course, too far to do any damage, but the whistling of shot through the olive-leaves and the splashing as it pattered into the sea would, he felt, act as a fairly good deterrent. So carried away was he by his own brilliance that he omitted to mention to anyone that he had constructed his burglar trap.

We had all retired to our rooms and were variously occupied. The house was silent. Outside came the gentle whispering of crickets in the hot night air. Suddenly there came a rapid series of colossal explosions that rocked the house and set all the dogs barking downstairs. I rushed out on to the landing, where pandemonium reigned: the dogs had rushed upstairs in a body to join in the fun, and were leaping about, yelping excitedly. Mother, looking wild and distraught, had rushed out of her bedroom in her voluminous nightie, under the impression that Margo had committed suicide. Larry burst angrily from his room to find out what the row was about, and Margo, under the impression that Peter had returned to claim her and was being slaughtered by Leslie, was fumbling at the lock on the attic door and screaming at the top of her voice.

'She's done something silly ... she's done something

silly . . .' wailed Mother, making frantic endeavours to get herself free from Widdle and Puke, who, thinking this was all a jolly nocturnal romp, had seized the end of her nightie and were tugging at it, growling ferociously.

'It's the limit . . . You can't even sleep in peace . . . This family's driving me mad . . .' bellowed Larry.

'Don't hurt him . . . leave him alone . . . you cowards,' came Margo's voice, shrill and tearful, as she scrabbled wildly in an attempt to get the attic door opened.

'Burglars . . . Keep calm . . . it's only burglars,' yelled Leslie, opening his bedroom door.

'She's still alive . . . she's still alive . . . Get these dogs away . . .'

'You brutes . . . how dare you shoot him? . . . Let me out, *let me out* . . .'

'Stop fussing; it's only burglars . . .'

'Animals and explosions all day, and then bloody great twelve-gun salutes in the middle of the night . . . It's carrying eccentricity too far . . .'

Eventually Mother struggled up to the attic, trailing Widdle and Puke from the hem of her night attire, and, white and shaking, threw open the door to find an equally white and shaking Margo. After a lot of confusion we discovered what had happened, and what each of us had thought. Mother, trembling with shock, reprimanded Leslie severely.

'You mustn't do things like that dear,' she pointed out. 'It's really stupid. If you fire your guns off do at least let us *know*.'

'Yes,' said Larry bitterly, 'just give us a bit of warning, will you? Shout "Timber", or something of the sort.'

'I don't see how I can be expected to take burglars by surprise if I've got to shout out warnings to you all,' said Leslie aggrievedly.

'I'm damned if I see why we should be taken by surprise too,' said Larry.

'Well, ring a bell or something, dear. Only please don't do that again . . . it's made me feel quite queer.'

But the episode got Margo out of the attic, which, as Mother said, was one mercy.

In spite of being on nodding acquaintance with the family once again, Margo still preferred to nurse her broken heart in private, so she took to disappearing for long periods with only the dogs for company. She waited until the sudden, fierce siroccos of autumn had started before deciding that the ideal place for her to be alone was a small island situated in the bay opposite the house, about half a mile out. One day, when her desire for solitude became overwhelming, she borrowed the *Bootle-Bumtrinket* (without my permission), piled the dogs into it, and set off to the island to lie in the sun and meditate on Love.

It was not until tea-time, and with the aid of field-glasses, that I discovered where my boat and Margo had got to. Irately, and somewhat unwisely, I told Mother of Margo's whereabouts, and pointed out that she had no business to borrow my boat without permission. Who, I asked acidly, was going to build me a new boat if the *Bootle-Bumtrinket* was wrecked? By now the sirocco was howling round the house like a pack of wolves, and Mother, actuated by what I at first considered to be acute worry regarding the fate of the *Bootle-Bumtrinket*, panted upstairs and hung out of the bedroom window, scanning the bay with the field-glasses. Lugaretzia, sobbing and wringing her hands, hobbled up as well, and the two of them, trembling and anxious, kept chasing from window to window peering out at the foam-flecked bay. Mother was all for sending someone out to rescue Margo, but there was no one available. So all she could do was to squat at the window with the glasses glued to her eyes while Lugaretzia offered up prayers to Saint Spiridion and kept telling Mother a long and involved story about her uncle who had been drowned in just such a sirocco. Fortunately, Mother could only understand about one word in seven of Lugaretzia's tale.

Eventually it apparently dawned on Margo that she had better start for home before the sirocco got any worse, and we saw her come down through the trees to where the *Bootle-Bumtrinket* bobbed and jerked at her moorings. But Margo's progress was slow and, to say the least, curious; first she fell down twice, then she ended up on the shore about fifty yards away from the boat, and wandered about in circles for some time, apparently looking for it. Eventually, attracted by barks from Roger, she stumbled along the shore and found the boat. Then she had great difficulty in persuading Widdle and Puke to get into it. They did not mind boating when the weather was calm, but they had never been in a rough sea and they had no intention of starting now. As soon as Widdle was safely installed in the boat she would turn to catch Puke, and by the time she had caught him, Widdle had leapt ashore again. This went on for some time. At last she managed to get them both in together, leapt in after them, and rowed strenuously for some time before realizing that she had not untied the boat.

Mother watched her progress across the bay with bated breath. The *Bootle-Bumtrinket*, being low in the water, was not always visible, and whenever it disappeared behind a particularly large wave Mother would stiffen anxiously, convinced that the boat had foundered with all hands. Then the brave orange-and-white blob would appear once more on the crest of a wave and Mother would breathe again. The course Margo steered was peculiar, for the *Bootle-Bumtrinket* tacked to and fro across the bay in a haphazard fashion, occasionally even reappearing above the waves with her nose pointing towards Albania. Once or twice Margo rose unsteadily to her feet and peered around the horizon, shading her eyes with her hand; then she would sit down and start rowing once more. Eventually, when the boat had, more by accident than design, drifted within hailing distance, we all went down to the jetty and yelled instructions above the hiss and splash of the waves and the roar of the wind. Guided by our shouts Margo pulled valiantly for the shore, hitting the jetty with such violence that she almost knocked Mother off into the sea. The dogs scrambled out and fled up the hill, obviously scared that we might make them undertake another trip with the same captain. When we had helped Margo ashore we discovered the reason for her unorthodox navigation. Having reached the island, she had draped herself out in the sun and fallen into a deep sleep, to be woken by the noise of the wind. Having slept for the better part of three hours in the fierce sun, she found her eyes so puffy and swollen that she could hardly see out of them. The wind and spray had made them worse, and by the time she reached the jetty she cold hardly see at all. She was red and raw with sunburn and her eyelids so puffed out that she looked like a particularly malevolent Mongolian pirate.

'Really, Margo, I sometimes wonder if you're quite *right*,' said Mother, as she bathed Margo's eyes with cold tea; 'you do the most stupid things.'

'Oh, rubbish, Mother. You do fuss,' said Margo. 'It could have happened to anyone.'

But this incident seemed to cure her broken heart, for she no longer took solitary walks, nor did she venture out in the boat again; she behaved once more as normally as it was possible for her to do.

Winter came to the island gently as a rule. The sky was still clear, the sea blue and calm, and the sun warm. But there would be an uncertainty in the air. The gold and scarlet leaves that littered the countryside in great drifts whispered and chuckled among themselves, or took experimental runs from place to place, rolling like coloured hoops among the trees. It was as if they were practising something, preparing for something, and they would discuss it excitedly in rusty voices as they crowded round the tree-trunks. The birds, too, congregated in little groups, puffing out their feathers, twittering thoughtfully. The whole air was one of expectancy, like a vast audience waiting for the curtain to go up. Then one morning you threw back the shutters and looked down over the olive-trees, across the blue bay to the russet mountains of the mainland and became aware that winter had arrived, for each mountain peak would be wearing a tattered skull-cap of snow. Now the air of expectancy grew almost hourly.

In a few days small white clouds started their winter parade, trooping across the sky, soft and chubby, long, languorous, and unkempt, or small and crisp as feathers, and driving them before it, like an ill-assorted flock of sheep, would come the wind. This was warm at first, and came in gentle gusts, rubbing through the olive-groves so that the leaves trembled and turned silver with excitement, rocking the cypresses so that they undulated gently, and stirring the dead leaves into gay, swirling little dances that died as suddenly as they began. Playfully it ruffled the feathers on the sparrows' backs, so that they shuddered and fluffed themselves; and it leapt without warning at the gulls, so that they were stopped in mid-air and had to curve their white wings against it. Shutters started to bang and doors chattered suddenly in their frames. But still the sun shone, the sea remained placid, and the mountains sat complacently, summer bronzed, wearing their splintered snow hats.

For a week or so the wind played with the island, patting it, humming to itself among the bare branches. Then there was a lull, a few days' strange calm; suddenly, when you least expected it, the wind would be back. But it was a changed wind, a mad, hooting, bellowing wind that leapt down on the island and tried to blow it into the sea. The blue sky vanished as a cloak of fine grey cloud was thrown over the island. The sea turned a deep blue, almost black, and became crusted with foam. The cypress-trees were whipped like dark pendulums against the sky, and the olives (so fossilized all summer, so still and witch-like) were infected with the madness of the wind and swayed creaking on their misshapen, sinewy trunks, their leaves hissing as they turned, like mother of pearl, from green to silver. This is what the dead leaves had whispered about, this is what they had practised for; exultantly they rose in the air and danced, whirligiging about, dipping, swooping, falling exhausted when the wind tired of them and passed on. Rain followed the wind, but it was a warm rain that you could walk in and enjoy, great fat drops that rattled on the shutters, tapped on the vine leaves like drums, and gurgled musically in the gutters. The rivers up in the Albanian mountains became swollen and showed white teeth in a snarl as they rushed down to the sea, tearing at their banks, grabbing the summer debris of sticks, logs, grass tussocks, and other things, and disgorging them into the bay, so that the dark-blue waters became patterned with great coiling veins of mud and other flotsam. Gradually all these veins burst, and the sea changed from blue to yellow-brown; then the wind tore at the surface, piling the water into ponderous waves, like great tawny lions with white manes that stalked and leaped upon the shore.

This was the shooting season: on the mainland the great lake of Butrinto had a fringe of tinkling ice round its rim, and its surface was patterned with flocks of wild duck. On the brown hills, damp and crumbling with rain, the hares, roe deer, and wild boar gathered in the thickets to stamp and gnaw at the frozen ground, unearthing the bulbs and roots beneath. On the island the swamps and pools had their wisps of snipe, probing the mushy earth with their long rubbery beaks, humming like arrows as they flipped up from under your feet. In the olive-groves, among the myrtles, the woodcock lurked, fat and ungainly, leaping away when disturbed with a tremendous purring of wings, looking like bundles of wind-blown autumn leaves.

Leslie, of course, was in his element at this time. With a band of fellow enthusiasts he made trips over to the mainland once a fortnight, returning with the great bristly carcase of wild boar, cloaks of bloodstained hares, and huge baskets brimming over with the iridescent carcases of ducks. Dirty, unshaven, smelling strongly of gun-oil and blood, Leslie would give us the details of the hunt, his eyes gleaming as he strode about the room demonstrating where and how he had stood, where and how the boar had broken cover, the crash of the gun rolling and bouncing among the bare mountains, the thud of the bullet, and the skidding somersault that the boar took into the heather. He described it so vividly that we felt we had been present at the hunt. Now he was the boar, testing the wind, shifting uneasily in the cane thicket, glaring under its bristling eyebrows, listening to the sound of the beaters and dogs; now he was one of the beaters, moving cautiously through waist-high undergrowth, looking from side to side, making the curious bubbling cry to drive the game from cover; now, as the boar broke cover and started down the hill, snorting, he flung the imaginary gun to his shoulder and fired, the gun kicked realistically, and in the corner of the room the boar somersaulted and rolled to his death.

Mother thought little about Leslie's hunting trips until he brought the first wild boar back. Having surveyed the ponderous, muscular body and the sharp tusks that lifted the upper lip in a snarl, she gasped faintly.

'Goodness! I never realized they were so big,' she said. 'I do hope you'll be careful, dear.'

'Nothing to worry about,' said Leslie, 'unless they break cover right at your feet; then it's a bit of a job, because if you miss they're on you.'

'Most *dangerous*,' said Mother. 'I never realized they were so big . . . you might easily be injured or killed by one of those brutes, dear.'

'No, no, Mother; it's perfectly safe unless they break right under your feet.'

'I don't see why it should be dangerous even then,' said Larry.

'Why not?' asked Leslie.

'Well, if they charge you, and you miss, why not just jump over them?'

'Don't be ridiculous,' said Leslie, grinning. 'The damn' things stand about three feet at the shoulder, and they're hellish fast. You haven't got time to jump over them.'

'I really don't see why not,' said Larry; 'after all, it would be no more difficult than jumping over a chair. Anyway, if you couldn't jump over them, why not vault over them?'

'You do talk nonsense, Larry; you've never seen these things move. It would be impossible to vault *or* jump.'

'The trouble with you hunting blokes is lack of imagination,' said Larry critically. 'I supply magnificent ideas – all you have to do is to try them out. But no, you condemn them out of hand.'

'Well, you come on the next trip and demonstrate how to do it,' suggested Leslie.

'I don't profess to being a hairy-chested man of action,' said Larry austerely. 'My place is in the realm of ideas – the brain-work, as it were. I put my brain at your disposal for the formation of schemes and stratagems, and then you, the muscular ones, carry them out.'

'Yes; well, I'm not carrying *that* one out,' said Leslie with conviction.

'It sounds most foolhardy,' said Mother. 'Don't you do anything silly, dear. And, Larry, stop putting dangerous ideas into his head.'

Larry was always full of ideas about things of which he had no experience. He advised me on the best way to study nature, Margo on clothes, Mother on how to manage the family and pay up her overdraft, and Leslie on shooting. He was perfectly safe, for he knew that none of us could retaliate by telling him the best way to write. Invariably, if any member of the family had a problem, Larry knew the best way to solve it; if any one boasted of an achievement, Larry could never see what the fuss was about – the thing was perfectly easy to do, providing one used one's brain. It was due to this attitude of pomposity that he set the villa on fire.

Leslie had returned from a trip to the mainland, loaded with game, and puffed up with pride. He had, he explained to us, pulled off his first left and right. He had to explain in detail, however, before we grasped the full glory of his action. Apparently a left-and-a-right in hunting parlance meant to shoot and kill two birds or animals in quick succession, first with your left barrel and then with your right. Standing in the great stone-flagged kitchen, lit by the red glow of the charcoal fires, he explained how the flock of ducks had come over in the wintry dawn, spread out across the sky. With a shrill whistle of wings they had swept overhead, and Leslie had picked out the leader, fired, turned his gun on to the second bird, and fired again with terrific speed, so that when he lowered his smoking barrels the two ducks splashed into the lake almost as one. Gathered in the kitchen, the family listened spellbound to his graphic description. The broad wooden table was piled high with game, Mother and Margo were plucking a brace of ducks for dinner, I was examining the various species and making notes on them in my diary (which was rapidly becoming more bloodstained and feather-covered), and Larry was sitting on a chair, a neat, dead mallard in his lap, stroking its crisp wings and watching, as Leslie, up to the waist in an imaginary swamp, for the third time showed us how he achieved his left-and-a-right.

'Very good, dear,' said Mother, when Leslie had described the scene for the fourth time. 'It must have been very difficult.'

'I don't see why,' said Larry.

Leslie, who was just about to describe the whole thing over again, broke off and glared at him.

'Oh, you don't?' he asked belligerently. 'And what d'you know about it? You couldn't hit an olive-tree at three paces, let alone a flying bird.'

'My dear fellow, I'm not belittling you,' said Larry in his most irritating and unctuous voice. 'I just don't see why it is considered so difficult to perform what seems to me a simple task.'

'*Simple*? If you'd had any experience of shooting you wouldn't call it simple.'

'I don't see that it's necessary to have had shooting experience. It seems to me to be merely a matter of keeping a cool head and aiming reasonably straight.'

'Don't be silly,' said Les disgustedly. 'You always think the things other people do are simple.

'It's the penalty of being versatile,' sighed Larry. 'Generally they turn out to be ridiculously simple when I try them. That's why I can't see what you're making a fuss for, over a perfectly ordinary piece of markmanship.'

'Ridiculously simple when *you* try them?' repeated Leslie incredulously. 'I've never seen you carry out one of your suggestions yet.'

'A gross slander,' said Larry, nettled. 'I'm always ready to prove my ideas are right.'

'All right, let's see you pull off a left-and-a-right, then.'

'Certainly. You supply the gun and the victims and I'll show you that it requires no ability whatsoever: it's a question of a mercurial mind that can weigh up the mathematics of the problem.'

'Right. We'll go after snipe down in the marsh tomorrow. You can get your mercurial mind to work on those.'

'It gives me no pleasure to slaughter birds that have every appearance of having been stunted from birth,' said Larry, 'but, since my honour is at stake, I suppose they must be sacrificed.'

'If you get *one* you'll be lucky,' said Leslie with satisfaction.

'Really, you children do argue about the stupidest things,' said Mother philosophically, wiping the feathers off her glasses.

'I agree with Les,' said Margo unexpectedly; 'Larry's too fond of telling people how to do things, and doing nothing himself. It'll do him good to be taught a lesson. I think it was jolly clever of Les to kill two birds with one stone, or whatever it's called.'

Leslie, under the impression that Margo had misunderstood his feat, started on a new and more detailed recital of the episode.

It had rained all night, so early next morning, when we set off to see Larry perform his feat, the ground was moist and squelchy underfoot, and smelt as rich and fragrant as plum cake. To honour the occasion Larry had placed a large turkey feather in his tweed hat, and he looked like a small, portly, and immensely dignified Robin Hood. He complained vigorously all the way down to the swamp in the valley where the snipe congregated. It was cold, it was extremely slippery, he didn't see why Leslie couldn't take his word for it without this ridiculous farce, his gun was heavy, there probably wouldn't be any game at all, for he couldn't see anything except a mentally defective penguin being out on a day like this. Coldly and relentlessly we urged him down to the swamp, turning a deaf ear to all his arguments and protests.

The swamp was really the level floor of a small valley, some ten acres of flat land which were cultivated during the spring and summer months. In the winter it was allowed to run wild, and it became a forest of bamboos and grass, intersected by the brimming irrigation ditches. These ditches that criss-crossed about the swamp made hunting difficult, for most of them were too wide to jump, and you could not wade them, since they consisted of about six feet of liquid mud and four feet of dirty water. They were spanned, here and there, by narrow plank bridges, most of which were rickety and decayed, but which were the only means of getting about the swamp. Your time during a hunt was divided between looking for game and looking for the next bridge.

We had hardly crossed the first little bridge when three snipe purred up from under our feet and zoomed away, swinging from side to side as they flew. Larry flung the gun to his shoulder and pulled the trigger excitedly. The hammers fell, but there was no sound.

'It would be an idea to load it,' said Leslie with a certain quiet triumph.

'I thought *you'd* done that,' Larry said bitterly; 'you're acting as the blasted gunbearer, after all. I'd have got that pair if it hadn't been for your inefficiency.'

He loaded the gun and we moved slowly on through the bamboos. Ahead we could hear a pair of magpies cackling fiendishly whenever we moved. Larry muttered threats and curses on them for warning the game. They kept flying ahead of us, cackling loudly, until Larry was thoroughly exasperated. He stopped at the head of a tiny bridge that sagged over a wide expanse of placid water.

'Can't we do something about those birds?' he inquired heatedly. 'They'll scare everything for miles.'

'Not the snipe,' said Leslie; 'the snipe stick close until you almost walk on them.'

'It seems quite futile to continue,' said Larry. 'We might as well send a brass band ahead of us.'

He tucked the gun under his arm and stamped irritably on to the bridge. It was then that the accident occurred. He was in the middle of the groaning, shuddering plank when two snipe which had been lying concealed in the long grass at the other end of the bridge rocketed out of the grass and shot skywards. Larry, forgetting in his excitement his rather peculiar situation, shipped the gun to his shoulder and, balancing precariously on the swaying bridge, fired both barrels. The gun roared and kicked, the snipe flew away undamaged, and Larry with a yell of fright fell backwards into the irrigation ditch.

'Hold the gun above your head! . . . Hold it above your head!' roared Leslie.

'Don't stand up or you'll sink,' screeched Margo. 'Sit still.'

But Larry, spreadeagled on his back, had only one idea, and that was to get out as quickly as possible. He sat up and then tried to get to his feet, using, to Leslie's anguish, the gun barrels as a support. He raised himself up, the liquid mud shuddered and boiled, the gun sank out of sight, and Larry disappeared up to his waist.

'Look what you've done to the gun,' yelled Leslie furiously; 'you've choked the bloody barrels.'

'What the hell do you expect me to do?' snarled Larry. 'Lie here and be sucked under? Give me a hand for heaven's sake.'

'Get the gun out,' said Leslie angrily.

'I refuse to save the gun if you don't save me,' Larry yelled. 'Damn it, I'm not a seal . . . *get me out*!'

'If you give me the end of the gun I can pull you out, you idiot,' shouted Leslie. 'I can't reach you otherwise.'

Larry groped wildly under the surface for the gun, and sank several inches before he retrieved it, clotted with black and evil-smelling mud.

'Dear God! just *look* at it,' moaned Leslie, wiping the mud off it with his handkerchief, 'just look at it.'

'Will you stop carrying on over that beastly weapon and get me out of here?' asked Larry vitriolically. 'Or do you want me to sink beneath the mud like a sort of sportsmen's Shelley?'

Leslie handed him the ends of the barrels, and we all heaved mightily. It seemed to make no impression whatsoever, except that when we stopped, exhausted, Larry sank a little deeper.

'The idea is to *rescue* me,' he pointed out, panting, 'not deliver the *coup de grâce*.'

'Oh, stop yapping and try to heave yourself out,' said Leslie.

'What d'you think I've been doing, for heaven's sake? I've ruptured myself in three places as it is.'

At last, after much effort, there came a prolonged belch from the mud and Larry shot to the surface and we hauled him up the bank. He stood there, covered with the black and stinking slush, looking like a chocolate statue that has come in contact with a blast furnace; he appeared to be melting as we approached.

'Are you all right?' asked Margo.

Larry glared at her.

'I'm fine,' he said sarcastically, 'simply fine. Never enjoyed myself more. Apart from a slight touch of pneumonia, a ricked back, and the fact that one of my shoes lies full fathoms five, I'm having a wonderful time.'

As he limped homewards he poured scorn and wrath on our heads, and by the time we reached home he was convinced that the whole thing had been a plot. As he entered the house, leaving a trail like a ploughed field, Mother uttered a gasp of horror.

'What *have* you been doing, dear?' she asked.

'Doing? What do you think I've been doing? I've been shooting.'

'But how did you get like that, dear? You're *sopping*. Did you fall in?'

'Really, Mother, you and Margo have such remarkable perspicacity I sometimes wonder how you survive.'

'I only *asked*, dear,' said Mother.

151

'Well, of course I fell in; what did you think I'd been doing?'

'You must change, dear, or you'll catch cold.'

'I can manage,' said Larry with dignity; 'I've had quite enough attempts on my life for one day.'

He refused all offers of assistance, collected a bottle of brandy from the larder, and retired to his room, where, on his instructions, Lugaretzia built a huge fire. He sat muffled up in bed, sneezing and consuming brandy. By lunch-time he sent down for another bottle, and at tea-time we could hear him singing lustily, interspersed with gigantic sneezes. At supper-time Lugaretzia had paddled upstairs with the third bottle, and Mother began to get worried. She sent Margo up to see if Larry was all right. There was a long silence, followed by Larry's voice raised in wrath, and Margo's pleading plaintively. Mother, frowning, stumped upstairs to see what was happening, and Leslie and I followed her.

In Larry's room a fire roared in the grate, and Larry lay concealed under a towering pile of bedclothes. Margo, clasping a glass, stood despairingly by the bed.

'What's the matter with him?' asked Mother, advancing determinedly.

'He's drunk,' said Margo despairingly, 'and I can't get any sense out of him. I'm trying to get him to take his Epsom salts, otherwise he'll feel awful tomorrow, but he won't touch it. He keeps hiding under the bedclothes and saying I'm trying to poison him.'

Mother seized the glass from Margo's hand and strode to the bedside.

'Now come on, Larry, and stop being a fool,' she snapped briskly; 'drink this down at *once*.'

The bedclothes heaved and Larry's tousled head appeared from the depths. He peered blearily at Mother, and blinked thoughtfully to himself.

'You're a horrible old woman ... I'm sure I've seen you somewhere before,' he remarked, and before Mother had recovered from the shock of this observation he had sunk into a deep sleep.

'Well,' said Mother, aghast, 'he must have had a lot. Anyway, he's asleep now, so let's just build up the fire and leave him. He'll feel better in the morning.'

It was Margo who discovered, early the following morning, that a pile of glowing wood from the fire had slipped down between the boards of the room and set fire to the beam underneath. She came flying downstairs in her nightie, pale with emotion, and burst into Mother's room.

'The house is on fire ... Get out ... get out ...' she yelled dramatically.

Mother leapt out of bed with alacrity.

'Wake Gerry ... wake Gerry,' she shouted, struggling, for some reason best known to herself, to get her corsets on over her nightie.

'Wake up ... wake up ... Fire ... fire!' screamed Margo at the top of her voice.

Leslie and I tumbled out on to the landing.

'What's going on?' demanded Leslie.

'Fire!' screamed Margo in his ear. 'Larry's on fire!'

Mother appeared, looking decidedly eccentric with her corsets done up crookedly over her nightie.

'Larry's on fire? Quickly, save him,' she screamed, and rushed upstairs to the attic, closely followed by the rest of us. Larry's room was full of acrid smoke, which poured up from between the floorboards. Larry himself lay sleeping peacefully. Mother dashed over to the bed and shook him vigorously.

'Wake *up*, Larry; for heaven's sake wake up.'

'What's the matter?' he asked, sitting up sleepily.

'The room's on fire.'

'I'm not surprised,' he said, lying down again. 'Ask Les to put it out.'

'Pour something on it,' shouted Les, 'get something to pour on it.'

Margo, acting on these instructions, seized a half-empty brandy bottle and scattered the contents over a wide area of floor. The flames leapt up and crackled merrily.

'You fool, not *brandy*!' yelled Leslie; 'water ... get some water.'

But Margo, overcome at her contribution to the holocaust, burst into tears. Les, muttering wrathfully, hauled the bedclothes off the recumbent Larry and used them to smother the flames. Larry sat up indignantly.

'What the hell's going on?' he demanded.

'The room's on fire, dear.'

'Well, I don't see why I should freeze to death ... why tear all the bedclothes off? Really, the fuss you all make. It's quite simple to put out a fire.'

'Oh, shut up,' snapped Leslie, jumping up and down on the bedclothes.

'I've never known people for panicking like you all do,' said Larry; 'it's simply a matter of keeping your head. Les has the worst of it under control; now if Gerry fetches the hatchet, and you, Mother, and Margo fetch some water, we'll soon have it out.'

Eventually, while Larry lay in bed and directed operations, the rest of us managed to rip up the planks and put out the smouldering beam. It must have been smouldering throughout the night, for the beam, a twelve-inch-thick slab of olive wood, was charred half-way through. When, eventually, Lugaretzia appeared and started to clean up the mass of smouldering bedclothes, wood splinters, water, and brandy, Larry lay back on the bed with a sigh.

'There you are,' he pointed out; 'all done without fuss and panic. It's just a matter of keeping your head. I would like someone to bring me a cup of tea, please; I've got the most splitting headache.'

'I'm not surprised; you were as tiddled as an owl last night,' said Leslie.

'If you can't tell the difference between a high fever due to exposure and a drunken orgy it's hardly fair to besmirch my character,' Larry pointed out.

'Well, the fever's left you with a good hangover, anyway,' said Margo.

'It's not a hangover,' said Larry with dignity, 'it's just the strain of being woken up at the crack of dawn by an hysterical pack of people and having to take control of a crisis.'

'Fat lot of controlling you did, lying in bed,' snorted Leslie.

'It's not the action that counts, it's the brainwork behind it, the quickness of wit, the ability to keep your head when all about you are losing theirs. If it hadn't been for me you would probably all have been burnt in your beds.'

# Conversation

Spring had arrived and the island was sparkling with flowers. Lambs with flapping tails gambolled under the olives, crushing the yellow crocuses under their tiny hooves. Baby donkeys with bulbous and uncertain legs munched among the asphodels. The ponds and streams and ditches were tangled in chains of spotted toads' spawn, the tortoises were heaving aside their winter bedclothes of leaves and earth, and the first butterflies, winter-faded and frayed, were flitting wanly among the flowers.

In the crisp, heady weather the family spent most of its time on the veranda, eating, sleeping, reading, or just simply arguing. It was here, once a week, that we used to congregate to read our mail which Spiro had brought out to us. The bulk of it consisted of gun catalogues for Leslie, fashion magazines for Margo, and animal journals for myself. Larry's post generally contained books and interminable letters from authors, artists, and musicians, about authors, artists, and musicians. Mother's contained a wedge of mail from various relatives, sprinkled with a few seed catalogues. As we browsed we would frequently pass remarks to one another, or read bits aloud. This was not done with any motive of sociability (for no other member of the family would listen, anyway), but merely because we seemed unable to extract the full flavour of our letters and magazines unless they were shared. Occasionally, however, an item of news would be sufficiently startling to rivet the family's attention on it, and this happened one day in spring when the sky was like blue glass, and we sat in the dappled shade of the vine, devouring our mail.

'Oh, this is nice ... Look ... organdie with puffed sleeves

... I think I would prefer it in *velvet*, though ... or maybe a brocade top with a *flared* skirt. Now, that's nice ... it would look good with long white gloves and one of those sort of summery hats, wouldn't it?'

A pause, the faint sound of Lugaretzia moaning in the dining-room mingled with the rustle of paper. Roger yawned loudly, followed in succession by Puke and Widdle.

'God! What a beauty! ... Just *look* at her ... telescopic sight, bolt action ... What a beaut! Um ... a hundred and fifty ... not really expensive, I suppose ... Now *this* is good value ... Let's see ... double-barrelled ... choke ... Yes ... I suppose one really needs something a bit heavier for ducks.'

Roger scratched his ears in turn, twisting his head on one side, a look of bliss on his face, groaning gently with pleasure. Widdle lay down and closed his eyes. Puke vainly tried to catch a fly, his jaws clopping as he snapped at it.

'Ah! Antoine's had a poem accepted at last! Real talent there, if he can only dig down to it. Varlaine's starting a printing press in a stable ... Pah! limited editions of his own works. Oh, God. George Bullock's trying his hand at portraits ... portraits, I ask you! He couldn't paint a candlestick. Good book here you should read, Mother: *The Elizabethan Dramatists* ... a wonderful piece of work ... some fine stuff in it ...'

Roger worked his way over his hind-quarters in search of a flea, using his front teeth like a pair of hair-clippers, snuffling noisily to himself. Widdle twitched his legs and tail minutely, his ginger eyebrows going up and down in astonishment at his own dream. Puke lay down and pretended to be asleep, keeping an eye cocked for the fly to settle.

'Aunt Mabel's moved to Sussex ... She says Henry's passed all his exams and is going into a bank ... at least I *think* it's a bank ... her writing really is awful, in spite of that expensive education she's always boasting about ... Uncle Stephen's broken his leg, poor old dear ... and done something to his *bladder*? ... Oh, no, I see ... really this writing ... he broke his leg falling off a ladder ... You'd think he'd have more sense than to go up a ladder at his age ... ridiculous ... Tom's married ... one of the Garnet girls ...'

Mother always left until the last a fat letter, addressed in large firm, well-rounded handwriting, which was the monthly instalment from Great-aunt Hermione. Her letters invariably created an indignant uproar among the family, so we all put aside our mail and concentrated when Mother, with a sigh of resignation, unfurled the twenty-odd pages, settled herself comfortably and began to read.

'She says that the doctors don't hold out much hope for her,' observed Mother.

'They haven't held out any hope for her for the last forty years and she's still as strong as an ox,' said Larry.

'She says she always thought it a little peculiar of us, rushing off to Greece like that, but they've just had a bad winter and she thinks that perhaps it was wise of us to choose such a salubrious climate.'

'Salubrious! What a word to use!'

'Oh, heavens! . . . oh, no . . . oh, Lord! . . .'

'What's the matter?'

'She says she wants to come and stay . . . the doctors have advised a warm climate!'

'No, I refuse! I couldn't bear it,' shouted Larry, leaping to his feet; 'it's bad enough being shown Lugaretzia's gums every morning, without having Great-aunt Hermione dying by inches all over the place. You'll have to put her off, Mother . . . tell her there's no room.'

'But I can't, dear; I told her in the last letter what a big villa we had.'

'She's probably forgotten,' said Leslie hopefully.

'She hasn't. She mentions it here . . . where is it? . . . oh, yes, here you are: "As you now seem able to afford such an extensive establishment, I am sure, Louise dear, that you would not begrudge a small corner to an old woman who has not much longer to live." There you are! What on earth can we *do*?'

'Write and tell her we've got an epidemic of smallpox raging out here, and send her a photograph of Margo's acne,' suggested Larry.

'Don't be silly, dear. Besides, I told her how healthy it is here.'

'Really, Mother, you are impossible!' exclaimed Larry angrily. 'I was looking forward to a nice quiet summer's work, with just a few select friends, and now we're going to be invaded by that evil old camel, smelling of mothballs and singing hymns in the lavatory.'

'Really, dear, you do *exaggerate*. And I don't know why you have to bring lavatories into it – I've never heard her sing hymns anywhere.'

'She does nothing else *but* sing hymns . . . "Lead, Kindly Light", while everyone queues on the landing.'

157

Well, anyway, we've got to think of a good excuse. I can't write and tell her we don't want her because she sings hymns.'

'Why not?'

'Don't be unreasonable, dear; after all, she *is* a relation.'

'What on earth's that got to do with it? Why should we have to fawn all over the old hag because she's a relation, when the really sensible thing to do would be burn her at the stake.'

'She's not as bad as that,' protested Mother half-heartedly.

'My dear Mother, of all the foul relatives with which we are cluttered, she is definitely the worst. Why you keep in touch with her I cannot, for the life of me, imagine.'

'Well, I've got to answer her *letters*, haven't I?'

'Why? Just write "Gone away" across them and send them back.'

'I couldn't do that, dear; they'd recognize my handwriting,' said Mother vaguely; 'besides, I've opened this now.'

'Can't one of us write and say you're ill?' suggested Margo.

'Yes, we'll say the doctors have given up hope,' said Leslie.

'*I'll* write the letter,' said Lzrry with relish. 'I'll get one of those lovely black-edged envelopes . . . that will add an air of verisimilitude to the whole thing.'

'You'll do nothing of the sort,' said Mother firmly. 'If you did that she'd come straight out to nurse me. You know what she is.'

'Why keep in touch with them? that's what I want to know,' asked Larry despairingly. 'What satisfaction does it give you? They're all either fossilized or mental.'

'Indeed, they're *not* mental,' said Mother indignantly.

'Nonsense, Mother . . . Look at Aunt Bertha, keeping flocks of imaginary cats . . . and there's Great-uncle Patrick, who wanders about nude and tells complete strangers how he killed whales with a pen-knife . . ., They're *all* bats.'

'Well, they're *queer*; but they're all very old, and so they're bound to be. But they're not *mental*,' explained Mother; adding candidly, 'Anyway, not enough to be put away.'

'Well, if we're going to be invaded by relations, there's only one thing to do,' said Larry resignedly.

'What's that?' inquired Mother, peering over her spectacles expectantly.

'We must move, of course.'

'Move? Move where?' asked Mother, bewildered.

'Move to a smaller villa. Then you can write to all these zombies and tell them we haven't any room.'

'But don't be stupid, Larry. We can't *keep* moving. We moved here in order to cope with your friends.'

'Well, now we'll have to move to cope with the relations.'

'But we can't *keep* rushing to and fro about the island . . . people will think we've gone mad.'

'They'll think we're even madder if that old harpy turns up. Honestly, Mother, I couldn't stand it if she came. I should probably borrow one of Leslie's guns and blow a hole in her corsets.'

'Larry! I do wish you *wouldn't* say things like that in front of Gerry.'

'I'm just warning you.'

There was a pause, while Mother polished her spectacles feverishly.

'But it seems so . . . so . . . *eccentric* to keep changing villas like that, dear,' she said at last.

'There's nothing eccentric about it,' said Larry, surprised; 'it's a perfectly logical thing to do.'

'Of course it is,' agreed Leslie; 'it's a sort of self-defence, anyway.'

'Do be sensible, Mother,' said Margo; 'after all, a change is as good as a feast.'

So, bearing that novel proverb in mind, we moved.

# PART III

As long liveth the merry man (they say)
As both the sorry man, and longer by a day.
UDALL, *Ralph Roister Doister*

# 13

# The Snow-White Villa

Perched on a hill-top among olive-trees, the new villa, white as snow, had a broad veranda running along one side, which was hung with a thick pelmet of grape-vine. In front of the house was a pocket-handkerchief-sized garden, neatly walled, which was a solid tangle of wild flowers. The whole garden was overshadowed by a large magnolia tree, the glossy dark green leaves of which cast a deep shadow. The rutted driveway wound away from the house, down the hillside through the olive-groves, vineyards, and orchards, before reaching the road. We had liked the villa the moment Spiro had shown it to us. It stood, decrepit but immensely elegant, among the drunken olives, and looked rather like an eighteenth-century exquisite reclining among a congregation of charladies. Its charms had been greatly enhanced, from my point of view, by the discovery of a bat in one of the rooms, clinging upside down to a shutter and chittering with dark malevolence. I had hoped that he would continue to spend the day in the house, but as soon as we moved in he decided that the place was getting overcrowded and departed to some peaceful olive trunk. I regretted his decision, but having many other things to occupy me, I soon forgot about him.

It was at the white villa that I got on really intimate terms with the mantids; up till then I had seen them, occasionally, prowling through the myrtles, but I had never taken very much notice of them. Now they forced me to take notice of them, for the hill-top on which the villa stood contained hundreds, and most of them were much larger than any I had seen before. They squatted disdainfully on the olives, among the myrtles, on the smooth green magnolia leaves, and at night they would converge on the house, whirring into the lamplight with their green wings churning like the wheels of ancient paddle-steamers, to alight on the tables or chairs and stalk mincingly about, turning their heads from side to side in search of prey, regarding us fixedly from bulbous eyes in chinless faces. I had never realized before that mantids could grow so large, for some of the specimens that visited us were fully four and a half inches long; these monsters feared nothing, and would, without hesitation, attack something as big as or bigger than themselves. These insects seemed to consider that the house was their property, and the walls and ceilings their legitimate hunting grounds. But the geckos that lived in the cracks in the garden wall also considered the house their hunting ground, and so the mantids and the geckos waged a constant war against each other. Most of the battles were mere skirmishes between individual members of the two forms of animals, but as they were generally well matched the fights rarely came to much. Occasionally, however, there would be a battle really worth watching. I was lucky enough to have a grandstand view of such a fight, for it took place above, on, and in my bed.

During the day most of the geckos lived under the loose plaster on the garden wall. As the sun sank and the cool shadow of the magnolia tree enveloped the house and garden they would appear, thrusting their small heads out of the cracks and staring interestedly around with their golden eyes. Gradually, they slid out on to the wall, their flat bodies and stubby, almost conical tails looking ash-grey in the twilight. They would move cautiously across the moss-patched wall until they reached the safety of the vine over the veranda, and there wait patiently until the sky grew dark and the lamps were lit. Then they would choose their hunting areas and make their way to them across the wall of the house, some to the bedrooms, some to the kitchen, while others remained on the veranda among the vine leaves.

There was a particular gecko that had taken over my bedroom as his hunting ground, and I grew to know him quite well and christened him Geronimo, since his assaults on the insect life seemed to me as cunning and well-planned as anything that famous Red Indian had achieved. Geronimo seemed to be a cut above the other geckos. To begin with, he lived alone, under a large stone in the zinnia bed beneath my window, and he would not tolerate another gecko anywhere near his home; nor, for that matter, would he allow any strange gecko to enter my bedroom. He rose earlier than the others of his kind, coming out from beneath his stone while the wall and house were still suffused with pale sunset-light. He would scuttle up the flaky white plaster precipice until he reached my bedroom window, and poke his head over the sill, peering about curiously and nodding his head rapidly, two or three times, whether in greeting to me or in satisfaction at finding the room as he had left it, I could never make up my mind. He would sit on the window-sill, gulping to himself, until it got dark and a light was brought in; in the lamp's golden gleam he seemed to change colour, from ash-grey to a pale, translucent pinky pearl that made his neat pattern of goose-pimples stand out, and made his skin look so fine and thin that you felt it should be transparent so that you could see the viscera, coiled neatly as a butterfly's proboscis, in his fat tummy. His eyes glowing with enthusiasm, he would waddle up the wall to his favourite spot, the left-hand outside corner of the ceiling, and hang there upside down, waiting for his evening meal to appear.

The food was not long in arriving. The first shoal of gnats, mosquitoes, and lady-birds, which Geronimo ignored, was very soon followed by the daddy-longlegs, the lacewing-flies, the smaller moths, and some of the more robust beetles. Watching Geronimo's stalking tactics was quite an education. A lacewing or a moth, having spun round the lamp until it was dizzy, would flutter up and settle on the ceiling in the white circle of lamplight printed there. Geronimo, hanging upside down in his corner, would stiffen. He would nod his head two or three times very rapidly, and then start to edge across the ceiling cautiously, millimetre by millimetre, his bright eyes on the insect in a fixed stare. Slowly he would slide over the plaster until he was six inches or so away from his prey, whereupon he stopped for a second and you could see his padded toes moving as he made his grip on the plaster more secure. His eyes would become more protuberant with excitement, what he imagined to be a look of blood-curdling ferocity would spread over his face, the tip of his tail would twitch minutely, and then he would skim across the ceiling as smoothly as a drop of water, there would be a faint snap, and he would turn round, an expression of smug happiness on his face, the lacewing inside his mouth with its legs and wings trailing over his lips like a strange, quivering walrus moustache. He would wag his tail vigorously, like an excited puppy, and then trot back to his resting place to consume his meal in comfort. He had incredibly sharp eyesight, for I frequently saw him spot a minute moth from the other side of the room, and circle the ceiling in order to get near enough for the capture.

His attitude towards rivals who tried to usurp his territory was very straightforward. No sooner had they hauled themselves over the edge of the sill and settled down for a short rest after the long climb up the side of the villa, than there would be a scuffling noise, and Geronimo would flash across the ceiling and down the wall, to land on the window-sill with a faint thump. Before the newcomer could make a move, Geronimo would rush forward and leap on him. The curious thing was that, unlike the other geckos, he did not attack the head or body of his enemy. He made straight for his opponent's tail, and seizing it in his mouth, about half an inch from the tip, he would hang on like a bulldog and shake it from side to side. The newcomer, unnerved by this dastardly and unusual mode of attack, immediately took refuge in the time-honoured protective device of the lizards: he would drop his tail and scuttle over the edge of the sill and down the wall to the zinnia bed as fast as he could. Geronimo, panting a little from the exertion, would be left standing triumphantly on the sill, his opponent's tail hanging out of his mouth and thrashing to and fro like a snake. Having made sure his rival had departed, Geronimo would then settle down and proceed to eat the tail, a disgusting habit of which I strongly disapproved. However, it was apparently his way of celebrating a victory, and he was not really happy until the tail was safely inside his bulging stomach.

Most of the mantids that flew into my room were fairly small. Geronimo was always eager to tackle them, but they were too quick for him. Unlike the other insects the mantids seemed unaffected by the lamplight: instead of whirling round and round drunkenly, they would calmly settle in a convenient spot and proceed to devour the dancers whenever they settled to regain their strength. Their bulbous eyes seemed just as keen as the gecko's, and they would always spot him and move hurriedly, long before he had crept within fighting range. The night of the great fight, however, he met a mantis that not only refused to fly away, but actually went to meet him, and it was almost more than he could cope with.

I had for some time been intrigued by the breeding habits of the mantids. I had watched the unfortunate male crouching on the back of a female who, with complete equanimity, was browsing on him over her shoulder. Even after his head and thorax had disappeared into the female's neat mouth his hinder end continued to do its duty. Having watched their rather savage love life, I was now very anxious to see the laying and hatching of the eggs. My chance came one day when I was in the hills and I came face to face, as it were, with an exceptionally large female mantis who was stalking regally through the grass. Her belly was distended, and I felt sure that she was expecting a happy event. Having paused, swaying from side to side on her slender legs, and surveyed me coldly, she continued on her way, mincing through the grass-stalks. I decided that the best thing to do would be to capture her so that she could lay her eggs in a box where I could watch over them in comfort. As soon as she realized that I was attempting to capture her, she whirled round amd stood up on end, her pale, jade-green wings outspread, her toothed arms curved upwards in a warning gesture of defiance. Amused at her belligerence towards a creature so much bigger than herself, I casually caught her round the thorax between finger and thumb. Instantly, her long, sharp arms reached over her back and closed on my thumb, and it felt as though half a dozen needles had been driven through the skin. In my surprise I dropped her and sat back to suck my wound: I found that three of the little punctures had gone really deep, and that, by squeezing, tiny drops of blood appeared. My respect for her increased; she was obviously an insect to be reckoned with. At the next attempt I was more cautious and used two hands, grabbing her round the thorax with one and holding on to her dangerous front arms with the other. She wiggled ineffectually, and tried to bite me with her jaws, lowering her evil little pointed face and nibbling at my skin, but her jaws were too weak to have any effect. I carried her home and imprisoned her in a large gauze-covered cage in my bedroom, tastefully decorated with ferns, heather, and rocks among which she moved with light-footed grace. I christened her Cicely, for no obvious reason, and spent a lot of time catching butterflies for her, which she ate in large quantities and with apparently undiminishing appetite, while her stomach got bigger and bigger. Just when I was certain that at any moment she would lay her eggs, she somehow or other found a hole in her cage and escaped.

I was sitting in bed reading one night when, with a great whirring of wings, Cicely flew across the room and landed heavily on the wall, some ten feet away from where Geronimo was busily cleaning up the last bits of an exceptionally furry moth. He paused with bits of fluff adhering to his lips, and gazed in astonishment at Cicely. He had, I am sure, never seen such a large mantis before, for Cicely was a good half-inch longer than he was. Amazed by her size and taken aback by her effrontery at settling in his room, Geronimo could do nothing but stare at her for a few seconds. Meanwhile Cicely turned her head from side to side and looked about with an air of grim interest, like an angular spinster in an art gallery. Recovering from his surprise, Geronimo decided that this impertinent insect would have to be taught a lesson. He wiped his mouth on the ceiling, and then nodded his head rapidly and lashed his tail from side to side, obviously working himself up into a death-defying fury. Cicely took no notice at all, but continued to stare about her, swaying slightly on her long, slender legs. Geronimo slid slowly from the wall, gulping with fury, until about three feet away from the mantis he paused and shifted his feet in turn to make sure that his grip was good. Cicely, with well-simulated astonishment, appeared to notice him for the first time. Without changing her position she turned her head round and peered over her shoulder. Geronimo glared at her and gulped harder. Cicely, having surveyed him coolly with her bulging eyes, continued her inspection of the ceiling as if the gecko did not exist. Geronimo edged forward a few inches, and scuffled his toes once more, and the tip of his tail twitched. Then he launched himself forward, and a strange thing happened. Cicely, who up till then was apparently absorbed in the inspection of a crack in the plaster, leapt suddenly into the air, turned round, and landed in the same spot, but with her wings spread out like a cloak, reared up on her hind legs, and curved both serviceable forefeet at the ready. Geronimo had not been prepared for this spiky reception, and he skidded to a halt about three inches away and stared at her. She returned his stare with one of scornful belligerence. Geronimo seemed a little puzzled by the whole thing; according to his experience the mantis should have taken flight and zoomed away across the room at his approach, and yet here she was standing on end, arms ready to stab, her green cloak of wings rustling gently as she swayed from side to side. However, he could not back out now, having got so far, so he braced himself and leapt in for the kill.

His speed and weight told, for he crashed into the mantis and made her reel, and grabbed the underside of her thorax in his jaws. Cicely retaliated by snapping both her front legs shut on Geronimo's hind legs.They rustled and staggered across the ceiling and down the wall, each seeking to gain some advantage. Then there was a pause while the contestants had a rest and prepared for the second round, without either losing their grips. I wondered whether I ought to interfere; I did not want either of them to get killed, but at the same time the fight was so intriguing that I was loath to separate them. Before I could decide, they started once again.

For some reason or other Cicely was bent on trying to drag Geronimo down the wall to the floor, while he was equally determined that he should drag her up to the ceiling. They lurched to and fro for some time, first one and then the other gaining the upper hand, but nothing decisive really happening. Then Cicely made her fatal mistake: seizing the opportunity during one of their periodic pauses, she hurled herself into the air in what seemed to be an attempt to fly across the room with Geronimo dangling from her claws, like an eagle with a lamb. But she had not taken his weight into consideration. Her sudden leap took the gecko by surprise and tore the suction-pads on his toes free from their grip on the ceiling, but no sooner were they in mid-air than he became a dead weight, and a weight that not even Cicely could cope with. In an intricate tangle of tail and wings they fell on to the bed.

The fall surprised them both so much that they let go of each other, and sat on the blanket regarding each other with blazing eyes. Thinking this was a suitable opportunity to come between them and call it a draw, I was just about to grab the contestants when they launched themselves at each other once again. This time Geronimo was wiser and grasped one of Cicely's sharp forearms in his mouth. She retaliated by grabbing him round the neck with the other arm. Both were at an equal disadvantage on the blanket, for their toes and claws got caught in it and tripped them up. They struggled to and fro across the bed, and then started to work their way up towards the pillow. By now they were both looking very much the worse for wear: Cicely had a wing crushed and torn and one leg bent and useless, while Geronimo had a great number of bloody scratches across his back and neck caused by Cicely's front claws. I was now far too interested to see who was going to win to dream of stopping them, so I vacated the bed as they neared the pillow, for I had no desire to have one of Cicely's claws dug into my chest.

It looked as though the mantis was tiring, but as her feet

made contact with the smooth surface of the sheet it seemed as if she was given a new lease of life. It was a pity that she applied her new-found strength towards the wrong objective. She released her grip on Geronimo's neck and seized his tail instead; whether she thought that by doing so she could hoist him into the air and thus immobilize him, I don't know, but it had the opposite effect. As soon as the claws dug into his tail Geronimo dropped it, but the furious wiggle he gave to accomplish this made his head wag rapidly from side to side, and the result was that he tore Cicely's forearm off in his mouth. So there was Cicely with Geronimo's lashing tail clasped in one claw, while Geronimo, tailless and bloody, had Cicely's left forearm twitching in his mouth. Cicely might still have saved the fight if she had grabbed Geronimo quickly, before he spat out his mouthful of arm; but she was too wrapped up in the thrashing tail, which I think she thought was a vital part of her adversary, and with her one claw she maintained a firm grip on it. Geronimo spat out the forearm and leapt forward, his mouth snapped, and Cicely's head and thorax disappeared into his mouth.

This was really the end of the fight; now it was merely a matter of Geronimo hanging on until Cicely was dead. Her legs twitched, her wings unfurled like green fans and rustled crisply as they flapped, her great abdomen pulsed, and the movements of her dying body toppled them both into a cleft in the rumpled bedclothes. For a long time I could not see them; all I could hear was the faint crackle of the mantis's wings, but presently even this ceased. There was a pause, and then a small, scratched, and bloodstained head poked above the edge of the sheet, and a pair of golden eyes contemplated me triumphantly as Geronimo crawled tiredly into view. A large piece of skin had been torn from his shoulder, leaving a raw, red patch; his back was freckled with beads of blood where the claws had dug into him, and his gory tail-stump left a red smear on the sheet when he moved. He was batterd, limp, and exhausted, but victorious. He sat there for some time, gulping to himself, and allowed me to mop his back with a ball of cotton wool on the end of a match-stick. Then, as a prize, I caught five fat flies and gave them to him, and he ate them with enjoyment. Having recovered his strength somewhat, he made his way slowly round the wall, over the window-sill, and down the outside wall of the house to his home under the stone in the zinnia bed. Obviously he had decided that a good night's rest was needed after such a hectic brawl. The following night he was back in his usual corner, perky as ever, wagging his stump of a tail with pleasure as he eyed the feast of insects drifting about the lamp.

It was a couple of weeks after his great battle that Geronimo appeared one night over the window-sill and, to my astonishment, he had with him another gecko. The newcomer was quite tiny, only about half Geronimo's size, and a very delicate pearly pink with large and lustrous eyes. Geronimo took up his usual stand in one corner while the newcomer chose a spot in the centre of the ceiling. They set about the task of insect-hunting with immense concentration, completely ignoring each other. I thought at first that the newcomer, being so dainty, was Geronimo's bride, but investigation in the zinnia bed proved that he still maintained a bachelor establishment under his stone. The new gecko apparently slept elsewhere, appearing only at night to join Geronimo as he shinned up the wall to the bedroom. In view of his pugnacious attitude towards other geckos I found it difficult to understand his toleration of this newcomer. I toyed with the idea that it might be Geronimo's son or daughter, but I knew that geckos had no family life whatsoever, simply laying their eggs and leaving the young (when hatched) to fend for themselves, so this did not seem probable. I was still undecided as to what name I should bestow on this new inhabitant of my bedroom when it met with a dreadful fate.

To the left of the villa was a large valley like a bowl of greensward, thickly studded with the twisted columns of the olive-trunks. This valley was surrounded by clay and gravel cliffs about twenty feet high, along the base of which grew a thick bed of myrtles that covered a tumbled mass of rocks. This was a fertile hunting ground from my point of view, for a great quantity of various animals lived in and round this area. I was hunting among these boulders one day when I found a large, half-rotten olive-trunk lying under the bushes. Thinking there might be something of interest beneath it, I heaved valiantly until it rolled over and settled on its back soggily. In the trough left by its weight crouched two creatures that made me gasp with astonishment.

They were, as far as I could see, common toads, but they were the largest I had ever seen. Each one had a girth greater than the average saucer. They were greyish-green, heavily carunculated, and with curious white patches here and there on their bodies where the skin was shiny and lacking in pigment. They squatted there like two obese, leprous Buddhas, peering at me and gulping in that guilty way that toads have. Holding one in each hand, it was like handling two flaccid, leathery balloons, and the toads blinked their fine golden filigreed eyes at me, and settled themselves more comfortably on my fingers, gazing at me trustfully, their wide, thick-lipped mouths seeming to spread in embarrassed and uncertain grins. I was delighted with them, and so excited at their discovery that I felt I must immediately share them with someone or I would burst with suppressed joy. I tore back to the villa, clutching a toad in each hand, to show my new acquisitions to the family.

Mother and Spiro were in the larder checking the groceries when I burst in. I held the toads aloft and implored them to look at the wonderful amphibians. I was standing fairly close to Spiro so that when he turned round he found himself staring into a toad's face. Spiro's scowl faded, his eyes bulged, and his skin took on a greenish hue; the resemblance between him and the toad was quite remarkable. Whipping out his handkerchief and holding it to his mouth, Spiro waddled uncertainly out on to the veranda and was violently sick.

'You shouldn't show Spiro things like that, dear,' Mother remonstrated. 'You know he's got a weak stomach.'

I pointed out that although I was aware of Spiro's weak stomach I had not thought that the sight of such lovely creatures as the toads would affect him so violently. What was wrong with them? I asked, greatly puzzled.

'There's nothing wrong with them, dear; they're lovely,' said Mother, eyeing the toads suspiciously. 'It's just that *everyone* doesn't like them.'

Spiro waddled in again, looking pale, mopping his forehead with his handkerchief. I hastily hid the toads behind my back.

'Gollys, Master Gerrys,' he said dolefully, 'whys you shows me things like that? I'm sorrys I had to rush outs, Mrs Durrells, but honest to Gods when I sees one of them bastards I haves to throws, and I thought it was betters if I throws out theres than in heres. Donts you ever shows me them things again, Master Gerrys, please.'

To my disappointment the rest of the family reacted in much the same way as Spiro had done to the toad twins, and so, finding that I could not stir up any enthusiasm among the others, I sadly took the creatures up to my room and placed them carefully under my bed.

That evening, when the lamps were lit, I let the toads out for a walk about the room, and amused myself by knocking down insects that swirled round the lamp for them to eat. They flopped ponderously to and fro, gulping up these offerings, their wide mouths snapping shut with a faint clopping sound as their sticky tongues flipped the insect inside. Presently an exceptionally large and hysterical moth came barging into the room, and thinking what a fine titbit it would make, I pursued it relentlessly. Presently it settled on the ceiling, out of my reach, within a few inches of Geronimo's friend. Since the moth was at least twice its size, the gecko wisely ignored it. In an effort to knock it down for the toads I hurled a magazine at it, which was a stupid thing to do. The magazine missed the moth but caught the gecko amidships, just as it was staring at an approaching lacewing-fly. The book flew into the corner of the room, and the gecko fell with a plop on to the carpet right in front of the larger of the two toads. Before the reptile had recovered its breath, and before I could do anything to save it, the toad leant forward with a benign expression on its face, the wide mouth fell open like a draw-bridge, the tongue flicked out and in again, carrying the gecko with it, and the toad's mouth closed once more and assumed its expression of shy good humour. Geronimo, hanging upside down in his corner, seemed quite indifferent to the fate of his companion, but I was horrified by the whole incident and mortified to feel that it was my fault. I hastily gathered up the toads and locked them in their box, for fear that Geronimo himself might be the next victim of their ferocity.

I was very intrigued by these giant toads for a number of reasons. First, they appeared to be the common species, yet they were blotched with the curious white patches on body and legs. Also all the other common toads I had seen had been only a quarter of the size of these monsters. Another curious thing was that I had found them together under the log; to find one such monster would have been unusual, but to find a pair sitting side by side like that was, I felt sure, a unique discovery. I even wondered if they might turn out to be something quite new to science. Hopefully I kept them imprisoned under my bed until the following Thursday, when Theodore arrived. Then I rushed breathlessly up to the bedroom and brought them down for him to see.

'Ah ha!' Theodore observed, peering at them closely and prodding one with his forefinger; 'yes, they are certainly very large specimens.'

171

He lifted one out of the box and placed it on the floor, where it sat staring at him mournfully, bulging and sagging like a blob of mildewed dough.

'Um ... yes,' said Theodore; 'they seem to be ... er ... the common toad, though, as I say, they are exceptionally *fine* specimens. These curious marks are due to lack of pigmentation. I should think it's due to age, though of course I ... er ... I may be wrong. They must be a considerable age to have reached ... er ... to have attained such proportions.'

I was surprised, for I had never looked upon toads as being particularly long-lived creatures. I asked Theodore what the usual age was that they attained.

'Well, it's difficult to say ... um ... there are no statistics to go on,' he pointed out, his eyes twinkling, 'but I should imagine that ones as large as these might well be twelve or even twenty years old. They seem to have a great tenacity for life. I have read somewhere of toads being walled up in houses and so forth, and it appears that they must have been confined like that for a number of years. In one case I believe it was something like twenty-five years.'

He lifted the other toad out of the box and set it down beside its companion. They sat side by side, gulping and blinking, their flabby sides wobbling as they breathed. Theodore contemplated them fully for a moment, and then took a pair of forceps out of his waistcoat pocket. He strode into the garden and overturned several rocks until he found a large, moist, and liver-coloured earthworm. He picked it up neatly with his forceps and strode back to the veranda. He stood over the toads and dropped the writhing earthworm on to the stone flags. It coiled itself into a knot, and then slowly started to unravel itself. The nearest toad lifted its head, blinked its eyes rapidly, and turned slightly so that it was facing the worm. The worm continued to writhe like a piece of wool on a hot coal. The toad bent forward, staring down at it with an expression of extreme interest on its broad face.

'Ah ha!' said Theodore, and smiled in his beard.

The worm performed a particularly convulsive figure of eight, and the toad leant further forward with excitement. Its great mouth opened, the pink tongue flicked out, and the forepart of the worm was carried into the gaping maw. The toad shut its mouth with a snap, and most of the worm, which hung outside, coiled about wildly. The toad sat back and with great care proceeded to stuff the tail end of the worm into its mouth, using its thumbs. As each section of thrashing worm was pushed in, the toad would gulp hard, closing its eyes with an expression as if of acute pain. Slowly, but surely, bit by bit, the worm disappeared between the thick lips, until at last there was only a fraction of an inch dangling outside, twitching to and fro.

'Um,' said Theodore in an amused tone of voice. 'I always like watching them do that. It reminds me of those conjurers, you know, that pull yards and yards of tapes or coloured ribbons out of their mouths ... er ... only, of course, the other way *round*.'

The toad blinked, gulped desperately, its eyes screwed up, and the last bit of worm disappeared inside its mouth.

'I wonder,' said Theodore meditatively, his eyes twinkling – 'I wonder if one could teach toads to swallow *swords*? It would be interesting to try.'

He picked up the toads carefully and replaced them in their box.

'Not sharp swords, of course,' he said, straightening up and rocking on his toes, his eyes gleaming. 'If the swords were sharp you might get your toad *in a hole*.'

He chuckled quietly to himself, rasping the side of his beard with his thumb.

# 14

# The Talking Flowers

It was not long before I received the unwelcome news that yet another tutor had been found for me. This time it was a certain individual named Kralefsky, a person descended from an intricate tangle of nationalities but predominantly English. The family informed me that he was a very nice man and one who was, moreover, interested in birds, so we should get on together. I was not, however, the least impressed by this last bit of information; I had met a number of people who professed to be interested in birds, and who had turned out (after careful questioning) to be charlatans who did not know what a hoopoe looked like, or could not tell the difference between a black red-start and an ordinary one. I felt certain that the family had invented this bird-loving tutor simply in an effort to make me feel happier about having to start work once again. I was sure that his reputation as an ornithologist would turn out to have grown from the fact that he once kept a canary when he was fourteen. Therefore I set off for town to my first lesson in the gloomiest possible frame of mind.

Kralefsky lived in the top two storeys of a square, mildewed old mansion that stood on the outskirts of town. I climbed the wide staircase and, with disdainful bravado, rapped a sharp tattoo on the knocker that decorated the front door. I waited, glowering to myself and digging the heel of my shoe into the wine-red carpet with considerable violence; presently, just as I was about to knock again, there came the soft pad of footsteps, and the front door was flung wide to reveal my new tutor.

I decided immediately that Kralefsky was not a human being at all, but a gnome who had disguised himself as one by donning an antiquated but very dapper suit. He had a large, egg-shaped head with flattened sides that were tilted back against a smoothly rounded hump-back. This gave him the appearance of being permanently in the middle of shrugging his shoulders and peering up into the sky. A long, fine-bridged nose with widely flared nostrils curved out of his face, and his extremely large eyes were liquid and of a pale sherry colour. They had a fixed, far-away look in them, as though their owner were just waking up out of a trance. His wide, thin mouth managed to combine primness with humour, and now it was stretched across his face in a smile of welcome, showing even but discoloured teeth.

'Gerry Durrell?' he asked, bobbing like a courting sparrow, and flapping his large, bony hands at me. 'Gerry Durrell, is it not? Come in, my dear boy, do come in.'

He beckoned me with a long forefinger, and I walked past him into the dark hall, the floorboards creaking protestingly under their mangy skin of carpet.

'Through here; this is the room we shall work in,' fluted Kralefsky, throwing open a door and ushering me into a small, sparsely furnished room. I put my books on the table and sat down in the chair he indicated. He leaned over the table, balancing on the tips of his beautifully manicured fingers, and smiled at me in a vague way. I smiled back, not knowing quite what he expected.

'Friends!' he exclaimed rapturously. 'It is most *important* that we are friends. I am quite, quite certain we will become friends, aren't you?'

I nodded seriously, biting the inside of my cheeks to prevent myself from smiling.

'Friendship,' he murmured, shutting his eyes in ecstasy at the thought, 'friendship! That's the ticket!'

His lips moved silently, and I wondered if he was praying, and if so whether it was for me, himself, or both of us. A fly circled his head, and then settled confidently on his nose. Kralefsky started, brushed it away, opened his eyes, and blinked at me.

'Yes, yes, that's it,' he said firmly; 'I'm sure we shall be friends. Your mother tells me you have a great love of natural history. This, you see, gives us something in common straight away . . . a bond, as it were, eh?'

He inserted a forefinger and thumb into his waistcoat pocket, drew out a large gold watch, and regarded it reproach-fully. He sighed, replaced the watch, and then smoothed the bald patch on his head that gleamed like a brown pebble through his licheny hair.

'I am by way of being an aviculturist, albeit an amateur,' he volunteered modestly. 'I thought perhaps you might care to see my collection. Half an hour or so with the feathered creatures will, I venture to think, do us no harm before we start work. Besides, I was a *little* late this morning, and one or two of them need fresh water.'

He led the way up a creaking staircase to the top of the house, and paused in front of a green baize door. He produced an immense bunch of keys that jangled musically as he searched for the right one; he inserted it, twisted it round, and drew open the heavy door. A dazzle of sunlight poured out of the room, blinding me, and with it came a deafening chorus of bird-song; it was as though Kralefsky had opened the gates of Paradise in the grubby corridor at the top of his house. The attic was vast, stretching away across almost the whole top of the house. It was uncarpeted, and the only piece of furniture was a large deal table in the centre of the room. But the walls were linked, from floor to ceiling, with row upon row of big, airy cages containing dozens of fluttering, chirruping birds. The floor of the room was covered with a fine layer of bird seed, so that as you walked your feet scrunched pleasantly, as though you were on a shingle beach. Fascinated by this mass of birds I edged slowly round the room, pausing to gaze into each cage, while Kralefsky (who appeared to have forgotten my existence) seized a large watering-can from the table and danced nimbly from cage to cage, filling water-pots.

My first impression, that the birds were all canaries, was quite wrong; to my delight I found there were goldfinches painted like clowns in vivid scarlet, yellow, and black; greenfinches as green and yellow as lemon leaves in midsummer; linnets in their neat chocolate-and-white tweed suiting; bullfinches with bulging, rose-pink breasts, and a host of other birds. In one corner of the room I found small french windows that led me out on to a balcony. At each end a large aviary had been built, and in one lived a cock blackbird, black and velvety with a flaunting banana-yellow beak; while in the other aviary opposite was a thrush-like bird which was clad in the most gorgeous blue feathering, a celestial combination of shades from navy to opal.

'Rock-thrush,' announced Kralefsky, poking his head round the door suddenly and pointing at this beautiful bird; 'I had it sent over as a nestling last year . . . from Albania, you know.

Unfortunately I have not, as yet, been able to obtain a lady for him.'

He waved the watering-can amiably at the thrush, and disappeared inside again. The thrush regarded me with a roguish eye, fluffed his breast out, and gave a series of little clucks that sounded like an amused chuckle. Having gazed long and greedily at him, I went back into the attic, where I found Kralefsky still filling water-pots.

'I wonder if you would care to assist?' he asked, staring at me with vacant eyes, the can drooping in his hand so that a fine stream of water dribbled on to the highly polished toe of one shoe. 'A task like this is so much easier if two pairs of hands work at it, I always think. Now, if you hold the watering-can ... so ... I will hold out the pots to be filled ... excellent! That's the ticket! We shall accomplish this in no time at all.'

So, while I filled the little earthenware pots with water, Kralefsky took them carefully between finger and thumb and inserted them deftly through the cage doors, as though he were popping sweets into a child's mouth. As he worked he talked both to me and the birds with complete impartiality, but as he did not vary his tone at all I was sometimes at a loss to know whether the remark was addressed to me or to some occupant of the cages.

'Yes, they're in fine fettle today; it's the sunshine, you know ... as soon as it gets to this side of the house they start to sing, don't you? You must lay more next time ... only two, my dear, only two. You wouldn't call *that* a clutch, with all the goodwill in the world. Do you like this new seed? Do you keep any yourself, eh? There are a number of most interesting seed-eaters found here ... Don't do that in your clean water ... Breeding some of them is, of course, a task, but a most rewarding one, I find, especially the crosses. I have generally had great success with crosses ... except when you only lay two, of course .., rascal, *rascal*!'

Eventually the watering was done and Kralefsky stood surveying his birds for a moment or so, smiling to himself and wiping his hands carefully on a small towel. Then he led me round the room, pausing before each cage to give me an account of the bird's history, its ancestors, and what he hoped to do with it. We were examining – in a satisfied silence – a fat, flushed, bullfinch, when suddenly a loud, tremulous ringing sound rose above the clamour of bird-song. To my astonishment the noise appeared to emanate from somewhere inside Kralefsky's stomach.

'By Jove!' he exclaimed in horror, turning agonized eyes on me, 'by Jove!'

He inserted finger and thumb into his waistcoat and drew out his watch. He depressed a tiny lever and the ringing sound ceased. I was a little disappointed that the noise should have such a commonplace source; to have a tutor whose inside chimed at intervals would, I felt, have added greatly to the charm of the lessons. Kralefsky peered eagerly at the watch and then screwed up his face in disgust.

'By Jove!' he repeated faintly, 'twelve o'clock already ... winged time indeed ... Dear me, and you leave at half past, don't you?'

He slipped the watch back into his pocket and smoothed his bald patch.

'Well,' he said at last, 'we cannot, I feel, achieve any scholastic advancement in half an hour. Therefore, if it would pass the time pleasantly for you, I suggest we go into the garden below and pick some groundsel for the birds. It's so good for them, you know, especially when they're laying.'

So we went into the garden and picked groundsel until Spiro's car honked its way down the street like a wounded duck.

'Your car, I believe,' observed Kralefsky politely. 'We have certainly managed to gather a good supply of green stuff in the time. Your assistance was invaluable. Now, tomorrow you will be here at nine o'clock sharp, won't you? That's the ticket! We may consider this morning was not wasted; it was a form of introduction, a measuring up of each other. And I hope a chord of friendship has been struck. By Jove, yes, that's very important! Well, *au revoir* until tomorrow, then.'

As I closed the creaking, wrought-iron gates he waved at me courteously and then wandered back towards the house, leaving a trail of golden-flowered groundsel behind him, his hump back bobbing among the rose-bushes.

When I got home the family asked me how I liked my new tutor. Without going into details, I said that I found him very nice, and that I was sure we should become firm friends. To the query as to what we had studied during our first morning I replied, with a certain amount of honesty, that the morning had been devoted to ornithology and botany. The family seemed satisfied. But I very soon found that Mr Kralefsky was a stickler for work, and he had made up his mind to educate me in spite of any ideas I might have on the subject. The lessons were boring to a degree, for he employed a method of teaching that must have been in fashion round about the middle of the eighteenth century. History was served in great, indigestible chunks, and the dates were learnt by heart. We would sit and repeat them in a monotonous, sing-song chorus, until they became like some incantation that we chanted automatically, our minds busy with other things. For geography I was confined, to my annoyance, to the British Isles, and innumerable maps had to be traced and filled in with the bevies of counties and the county towns. Then the counties and the towns had to be learnt by heart, together with the names of the important rivers, the main produce of places, the populations, and much other dreary and completely useless information.

'Somerset?' he would trill, pointing at me accusingly.

I would frown in a desperate attempt to remember something about that county. Kralefsky's eyes would grow large with anxiety as he watched my mental struggle.

'Well,' he would say at length, when it became obvious that my knowledge of Somerset was non-existent – 'well, let us leave Somerset and try Warwickshire. Now then, Warwickshire: county town? Warwick! That's the ticket! Now, what do they produce in Warwick, eh?'

As far as I was concerned they did not produce anything in Warwick, but I would hazard a wild guess at coal. I had discovered that if one went on naming a product relentlessly (regardless of the county or town under discussion), sooner or later you would find the answer to be correct. Kralefsky's anguish at my mistakes was very real; the day I informed him that Essex produced stainless steel there were tears in his eyes. But these long periods of depression were more than made up for by his extreme pleasure and delight when, by some strange chance, I answered a question correctly.

Once a week we tortured ourselves by devoting a morning to French. Kralefsky spoke French beautifully, and to hear me massacring the language was almost more than he could bear. He very soon found that it was useless to try to teach me from the normal text-books, so these were set aside in favour of a three-volume set of bird books; but even with these it was up-hill going. Occasionally, when we were reading the description of the robin's plumage for the twentieth time, a look of grim determination would settle on Kralefsky's face. He would slam the book shut, rush out into the hall, to reappear a minute later wearing a jaunty panama.

'I think it would freshen us up a little . . . blow the cobwebs away . . . if we went for a short *walk*,' he would announce, giving a distasteful glance at *Les Petits Oiseaux de l'Europe*. 'I think we will make our way through the town and come back along the esplanade, eh? Excellent! Now, we must not waste time, must we? It will be a good opportunity for us to practise our *conversational* French, won't it? So no English, please – everything to be said in French. It is in this way that we become familiar with a language.'

So, in almost complete silence, we would wend our way through the town. The beauty of these walks was that, no matter which direction we set out in, we invariably found ourselves, somehow or other, in the bird-market. We were rather like Alice in the Looking-glass garden: no matter how determinedly we strode off in the opposite direction, in no time at all we found ourselves in the little square where the stalls were piled high with wicker cages and the air rang with the song of birds. Here French would be forgotten; it would fade away into the limbo to join algebra, geometry, history dates, county towns, and similar subjects. Our eyes sparkling, our faces flushed, we would move from stall to stall, examining the birds carefully and bargaining fiercely with the vendors, and gradually our arms would become laden with cages.

Then we would be brought suddenly back to earth by the watch in Kralefsky's waistcoat pocket, chiming daintily, and he would almost drop his tottering burden of cages in his efforts to extract the watch and stop it.

'By Jove! Twelve o'clock! Who would have thought it, eh? Just hold this linnet for me, will you, while I stop the watch . . . Thank you . . . We will have to be quick, eh? I doubt whether we can make it on foot, laden as we are. Dear me! I think we had better have a cab. An extravagance, of course, but needs must where the devil drives, eh?'

So we would hurry across the square, pile our twittering, fluttering purchases into a cab, and be driven back to Kralefsky's house, the jingle of the harness and the thud of hooves mingling pleasantly with the cries of our bird cargo.

I had worked for some weeks with Kralefsky before I discovered that he did not live alone. At intervals during the morning he would pause suddenly, in the middle of a sum or a recitation of county towns, and cock his head on one side, as if listening.

'Excuse me a moment,' he would say. 'I must go and see Mother.'

At first this rather puzzled me, for I was convinced that Kralefsky was far too old to have a mother still living. After considerable thought, I came to the conclusion that this was merely his polite way of saying that he wished to retire to the lavatory, for 1 realized that not everyone shared my family's lack of embarrassment when discussing this topic. It never occurred to me that, if this was so, Kralefsky closeted himself more often than any other human being I had met. One morning I had consumed for breakfast a large quantity of loquats, and they had distressing effects on me when we were in the middle of a history lesson. Since Kralefsky was so finicky about the subject of lavatories I decided that I would have to phrase my request politely, so I thought it best to adopt his own curious term. I looked him firmly in the eye and said that I would like to pay a visit to his mother.

'My mother?' he repeated in astonishment. 'Visit my mother? Now?'

I could not see what the fuss was about, so I merely nodded.

'Well,' he said doubtfully, 'I'm sure she'll be delighted to see you, of course, but I'd better just go and see if it's convenient.'

He left the room, still looking a trifle puzzled, and returned after a few minutes.

'Mother would be delighted to see you,' he announced 'but she says will you please excuse her being a little untidy?'

I thought it was carrying politeness to an extreme to talk about the lavatory as if it were a human being, but, since Kralefsky was obviously a bit eccentric on the subject, I felt I had better humour him. I said I did not mind a bit if his mother was in a mess, as ours frequently was as well.

'Ah . . . er . . . yes, yes, I expect so,' he murmured, giving me rather a startled glance. He led me down the corridor, opened a door, and, to my complete surprise, ushered me into a large shadowy bedroom. The room was a forest of flowers; vases, bowls, and pots were perched everywhere, and each contained a mass of beautiful blooms that shone in the gloom, like walls of jewels in a green-shadowed cave. At one end of the room was an enormous bed, and in it, propped up on a heap of pillows, lay a tiny figure not much bigger than a child. She must have been very old, I decided as we drew nearer, for her fine, delicate features were covered with a network of wrinkles that grooved a skin as soft and velvety-looking as a baby mushroom's. But the astonishing thing about her was her hair. It fell over her shoulders in a thick cascade, and then spread halfway down the bed. It was the richest and most beautiful auburn colour imaginable, glinting and shining as though on fire, making me think of autumn leaves and the brilliant winter coat of a fox.

'Mother dear,' Kralefsky called softly, bobbing across the room and seating himself on a chair by the bed, 'Mother dear, here's Gerry come to see you.'

The minute figure on the bed lifted thin, pale lids and looked at me with great tawny eyes that were as bright and intelligent as a bird's. She lifted a slender, beautifully shaped hand, weighed down with rings, from the depths of the auburn tresses and held it out to me, smiling mischievously.

'I am so very flattered that you asked to see me,' she said in a soft, husky voice. 'So many people nowadays consider a person of my age a bore.'

Embarrassed, I muttered something, and the bright eyes looked at me, twinkling, and she gave a fluting blackbird laugh, and patted the bed with her hand.

'Do sit down,' she invited; 'do sit down and talk for a minute.'

Gingerly I picked up the mass of auburn hair and moved it to one side so that I could sit on the bed. The hair was soft, silky, and heavy, like a flame-coloured wave swishing through my fingers. Mrs Kralefsky smiled at me, and lifted a strand of it in her fingers, twisting it gently so that it sparkled.

'My one remaining vanity,' she said; 'all that is left of my beauty.'

She gazed down at the flood of hair as though it were a pet, or some other creature that had nothing to do with her, and patted it affectionately.

'It's strange,' she said, 'very strange. I have a theory, you know, that some beautiful things fall in love with themselves, as Narcissus did. When they do that, they need no help in order to live; they become so absorbed in their own beauty that they live for that alone, feeding on themselves, as it were. Thus, the more beautiful they become, the stronger they become; they live in a circle. That's what my hair has done. It is self-sufficient, it grows only for itself, and the fact that my old body has fallen to ruin does not affect it a bit. When I die they will be able to pack my coffin deep with it, and it will probably go on growing after my body is dust.'

'Now, now, Mother, you shouldn't talk like that,' Kralefsky chided her gently. 'I don't like these morbid thoughts of yours.'

She turned her head and regarded him affectionately, chuckling softly.

'But it's not morbid, John; it's only a theory I have,' she explained. 'Besides, think what a beautiful shroud it will make.'

She gazed down at her hair, smiling happily. In the silence Kralefsky's watch chimed eagerly, and he started, pulled it out of his pocket, and stared at it.

'By Jove!' he said, jumping to his feet, 'those eggs should have hatched. Excuse me a minute, will you, Mother? I really must go and see.'

'Run along, run along,' she said. 'Gerry and I will chat until you come back . . . don't worry about *us*.'

'That's the ticket!' exclaimed Kralefsky, and bobbed rapidly across the room between the banks of flowers, like a mole burrowing through a rainbow. The door sighed shut behind him, and Mrs Kralefsky turned her head and smiled at me.

'They say,' she announced – 'they *say* that when you get old, as I am, your body slows down. I don't believe it. No, I think that is quite wrong. I have a theory that you do *not* slow down at all, but that *life slows down for you*. You understand me? Everything becomes languid, as it were, and you can notice so much more when things are in slow motion. The things you see! The extraordinary things that happen all around you, that you never even suspected before. It is really a delightful adventure, quite delightful!'

She sighed with satisfaction, and glanced round the room. 'Take flowers,' she said, pointing at the blooms that filled the room. Have you heard flowers *talking*?'

Greatly intrigued, I shook my head; the idea of flowers talking was quite new to me.

'Well, I can assure you that they *do* talk,' she said. 'They hold long conversations with each other . . . at least I presume them to be conversations, for I don't understand what they're saying, naturally. When you're as old as I am you'll probably be able to hear them as well; that is, if you retain an open mind about such matters. *Most* people say that as one gets older one believes nothing and is surprised at nothing, so that one becomes more receptive to ideas. Nonsense! All the old people I know have had their minds locked up like grey, scaly oysters since they were in their teens.'

She glanced at me sharply.

'D'you think I'm queer? Touched, eh? Talking about flowers holding conversations?'

Hastily and truthfully I denied this. I said that I thought it was more than likely that flowers conversed with each other. I pointed out that bats produced minute squeaks which I was able to hear, but which would be inaudible to an elderly person, since the sound was too high-pitched.

'That's it, that's it!' she exclaimed delightedly. 'It's a question of wave-length. I put it all down to this slowing-up process. Another thing that you don't notice when you're young is that flowers have personality. They are different from each other, just as people are. Look, I'll show you. D'you see that rose over there, in the bowl by itself?'

On a small table in the corner, enshrined in a small silver bowl, was a magnificent velvety rose, so deep a garnet red that it was almost black. It was a gorgeous flower, the petals curled to perfection, the bloom in them as soft and unblemished as the down on a newly-hatched butterfly's wing.

'Isn't he a beauty?' inquired Mrs Kralefsky. 'Isn't he wonderful? Now, I've had him two weeks. You'd hardly believe it would you? And he was not a bud when he came. No, no, he was fully open. But, do you know, he was so sick that I did not think he would live? The person who plucked him was careless enough to put him in with a bunch of Michaelmas daisies. Fatal, absolutely fatal! You have no idea how cruel the daisy family is, on the whole. They are very rough-and-ready sort of flowers, very down to earth, and, of course, to put such an aristocrat as a rose amongst them is just *asking* for trouble. By the time he got here he had drooped and faded to such an extent that I did not even notice him among the daisies. But, luckily, I heard them at it. I was dozing here when they started, particularly, it seemed to me, the yellow ones, who always seem so belligerent. Well, of course, I didn't know what they were saying, but it sounded *horrible*. I couldn't think *who* they were talking to at first; I thought they were quarrelling amongst themselves. Then I got out of bed to have a look and I found that poor rose, crushed in the middle of them, being harried to death. I got him out and put him by himself and gave him half an aspirin. Aspirin is so good for roses. Drachma pieces for the chrysanthemums, aspirin for roses, brandy for sweet peas, and a squeeze of lemon-juice for the fleshy flowers, like begonias. Well, removed from the company of the daisies and given that pick-me-up, he revived in no time, and he seems so grateful; he's obviously making an effort to remain beautiful for as long as possible in order to thank me.'

She gazed at the rose affectionately, as it glowed in its silver bowl.

'Yes, there's a lot I have learnt about flowers. They're just like people. Put too many together and they get on each other's nerves and start to wilt. Mix some kinds and you get what appears to be a dreadful form of class distinction. And, of course, the water is so important. Do you know that some people think it's kind to change the water every day? Dreadful! You can *hear* the flowers dying if you do that. I change the water once a week, put a handful of earth in it, and they thrive.'

The door opened and Kralefsky came bobbing in, smiling triumphantly.

'They've all hatched!' he announced, 'all four of them. I'm so glad. I was quite worried, as it's her first clutch.'

'Good, dear; I'm so glad,' said Mrs Kralefsky delightedly. 'That is nice for you. Well, Gerry and I have been having a most interesting conversation. At least, I found it interesting anyway.'

Getting to my feet, I said that I had found it most interesting as well.

'You must come and see me again, if it would not bore you,' she said. 'You will find my ideas a little eccentric, I think, but they are worth listening to.'

She smiled up at me, lying on the bed under her great cloak of hair, and lifted a hand in a courteous gesture of dismissal. I followed Kralefsky across the room, and at the door I looked back and smiled. She was lying quite still, submissive under the weight of her hair. She lifted her hand again and waved. It seemed to me, in the gloom, that the flowers had moved closer to her, had crowded eagerly about her bed, as though waiting for her to tell them something. A ravaged old queen, lying in state, surrounded by her whispering court of flowers.

# 15

# The Cyclamen Woods

Half a mile or so from the villa rose a fairly large conical hill,
covered with grass and heather, and crowned with three tiny
olive-groves, separated from each other by wide beds of myrtle.
I called these three little groves the Cyclamen Woods, for
in the right season the ground beneath the olive-trees was
flushed magenta and wine-red with the flowers of cyclamen
that seemed to grow more thickly and more luxuriantly here
than anywhere else in the countryside. The flashy, circular
bulbs, with their flaky peeling skin, grew in beds like oysters,
each with its cluster of deep green, white-veined leaves, a
fountain of beautiful flowers that looked as though they had
been made from magenta-stained snow-flakes.

The Cyclamen Woods were an excellent place to spend an
afternoon. Lying beneath the shade of the olive-trunks, you
could look out over the valley, a mosaic of fields, vineyards,
and orchards, to where the sea shone between the olive-trunks,
a thousand fiery sparkles running over it as it rubbed itself
gently and languorously along the shore. The hill-top seemed
to have its own breeze, albeit a baby one, for no matter how hot
it was below in the valley, up in the three olive-groves the tiny
wind played constantly, the leaves whispered and the drooping
cyclamen flowers bowed to each other in endless greeting. It
was an ideal spot in which to rest after a hectic lizard hunt,
when your head was pounding with the heat, your clothes limp
and discoloured with perspiration, and the three dogs hung out
their pink tongues and panted like ancient, miniature railway
engines. It was while the dogs and I were resting after just
such a hunt that I acquired two new pets, and, indirectly,
started off a chain of coincidences that affected both Larry

and Mr Kralefsky.

The dogs, tongues rippling, had flung themselves down among the cyclamens, and lay on their stomachs, hindlegs spread out in order to get as much of the cool earth against their bodies as possible. Their eyes were half-closed and their jowls dark with saliva. I was leaning against an olive-trunk that had spent the past hundred years growing itself into the right shape for a perfect back-rest, and gazing out over the fields and trying to identify my peasant friends among the tiny coloured blobs that moved there. Far below, over a blond square of ripening maize, a small black and white shape appeared, like a piebald Maltese cross, skimming rapidly across the flat areas of cultivation, heading determinedly for the hill-top on which I sat. As it flew up towards me the magpie uttered three brief, harsh chucks, that sounded rather muffled as though its beak were full of food. It dived as neatly as an arrow into the depths of an olive-tree some distance away; there was a pause, and then there arose a chorus of shrill wheezing shrieks from among the leaves, which swept to a crescendo and died slowly away. Again I heard the magpie chuck, softly and warningly, and it leapt out of the leaves and glided off down the hillside once more. I waited until the bird was a mere speck, like a dust-mote floating over the frilly tangle of vineyard on the horizon, and then got to my feet and cautiously circled the tree from which the curious sounds had come. High up among the branches, half hidden by the green silver leaves, I could make out a large, oval bundle of twigs, like a huge, furry football wedged among the branches. Excitedly I started to scramble up the tree, while the dogs gathered at the bottom of the trunk and watched me with interest; when I was near to the nest I looked down and my stomach writhed, for the dogs' faces, peering up at me eagerly, were the size of pimpernel flowers. Carefully, my palms sweating, I edged my way out along the branches until I crouched side by side with the nest among the breeze-ruffled leaves. It was a massive structure, a great basket of carefully interwoven sticks, a deep cup of mud and rootlets in its heart. The entrance hole through the wall was small, and the twigs that surrounded it bristled with sharp thorns, as did the sides of the nest and the neatly domed, wicker-work roof. It was the sort of nest designed to discourage the most ardent ornithologist.

Trying to avoid looking down, I lay on my stomach along the branch and pushed my hand carefully inside the thorny bundle, groping in the mud cup. Under my fingers I could feel soft, quivering skin and fluff, while a shrill chorus of wheezes rose from inside the nest. Carefully I curved my fingers round one fat, warm baby and drew it out. Enthusiastic though I was, even I had to admit it was no beauty. Its squat beak, with a yellow fold at each corner, the bald head, and the half-open and bleary eyes gave it a drunken and rather imbecile look. The skin hung in folds and wrinkles all over its body, apparently pinned loosely and haphazardly to its flesh by black feather-stubs. Between the lanky legs drooped a huge flaccid stomach, the skin of it so fine that you could dimly see the internal organs beneath. The baby squatted in my palm, its belly spreading out like a water-filled balloon, and wheezed hopefully. Groping about inside the nest I found that there were three other youngsters, each as revolting as the one I had in my hand. After some thought, and having examined each of them with care, I decided to take two and leave the other pair for the mother. This struck me as being quite fair, and I did not see how the mother could possibly object. I chose the largest (because he would grow up quickly) and the smallest (because he looked so pathetic), put them carefully inside my shirt and climbed cautiously back to the waiting dogs. On being shown the new additions to the menagerie Widdle and Puke immediately decided that they must be edible, and tried to find out if their conclusion was correct. After I had reprimanded them, I showed the birds to Roger. He sniffed at them in his usual way, and then retreated hastily when the babies shot their heads up on long, scrawny necks, red mouths gaping wide, and wheezed lustily.

As I carried my new pets back homewards I tried to decide what to call them; I was still debating this problem when I reached the villa and found the family, who had just been on a shopping expedition into town, disgorging from the car. Holding out the babies in my cupped hands, I inquired if anyone could think of a suitable pair of names for them. The family took one look and all reacted in their individual ways.

'Aren't they *sweet*?' said Margo.

'What are you going to feed them on?' asked Mother.

'What revolting things!' said Leslie.

'Not *more* animals?' asked Larry with distaste.

'Gollys, Master Gerrys,' said Spiro, looking disgusted, 'whats thems?'

I replied, rather coldly, that they were baby magpies, that I hadn't asked anyone's opinion on them, but merely wanted some help in christening them. What should I call them?

But the family were not in a helpful mood.

'Fancy taking them away from their mother, poor little things,' said Margo.

'I hope they're old enough to eat, dear,' said Mother.

'Honest to Gods! The things Master Gerrys *finds*,' said Spiro.

'You'll have to watch out they don't steal' said Leslie.

'Steal?' said Larry in alarm. 'I thought that was jackdaws?'

'Magpies too,' said Leslie; 'awful thieves, magpies.'

Larry took a hundred drachma note from his pocket and waved it over the babies, and they immediately shot their heads skywards, necks wavering, mouths gaping, wheezing and bubbling frantically. Larry jumped back hastily.

'You're right, by God!' he exclaimed excitedly. 'Did you see that? They tried to attack me and get the money!'

'Don't be ridiculous, dear; they're only hungry,' said Mother.

'Nonsense, Mother ... you saw them leap at me, didn't you? It's the money that did it ... even at that age they have criminal instincts. He can't possibly keep them; it will be like living with Arsène Lupin. Go and put them back where you found them, Gerry.'

Innocently and untruthfully I explained that I couldn't do that, as the mother would desert them, and they would then starve to death. This, as I had anticipated, immediately got Mother and Margo on my side.

'We can't let the poor little things starve,' protested Margo.

'I don't see that it would do any harm to keep them,' said Mother.

'You'll regret it,' said Larry; 'it's asking for trouble. Every room in the house will be rifled. We'll have to bury all our valuables and post an armed guard over them. It's lunacy.'

'Don't be silly, dear,' said Mother soothingly. 'We can keep them in a cage and only let them out for exercise.'

'Exercise!' exclaimed Larry. 'I suppose you'll call it exercise when they're flapping round the house with hundred drachma notes in their filthy beaks.'

I promised faithfully that the magpies should not, in any circumstances, be allowed to steal. Larry gave me a withering look. I pointed out that the birds had still to be named, but nobody could think of anything suitable. We stood and stared at the quivering babies, but nothing suggested itself.

'Whats you goings to do with them bastards?' asked Spiro.

Somewhat acidly I said that I intended to keep them as pets, and that, furthermore, they were not bastards, but magpies.

'*Whats* you calls them?' asked Spiro scowling.

'Magpies, Spiro, magpies,' said Mother, enunciating slowly and clearly.

Spiro turned this new addition to his English vocabulary over in his mind, repeating it to himself, getting it firmly embedded.

'Magenpies,' he said at last, 'magenpies, eh?'

'Magpies, Spiro,' corrected Margo.

'Thats what I says,' said Spiro indignantly, 'magenpies.'

So from that moment we gave up trying to find a name for them and they became known simply as the Magenpies.

By the time the Magenpies had gorged themselves to a size where they were fully fledged, Larry had become so used to seeing them around that he had forgotten their allegedly criminal habits. Fat, glossy, and garrulous, squatting on top of their basket and flapping their wings vigorously, the Magenpies looked the very picture of innocence. All went well until they learnt to fly. The early stages consisted in leaping off the table on the veranda, flapping their wings frantically, and gliding down to crash on to the stone flags some fifteen feet away. Their courage grew with the strength of their wings, and before very long they accomplished their first real flight, a merry go-round affair around the villa. They looked so lovely, their long tails glittering in the sun, their wings hissing as they swooped down to fly under the vine, that I called the family out to have a look at them. Aware of their audience, the Magenpies flew faster and faster, chasing each other, diving within inches of the wall before banking to one side, and doing acrobatics on the branches of the magnolia tree. Eventually one of them, made over-confident by our applause, misjudged his distance, crashed into the grape-vine, and fell on to the veranda, no longer a bold, swerving ace of the air, but a woebegone bundle of feathers that opened its mouth and wheezed plaintively at me when I picked it up and soothed it. But, once having mastered their wings, the Magenpies quickly mapped out the villa and then they were all set for their banditry.

The kitchen, they knew, was an excellent place to visit, providing they stayed on the doorstep and did not venture inside; the drawing-room and dining-room they never entered if someone was there; of the bedrooms they knew that the only one in which they were assured of a warm welcome was mine.

They would certainly fly into Mother's or Margo's but they were constantly being told not to do things, and they found this boring. Leslie would allow them on to his window-sill but no farther, but they gave up visiting him after the day he let off a gun by accident. It unnerved them, and I think they had a vague idea that Leslie had made an attempt on their lives. But the bedroom that really intrigued and fascinated them was, of course, Larry's, and I think this was because they never managed to get a good look inside. Before they had even touched down on the window-sill they would be greeted with such roars of rage, followed by a rapidly discharged shower of missiles, that they would be forced to flap rapidly away to the safety of the magnolia tree. They could not understand Larry's attitude at all; they decided that – since he made such a fuss – it must be that he had something to hide, and that it was their duty to find out what it was. They chose their time carefully, waiting patiently until one afternoon Larry went off for a swim and left his window open.

I did not discover what the Magenpies had been up to until Larry came back; I had missed the birds, but thought they had flown down the hill to steal some grapes. They were obviously well aware that they were doing wrong, for though normally loquacious they carried out their raid in silence and (according to Larry) took it in turns to do sentry duty on the window-sill. As he came up the hill he saw, to his horror, one of them sitting on the sill, and shouted wrathfully at it. The bird gave a chuck of alarm and the other one flew out of the room and joined it; they flapped off into the magnolia tree, chuckling hoarsely, like schoolboys caught raiding an orchard. Larry burst into the house, and swept up to his room, grabbing me *en route*. When he opened the door Larry uttered a moan like a soul in torment.

The Magenpies had been through the room as thoroughly as any Secret Service agent searching for missing plans. Piles of manuscript and typing paper lay scattered about the floor like drifts of autumn leaves, most of them with an attractive pattern of holes punched in them. The Magenpies never could resist paper. The typewriter stood stolidly on the table, looking like a disembowelled horse in a bull ring, its ribbon coiling out of its interior, its keys bespattered with droppings. The carpet, bed, and table were a-glitter with a layer of paper clips like frost. The Magenpies, obviously suspecting Larry of being a dope smuggler, had fought valiantly with the tin of bicarbonate of soda, and had scattered its contents along a line of books, so that they looked like a snow-covered mountain range. The table, the floor, the manuscript, the bed, and especially the pillow, were decorated with an artistic and unusual chain of footprints in green and red ink. It seemed almost as though each bird had overturned his favourite colour and walked in it. The bottle of blue ink, which would not have been so noticeable, was untouched.

'This is the last straw,' said Larry in a shaking voice, 'positively the last straw. Either you do something about those birds or I will personally wring their necks.'

I protested that he could hardly blame the Magenpies. They were interested in things, I explained; they couldn't help it, they were just made like that. All members of the crow tribe, I went on, warming to my defence work, were naturally curious. They didn't know they were doing wrong.

'I did not ask for a lecture on the crow tribe,' said Larry ominously, 'and I am not interested in the moral sense of magpies, either inherited or acquired. I am just telling you that you will have to either get rid of them or lock them up, otherwise I shall tear them wing from wing.'

The rest of the family, finding they could not siesta with the argument going on, assembled to find out the trouble.

'Good heavens! dear, what *have* you been doing?' asked Mother, peering round the wrecked room.

'Mother, I am in no mood to answer imbecile questions.'

'Must be the Magenpies,' said Leslie, with the relish of a prophet proved right. 'Anything missing?'

'No, nothing missing,' said Larry bitterly; 'they spared me that.'

'They've made an awful mess of your papers,' observed Margo.

Larry stared at her for a moment, breathing deeply.

'What a masterly understatement,' he said at last; 'you are always ready with the apt platitude to sum up a catastrophe. How I envy you your ability to be inarticulate in the face of Fate.'

'There's no need to be rude,' said Margo.

'Larry didn't mean it, dear,' explained Mother untruthfully; 'he's naturally upset.'

'Upset? *Upset?* Those scab-ridden vultures come flapping in here like a pair of critics and tear and be-spatter my manuscript before it's even finished, and you say I'm *upset?*'

'It's *very* annoying, dear,' said Mother, in an attempt to be vehement about the incident, 'but I'm sure they didn't mean it. After all, they don't understand ... they're only birds.'

'Now don't you start,' said Larry fiercely. 'I've already been treated to a discourse on the sense of right and wrong in the crow tribe. It's disgusting the way this family carries on over animals; all this anthropomorphic slush that's drooled out as an excuse. Why don't you all become Magpie Worshippers, and erect a prison to pray in? The way *you* all carry on one would think that *I* was to blame, and that it's *my* fault that my room looks as though it's been plundered by Attila the Hun. Well, I'm telling you: if something isn't done about those birds right away, I shall deal with them myself.'

Larry looked so murderous that I decided it would probably be safer if the Magenpies were removed from danger, so I lured them into my bedroom with the aid of a raw egg and locked them up in their basket while I considered the best thing to do. It was obvious that they would have to go into a cage of sorts, but I wanted a really large one for them, and I did not feel that I could cope with the building of a really big aviary by myself. It was useless asking the family to help me, so I decided that I would have to inveigle Mr Kralefsky into the constructional work. He could come out and spend the day, and once the cage was finished he would have the opportunity of teaching me how to wrestle. I had waited a long time for a favourable opportunity of getting these wrestling lessons, and this seemed to me to be ideal. Mr Kralefsky's ability to wrestle was only one of his many hidden accomplishments, as I had found out.

Apart from his mother and his birds I had discovered that Kralefsky had one great interest in life, and that was an entirely imaginary world he had evoked in his mind, a world in which rich and strange adventures were always happening, adventures in which there were only two major characters: himself (as hero) and a member of the opposite sex who was generally known as a Lady. Finding that I appeared to believe the anecdotes he related to me, he got bolder and bolder, and day by day allowed me to enter a little further into his private paradise. It all started one morning when we were having a break for coffee and biscuits. The conversation somehow got on to dogs, and I confessed to an overwhelming desire to possess a bulldog – creatures that I found quite irresistibly ugly.

'By Jove, yes! Bulldogs!' said Kralefsky. 'Fine beasts, trustworthy and brave. One cannot say the same of *bull-terriers*, unfortunately.'

He sipped his coffee and glanced at me shyly; I sensed that I was expected to draw him out, so I asked why he thought bull-terriers untrustworthy.

'Treacherous!' he explained, wiping his mouth. '*Most* treacherous.'

He leant back in his chair, closed his eyes, and placed the tips of his fingers together, as if praying.

'I recall that once – many years ago when I was in England – I was instrumental in saving a lady's life when she was attacked by one of those brutes.'

He opened his eyes and peered at me; seeing that I was all attention, he closed them again and continued:

'It was a fine morning in spring, and I was taking a constitutional in Hyde Park. Being so early, there was no one else about, and the park was silent except for the bird-songs. I had walked quite some distance when I suddenly became aware of a deep, powerful baying.'

His voice sank to a thrilling whisper and, with his eyes still closed, he cocked his head on one side as if listening. So realistic was it that I, too, felt I could hear the savage, regular barks echoing among the daffodils.

'I thought nothing of it at first. I supposed it to be some dog out enjoying itself chasing squirrels. Then, suddenly, I heard cries for help mingling with the ferocious baying.' He stiffened in his chair, frowned, and his nostrils quivered. 'I hurried through the trees, and suddenly came upon a terrible sight.'

He paused, and passed a hand over his brow, as though even now he could hardly bear to recall the scene.

'There, with her back to a tree, stood a Lady. Her skirt was torn and ripped, her legs bitten and bloody, and with a deckchair she was fending off a ravening bull-terrier. The brute, froth flecking its yawning mouth, leapt and snarled, waiting for an opening. It was obvious that the Lady's strength was ebbing. There was not a moment to be lost.'

Eyes still firmly closed, the better to see the vision, Kralefsky drew himself up in his chair, straightened his shoulders, and fixed his features into an expression of sneering defiance, a devil-may-care expression – the expression of a man about to save a Lady from a bull-terrier.

'I raised my heavy walking-stick and leapt forward, giving a loud cry to encourage the Lady. The hound, attracted by my voice, immediately sprang at me, growling horribly, and I struck it such a blow on the head that my stick broke in half. The animal, though of course dazed, was still full of strength;

I stood there, defenceless, as it gathered itself and launched itself at my throat with gaping jaws.'

Kralefsky's forehead had become quite moist during this recital, and he paused to take out his handkerchief and pat his brow with it. I asked eagerly what had happened then. Kralefsky reunited his finger-tips and went on.

'I did the only thing possible. It was a thousand-to-one chance, but I had to take it. As the beast leapt at my face I plunged my hand into his mouth, seized his tongue, and twisted it as hard as I could. The teeth closed on my wrist, blood spurted out, but I hung on grimly, knowing my life was at stake. The dog lashed to and fro for what seemed like an age. I was exhausted. I felt I could not hold on any longer. Then, suddenly, the brute gave a convulsive heave and went limp. I had succeeded. The creature had been suffocated by its own tongue.'

I sighed rapturously. It was a wonderful story, and might well be true. Even if it wasn't true, it was the sort of thing that *should* happen, I felt; and I sympathized with Kralefsky if, finding that life had so far denied him a bull-terrier to strangle, he had supplied it himself. I said that I thought he had been very brave to tackle the dog in that way. Kralefsky opened his eyes, flushed with pleasure at my obvious enthusiasm, and smiled deprecatingly.

'No, no, not really brave,' he corrected. 'The Lady was in distress, you see, and a gentleman could do nothing else. By Jove, no!'

Having found in me a willing and delighted listener, Kralefsky's confidence grew. He told me more and more of his adventures, and each became more thrilling than the last. I discovered that, by skilfully planting an idea in his mind one morning, I could be sure of an adventure dealing with it the following day, when his imagination had had a chance to weave a story. Enthralled, I heard how he, and a Lady, had been the sole survivors of a shipwreck on a voyage to Murmansk ('I had some business to attend to there'). For two weeks he and the Lady drifted on an iceberg, their clothes frozen, feeding on an occasional raw fish or seagull, until they were rescued. The ship that spotted them might easily have overlooked them if it had not been for Kralefsky's quick wit: he used the Lady's fur coat to light a signal fire.

I was enchanted with the story of the time he had been held up by bandits in the Syrian desert ('while taking a Lady to see some tombs'), and, when the ruffians threatened to carry his fair companion off and hold her to ransom, he offered to go in her place. But the bandits obviously thought the Lady would make a more attractive hostage, and refused. Kralefsky hated bloodshed, but, in the circumstances, what could a gentleman do? He killed all six of them with a knife he had concealed in his mosquito boot. During the First World War he had, naturally, been in the Secret Service. Disguised in a beard, he had been dropped behind the enemy lines to contact another English spy and obtain some plans. Not altogether to my surprise, the other spy turned out to be a Lady. Their escape (with the plans) from the firing squad was a masterpiece of ingenuity. Who but Kralefsky would have thought of breaking into the armoury, loading all the rifles with blanks, and then feigning death as the guns roared out?

I became so used to Kralefsky's extraordinary stories that on the rare occasions when he told me one that was faintly possible I generally believed it. This was his downfall. One day he told me a story of how, when he was a young man in Paris, he was walking along one evening and came across a great brute of a man ill-treating a Lady. Kralefsky, his gentlemanly instincts outraged, promptly hit the man on the head with his walking-stick. The man turned out to be the Champion Wrestler of France, and he immediately demanded that his honour be satisfied; Kralefsky agreed. The man suggested that they meet in the ring and wrestle it out; Kralefsky agreed. A date was fixed and Kralefsky started to go into training for the fight ('a vegetable diet and many exercises'), and when the great day came he had never felt fitter. Kralefsky's opponent – who, to judge from his description, bore a close resemblance, both in size and mentality, to Neanderthal Man – was surprised to find Kralefsky was a match for him. They struggled round the ring for an hour, neither succeeding in throwing the other. Then, suddenly, Kralefsky remembered a throw he had been taught by a Japanese friend of his. With a twist and a jerk he heaved his massive adversary up, twirled him round, and hurled him right out of the ring. The unfortunate man was in hospital for three months, so badly was he hurt. As Kralefsky rightly pointed out, this was a just and fitting punishment for a cad who was so low as to raise his hand to a Lady.

Intrigued by this tale, I asked Kralefsky if he would teach me the rudiments of wrestling, as I felt it would be most useful to me should I ever come across a Lady in distress. Kralefsky seemed rather reluctant; perhaps at some later date, when we had plenty of room, he might show me a few throws, he said. He had forgotten the incident, but I had not, and so the day he came out to help me build the Magenpies their new home I determined to remind him of his promise. During tea I waited until there was a suitable pause in the conversation and then reminded Kralefsky of his famous fight with the French Champion Wrestler. Kralefsky was not at all pleased to be reminded of this exploit, it appeared. He turned pale, and shushed me hurriedly.

'One does not boast in public about such things,' he whispered hoarsely.

I was quite willing to respect his modesty, providing he gave me a wrestling lesson. I pointed out that all I wanted was to be shown a few of the more simple tricks.

'Well,' said Kralefsky, licking his lips, 'I suppose I can show you a few of the more *elementary* holds. But it takes a long time to become a proficient wrestler, you know.'

Delighted, I asked him if we should wrestle out on the veranda, where the family could watch us, or in the seclusion of the drawing-room? Kralefsky decided on the drawing-room. It was important not to be distracted, he said. So we went into the house and moved the furniture out of the way, and Kralefsky reluctantly took off his coat. He explained that the basic and most important principle of wrestling was to try to throw your opponent off balance. You could do this by seizing him round the waist and giving a quick sideways twitch. He demonstrated what he meant, catching me and throwing me gently on to the sofa.

'Now!' he said, holding up a finger, 'have you got the idea?'

I said yes, I thought I'd got the idea all right.

'That's the ticket!' said Kralefsky. 'Now you throw *me.*'

Determined to be a credit to my instructor, I threw him with great enthusiasm. I hurled myself across the room, seized him round the chest, squeezed as hard as I could to prevent his escape, and then flung him with a dextrous twist of my wrist towards the nearest chair. Unfortunately, I did not throw him hard enough, and he missed the chair altogether and crashed on to the floor, uttering a yell that brought the family rushing in from the veranda. We lifted the white-faced, groaning wrestling champion on to the couch, and Margo went to bring some brandy.

'What on earth did you *do* to him?' Mother asked.

I said that all I had done was to follow instructions. I'd been invited to throw him and I had thrown him. It was

197

perfectly simple, and I didn't see that any blame could be attached to me.

'You don't know your own *strength*, dear,' said Mother; 'you should be more careful.'

'Damn' silly thing to do,' said Leslie. 'Might have killed him.'

'I knew a man once who was crippled for life by a wrestling throw,' remarked Larry conversationally.

Kralefsky groaned more loudly.

'Really, Gerry, you do some very silly things,' said Mother, distraught, obviously with visions of Kralefsky being confined to a wheelchair for the rest of his days.

Irritated by what I considered to be unfair criticisms, I pointed out again that it was not my fault. I had been shown how to throw a person, and then invited to demonstrate. So I had thrown him.

'I'm sure he didn't mean you to lay him out like *that*,' said Larry; 'you might have damaged his spine. Like this fellow I knew, his spine was split like a banana. Very curious. He told me that bits of the bone were sticking out . . .'

Kralefsky opened his eys and gave Larry an anguished look.

'I wonder if I might have some water?' he said faintly.

At this moment Margo returned with the brandy, and we made Kralefsky take some. A little colour came into his cheeks again, and he lay back and closed his eyes once more.

'Well, you can sit up, and that's one good sign,' said Larry cheerfully; 'though I believe it's not really a trustworthy indication. I knew an artist who fell off a ladder and broke his back, and he was walking round for a week before they discovered it.'

'Good God, really!' asked Leslie, deeply interested. 'What happened to him?'

'He died,' said Larry.

Kralefsky raised himself into a sitting position and gave a wan smile.

'I think perhaps, if you would be kind enough to let Spiro drive me, it would be wiser if I went into town and consulted a doctor.'

'Yes, of course Spiro will take you,' said Mother. 'I should go along to Theodore's laboratory and get him to take an X-ray, just to put your mind at rest.'

So we wrapped Kralefsky, pale but composed, in quantities of rugs and placed him tenderly in the back of the car.

'Tell Theodore to send us a note with Spiro to let us know how you are,' said Mother. 'I do hope you'll soon be better. I'm really so sorry this had to happen; it was so very careless of Gerry.'

It was Kralefsky's big moment. He smiled a smile of pain-racked nonchalance and waved a hand feebly.

'Please, please don't distress yourself. Think nothing more about it,' he said. 'Don't blame the boy; it was not his fault. You see, I'm a *little* out of practice.'

Much later that evening Spiro returned from his errand of mercy, bearing a note from Theodore.

Dear Mrs Durrell,

It appears from the X-ray photographs I have taken of Mr Kralefsky's *chest* that he has cracked two ribs: one of them, I'm sorry to say, quite severely. He was reticent as to the *cause* of the damage, but quite considerable force must have been employed. However, if he keeps them bound up for a week or so he should suffer no *permanent* injury.

With kindest regards to you all,
Yours,
Theodore.

P.S. I didn't by any chance leave a small black box at your house when I came out last Thursday, did I? It contains some very interesting Anopheles mosquitoes I had obtained, and it seems I must have mislaid it. Perhaps you would let me know?

# 16

# The Lake of Lilies

The Magenpies were most indignant at their imprisonment,
in spite of the large size of their quarters. Suffering from
insatiable curiosity as they did, they found it most frustrating
not to be able to investigate and comment on everything that
happened. Their field of view was limited to the front of the
house, and so if anything happened round the back they would
go almost frantic, cackling and chucking indignantly as they
flew round and round their cage, poking their heads through
the wire in an effort to see what was going on. Confined as
they were, they were able to devote a lot of time to their
studies, which consisted of getting a solid grounding in the
Greek and English language and producing skilful imitations
of natural sounds. Within a very short time they were able to
call all members of the family by name, and they would, with
extreme cunning, wait until Spiro had got into the car and
coasted some distance down the hill, before rushing to the
corner of their cage and screaming 'Spiro . . . *Spiro* . . . *Spiro*
. . .' making him cram on his brakes and return to the house
to find out who was calling him. They would also derive a lot of
innocent amusement by shouting 'Go away!' and 'Come here'
in rapid succession, in both Greek and English, to the complete
confusion of the dogs. Another trick, out of which they got
endless pleasure, was deluding the poor unfortunate flock of
chickens, which spent the day scratching hopefully round the
olive-groves. Periodically the maid would come to the kitchen
door and utter a series of piping noises, interspersed with
strange hiccoughing cries, which the hens knew was a signal
for food, and they would assemble at the backdoor like magic.
As soon as the Magenpies had mastered the chicken-food call

they worried the poor hens into a decline. They would wait until the most awkward time before using it; until the hens, with infinite effort and much squawking, had gone to roost in the smaller trees, or, in the heat of the day, when they had all settled down for a pleasant siesta in the shade of the myrtles. No sooner were they drowsing pleasantly than the Magenpies would start the food call, one doing the hiccoughs while the other did the piping. The hens would all glance nervously round, each waiting for one of the others to show signs of life. The Magenpies would call again, more seductively and urgently. Suddenly, one hen with less self-control than the rest would leap squawking to her feet and bounce towards the Magenpies' cage, and the rest, clucking and flapping, would follow her with all speed. They would rush up to the wire of the cage, barging and squawking, treading on each other's feet, pecking at each other, and then stand in a disorderly, panting crowd looking up into the cage where the Magenpies, sleek and elegant in their black and white suits, would stare down at them and chuckle, like a pair of city slickers that have successfully duped a crowd of bumbling and earnest villagers.

The Magenpies liked the dogs, although they seized every opportunity to tease them. They were particularly fond of Roger, and he would frequently go and call on them, lying down close to the wire netting, ears pricked, while the Magenpies sat on the ground inside the cage, three inches away from his nose, and talked to him in soft, wheezy chucks, with an occasional raucous guffaw, as though they were telling him dirty jokes. They never teased Roger as much as they teased the other two, and they never attempted to lure him close to the wire with soft blandishments so that they could flap down and pull his tail, as they frequently did with both Widdle and Puke. On the whole the Magenpies approved of dogs, but they liked them to look *and* behave like dogs; so when Dodo made her appearance in our midst the Magenpies absolutely refused to believe that she was a dog, and treated her from the beginning with a sort of rowdy, jeering disdain.

Dodo was a breed known as a Dandy Dinmont. They look like long, fat, hair-covered balloons, with minute bow legs, enormous and protuberant eyes, and long flopping ears. Strangely enough it was due to Mother that this curious misshapen breed of dog made its appearance among us. A friend of ours had a pair of these beasts which had suddenly (after years of barrenness) produced a litter of six puppies. The poor man was at his wits' end trying to find good homes for all these offspring, and so Mother, good-naturedly and unthinkingly, said she would have one. She set off one afternoon to choose her puppy and, rather unwisely, selected a female. At the time it did not strike her as imprudent to introduce a bitch into a household exclusively populated by very masculine dogs. So, clasping the puppy (like a dimly conscious sausage) under one arm, Mother climbed into the car and drove home in triumph to show the new addition to the family. The puppy, determined to make the occasion a memorable one, was violently and persistently sick from the moment she got in the car to the moment she got out. The family, assembled on the veranda, viewed Mother's prize as it waddled up the path towards them, eyes bulging, minute legs working frantically to keep the long, drooping body in motion, ears flapping wildly, passing now and then to vomit into a flower-bed.

'Oh, isn't he *sweet*?' cried Margo.

'Good God! It looks like a sea-slug,' said Leslie.

'Mother! Really!' said Larry, contemplating Dodo with loathing, 'where did you dig up that canine Frankenstein?'

'Oh, but he's *sweet*,' repeated Margo. 'What's wrong with him?'

'It's not a him, it's a her,' said Mother, regarding her acquisition proudly; 'she's called Dodo.'

'Well, that's two things wrong for a start,' said Larry. 'It's a ghastly name for an animal, and to introduce a bitch into the house with those other three lechers about is asking for trouble. Apart from that, just look at it! Look at the shape! How did it get like that? Did it have an accident, or was it born like that?'

'Don't be silly, dear; it's the breed. They're *meant* to be like that.'

'Nonsense, mother; it's a monster. Who would want to deliberately produce a thing that shape?'

I pointed out that dachshunds were much the same shape, and they had been bred specially to enable them to get down holes after badgers. Probably the Dandy Dinmont had been bred for a similar reason.

'She looks as though she was bred to go down holes after sewage,' said Larry.

'Don't be disgusting, dear. They're very nice little dogs, and very faithful, apparently.'

'I should imagine they have to be faithful to anyone who shows interest in them: they can't possible have many admirers in the world.'

'I think you're being very nasty about her, and, anyway, you're in no position to talk about beauty; it's only skin deep after all, and before you go throwing stones you should look for the beam in *your* eye,' said Margo triumphantly.

Larry looked puzzled.

'Is that a proverb, or a quotation from the *Builders' Gazette?'* he inquired.

'I think she means that it's an ill-wind that gathers no moss,' said Leslie.

'You make me sick,' said Margo, with dignified scorn.

'Well, join little Dodo in the flower-bed.'

'Now, now,' said Mother, 'don't argue about it. It's my dog and I like her, so that's all that matters.'

So Dodo settled in, and almost immediately showed faults in her make-up which caused us more trouble than all the other dogs put together. To begin with she had a weak hind-leg, and at any time during the day or night her hip joint was liable to come out of its socket, for no apparent reason. Dodo, who was no stoic, would greet this catastrophe with a series of piercing shrieks that worked up to a crescendo of such quivering intensity that it was unbearable. Strangely enough, her leg never seemed to worry her when she went out for walks, or gambolled with elephantine enthusiasm after a ball on the veranda. But invariably in the evening when the family were all sitting quietly, absorbed in writing or reading or knitting, Dodo's leg would suddenly leap out of its socket, she would roll on her back and utter a scream that would make everybody jump and lose control of whatever they were doing. By the time we had massaged her leg back into place Dodo would have screamed herself to exhaustion, and immediately fall into a deep and peaceful sleep, while we would be so unnerved that we would be unable to concentrate on anything for the rest of the evening.

We soon discovered that Dodo had an extremely limited intelligence. There was only room for one idea at a time in her skull, and once it was there Dodo would retain it grimly in spite of all opposition. She decided quite early in her career that Mother belonged to her, but she was not over-possessive at first until one afternoon Mother went off to town to do some shopping and left Dodo behind. Convinced that she would never see Mother again, Dodo went into mourning and waddled, howling sorrowfully, round the house, occasionally being so overcome with grief that her leg would come out of joint. She greeted Mother's return with incredulous joy, but made up her mind that from that moment she would not let Mother out of her sight, for fear she escaped again. So she attached herself to Mother with the tenacity of a limpet, never moving more than a couple of feet away at the most. If Mother sat down, Dodo would lie at her feet; if Mother had to get up and cross the room for a book or a cigarette, Dodo would accompany her, and then they would return together and sit down again, Dodo giving a deep sigh of satisfaction at the thought that once more she had foiled Mother's attempts at escape. She even insisted on being present when Mother had a bath, sitting dolefully by the tub and staring at Mother with embarrassing intensity. Any attempts to leave her outside the bathroom door resulted in Dodo howling madly and hurling herself at the door-panels, which almost invariably resulted in her hip slipping out of its socket. She seemed to be under the impression that it was not safe to let Mother go alone into the bathroom, even if she stood guard over the door. There was always the possibility, she seemed to think, that Mother might give her the slip by crawling down the plug-hole.

At first Dodo was regarded with tolerant scorn by Roger, Widdle, and Puke; they did not think much of her, for she was too fat and too low slung to walk far, and if they made any attempts to play with her it seemed to bring on an attack of persecution mania, and Dodo would gallop back to the house, howling for protection. Taken all round they were inclined to consider her a boring and useless addition to the household, until they discovered that she had one superlative and overwhelmingly delightful characteristic: she came into season with monotonous regularity. Dodo herself displayed an innocence about the facts of life that was rather touching. She seemed not only puzzled but positively scared at her sudden bursts of popularity, when her admirers arrived in such numbers that Mother had to go about armed with a massive stick. It was owing to this Victorian innocence that Dodo fell an easy victim to the lure of Puke's magnificent ginger eyebrows, and so met a fate worse than death when Mother inadvertently locked them in the drawing-room together while she supervised the making of tea. The sudden and unexpected arrival of the English padre and his wife, ushering them into the room in which the happy couple were disporting themselves, and the subsequent efforts to maintain a normal

204

conversation, left Mother feeling limp, and with a raging headache.

To everyone's surprise (including Dodo's) a puppy was born of this union, a strange, mewling blob of a creature with its mother's figure and its father's unusual liver-and-white markings. To suddenly become a mother like that, Dodo found, was very demoralizing, and she almost had a nervous breakdown, for she was torn between the desire to stay in one spot with her puppy and the urge to keep as close to Mother as possible. We were, however, unaware of this psychological turmoil. Eventually Dodo decided to compromise, so she followed Mother around and carried the puppy in her mouth. She had spent a whole morning doing this before we discovered what she was up to, the unfortunate baby hung from her mouth by its head, its body swinging to and fro as Dodo waddled along at Mother's heels. Scolding and pleading having no effect, Mother was forced to confine herself to the bedroom with Dodo and her puppy, and we carried their meals up on a tray. Even this was not altogether successful, for if Mother moved out of the chair, Dodo, ever alert, would seize her puppy and sit there regarding Mother with starting eyes, ready to give chase if necessary.

'If this goes on much longer that puppy'll grow into a giraffe,' observed Leslie.

'I know, poor little thing,' said Mother; 'but what can I *do*? She picks it up if she seems me lighting a cigarette.'

'Simplest thing would be to drown it,' said Larry. 'It's going to grow into the most horrifying animal, anyway. Look at its parents.'

'No, indeed you won't drown it!' exclaimed Mother indignantly.

'Don't be *horrible*,' said Margo; 'the poor little thing.'

'Well, I think it's a perfectly ridiculous situation, allowing yourself to be chained to a chair by a dog.'

'It's my dog, and if I want to sit here I *shall*,' said Mother firmly.

'But for how long? This might go on for months.'

'I shall think of something,' said Mother with dignity.

The solution to the problem that Mother eventually thought of was simple. She hired the maid's youngest daughter to carry the puppy for Dodo. This arrangement seemed to satisfy Dodo very well, and once more Mother was able to move about the house. She pottered from room to room like some Eastern potentate, Dodo pattering at her heels, and young Sophia

205

bringing up the end of the line, tongue protruding and eyes squinting with the effort, bearing in her arms a large cushion on which reposed Dodo's strange offspring. When Mother was going to be in one spot for any length of time Sophia would place the cushion reverently on the ground, and Dodo would surge on to it and sigh deeply. As soon as Mother was ready to go to another part of the house, Dodo would get off her cushion, shake herself, and take up her position in the cavalcade, while Sophia lifted the cushion aloft as though it carried a crown. Mother would peer over her spectacles to make sure the column was ready, giving a little nod, and they would wind their way off to the next job.

Every evening Mother would go for a walk with the dogs, and the family would derive much amusement from watching her progress down the hill. Roger, as senior dog, would lead the procession, followed by Widdle and Puke. Then came Mother, wearing an enormous straw hat, which made her look like an animated mushroom, clutching in one hand a large trowel with which to dig any interesting wild plants she found. Dodo would waddle behind, eyes protruding and tongue flapping, and Sophia would bring up the rear, pacing along solemnly, carrying the imperial puppy on its cushion. Mother's Circus, Larry called it, and would irritate her by bellowing out of the window:

'Oi! Lady, wot time does the big top go up, hay?'

He purchased a bottle of hair restorer for her so that, as he explained, she could conduct experiments on Sophia and try to turn her into a bearded lady.

'That's wot your show *needs*, lady,' he assured her in a hoarse voice – 'a bit of clarse, see? Nothing like a bearded lady for bringin' a bit o' clarse to a show.'

But in spite of all this Mother continued to lead her strange caravan off into the olive-groves at five o'clock every evening.

Up in the north of the island lay a large lake with the pleasant, jingling name of Antiniotissa, and this place was one of our favourite haunts. It was about a mile long, an elongated sheet of shallow water surrounded by a thick mane of cane and reed, and separated from the sea at one end by a wide, gently curving dune of fine white sand. Theodore always accompanied us when we paid our visits to the lake, for he and I would find a rich field of exploration in the ponds, ditches, and marshy pot-holes that lay around the shore of the lake. Leslie invariably took a battery of guns with him, since the cane forest rustled with game, while Larry insisted on taking an enormous harpoon, and would stand for hours in the stream that marked the lake's entry into the sea, endeavouring to spear the large fish that swam there. Mother would be laden with baskets full of food, empty baskets for plants, and various gardening implements for digging up her finds. Margo was perhaps the most simply equipped, with a bathing-costume, a large towel, and a bottle of sun-tan lotion. With all this equipment our trips to Antiniotissa were something in the nature of major expeditions.

There was, however, a certain time of the year when the lake was at its best, and that was the season of lilies. The smooth curve of the dune that ran between the bay and the lake was the only place on the island where these sand lilies grew, strange, misshapen bulbs buried in the sand, that once a year sent up thick green leaves and white flowers above the surface, so that the dune became a glacier of flowers. We always visited the lake at this time, for the experience was a memorable one. Not long after Dodo had become a mother, Theodore informed us that the time of the lilies was at hand, and we started to make preparations for our trip to Antiniotissa. We soon found that having a nursing mother in our midst was going to complicate matters considerably.

'We'll have to go by boat this time,' Mother said, frowning at a complicated, jigsaw-like jersey she was knitting.

'Why, by boat it takes twice as long,' said Larry.

'We can't go by car, dear, because Dodo will be sick, and anyway there wouldn't be room for all of us.'

'You're *not* going to take that animal, are you?' asked Larry in horror.

'But I have to, dear . . . purl two, cast off one . . . I can't leave her behind . . . purl three . . . you know what she's like.'

'Well, hire a special car for her then. I'm damned if I'm going to drive about the countryside looking as though I've just burgled Battersea Dogs' Home.'

'She can't travel by car. That's what I'm explaining to you. You know she gets car-sick . . . Now be quiet a minute, dear, I'm counting.'

'It's ridiculous . . .' began Larry exasperatedly.

'Seventeen, eighteen, *nineteen, twenty*,' said Mother loudly and fiercely.

'It's ridiculous that we should have to go the longest way round just because Dodo vomits every time she sees a car.'

'There!' said Mother irritably, 'you've made me lose count. I do wish you wouldn't argue with me when I'm knitting.'

'How d'you know she won't be sea-sick?' inquired Leslie interestedly.

'People who are car-sick are never sea-sick,' explained Mother.

'I don't believe it,' said Larry. 'That's an old wives' tale, isn't it, Theodore?'

'Well, I wouldn't like to say,' said Theodore judicially. 'I have heard it before, but whether there's any . . . um . . . you know . . . any *truth* in it, I can't say. All I know is that I have, so far, not felt sick in a car.'

Larry looked at him blankly. 'What does that prove?' he asked, bewildered.

'Well, I am always sick in a boat,' explained Theodore simply.

'That's wonderful!' said Larry. 'If we travel by car Dodo will be sick, and if we travel by boat Theodore will. Take your choice.'

'I didn't know you got sea-sick, Theodore,' said Mother.

'Oh, yes, unfortunately I do. I find it a great drawback.'

'Well, in weather like this the sea will be very calm, so I should think you'll be all right,' said Margo.

'Unfortunately,' said Theodore, rocking on his toes, 'that does not make any difference at all. I suffer from the . . . er . . . *slightest* motion. In fact on several occasions when I have been in the cinema and they have shown films of ships in rough seas I have been forced to . . . um . . . forced to leave my seat.'

'Simplest thing would be to divide up,' said Leslie; 'half go by boat and the other half go by car.'

'That's a brain-wave!' said Mother. 'The problem is solved.'

But it did not settle the problem at all, for we discovered that the road to Antiniotissa was blocked by a minor landslide, and so to get there by car was impossible. We would have to go by sea or not at all.

We set off in a warm pearly dawn that foretold a breathlessly warm day and a calm sea. In order to cope with the family, the dogs, Spiro, and Sophia, we had to take the *Bootle-Bumtrinket* as well as the *Sea Cow*. Having to trail the *Bootle-Bumtrinket*'s rotund shape behind her cut down on the *Sea Cow*'s speed, but it was the only way to do it. At Larry's suggestion the dogs, Sophia, Mother, and Theodore travelled in the *Bootle Bumtrinket* while the rest of us piled into the *Sea Cow*. Unfortunately Larry had not taken into consideration one important factor: the wash caused by the *Sea Cow*'s passage. The wave curved like a wall of blue glass from her stern and reached its maximum height just as it struck the broad breast of the *Bootle-Bumtrinket*, lifting her up into the air and dropping her down again with a thump. We did not notice the effect the wash was having for some considerable time, for the noise of the engine drowned the frantic cries for help from Mother. When we eventually stopped and let the *Bootle-Bumtrinket* bounce up to us, we found that not only were both Theodore and Dodo ill, but everyone else was as well, including such a hardened and experienced sailor as Roger. We had to get them all into the *Sea Cow* and lay them out in a row, and Spiro, Larry, Margo, and myself took up our positions in the *Bootle-Bumtrinket*. By the time we were nearing Antiniotissa everyone was feeling better, with the exception of Theodore, who still kept as close to the side of the boat as possible, staring hard at his boots and answering questions monosyllabically. We rounded the last headland of red and gold rocks, lying in wavy layers like piles of gigantic fossilized newspapers, or the rusty and mould-covered wreckage of a colossus's library, and the *Sea Cow* and the *Bootle-Bumtrinket* turned into the wide blue bay that lay at the mouth of the lake. The curve of pearl-white sand was backed by the great lily-covered dune behind, a thousand white flowers in the sunshine like a multitude of ivory horns lifting their lips to the sky and producing, instead of music, a rich, heavy scent that was the distilled essence of summer, a warm sweetness that made you breathe deeply time and again in an effort to retain it within you. The engine died away in a final splutter that echoed briefly among the rocks, and then the two boats whispered their way shorewards, and the scent of the lilies came out over the water to greet us.

Having got the equipment ashore and installed it on the white sand, we each wandered off about our own business. Larry and Margo lay in the shallow water half-asleep, being rocked by the faint, gentle ripples. Mother led her cavalcade off on a short walk, armed with a trowel and a basket. Spiro, clad only in his underpants and looking like some dark hairy prehistoric man, waddled into the stream that flowed from the lake to the sea and stood knee deep, scowling down into the transparent waters, a trident held at the ready as the shoals of fish flicked around his feet. Theodore and I drew lots with Leslie as to which side of the lake we should have, and then set off in opposite directions. The boundary marking the half-way mark on the lake-shore was a large and particularly misshapen olive. Once we reached there we would turn back and retrace our footsteps, and Leslie would do the same on his side. This cut out the possibility of his shooting us, by mistake, in some dense and confusing canebrake. So, while Theodore and I dipped and pottered among the pools and streamlets, like a pair of eager herons, Leslie strode stockily through the undergrowth on the other side of the lake, and an occasional explosion would echo across to us to mark his progress.

Lunch-time came and we assembled hungrily on the beach, Leslie with a bulging bag of game, hares damp with blood, partridge and quail, snipe and wood pigeons; Theodore and I with our test-tubes and bottles a-shimmer with small life. A fire blazed, the food was piled on the rugs, and the wine fetched from the sea's edge where it had been put to cool. Larry pulled his corner of the rug up the dune so that he could stretch full-length surrounded by the white trumpets of the lilies. Theodore sat upright and neat, his beard wagging as he chewed his food slowly and methodically. Margo sprawled elegantly in the sun, picking daintily at a pile of fruit and vegetables. Mother and Dodo were installed in the shade of a large umbrella. Leslie squatted on his haunches in the sand, his gun across his thighs, eating a huge hunk of cold meat with one hand and stroking the barrels of the weapon meditatively with the other. Nearby Spiro crouched by the fire, sweat running down his furrowed face and dropping in gleaming drops into the thick pelt of black hair of his chest, as he turned an improvised olive-wood spit, with seven fat snipe on it, over the flames.

'What a heavenly place!' mumbled Larry through a mouthful of food, lying back luxuriously among the shining flowers. 'I feel this place was designed for me. I should like to lie here forever, having food and wine pressed into my mouth by groups of naked and voluptuous dryads. Eventually, of course, over the centuries, by breathing deeply and evenly I should embalm myself with this scent, and then one day my faithful dryads would find me gone, and only the scent would remain. Will someone throw me one of those *delicious*-looking figs?'

'I read a most interesting book on embalming once,' said Theodore enthusiastically. 'They certainly seemed to go to a great deal of trouble to prepare the bodies in Egypt. I must say I thought the method of . . . er . . . extracting the brain through the nose was *most* ingenious.'

'Dragged them down through the nostrils with a sort of hook arrangement, didn't they?' inquired Larry.

'Larry, dear, not while we're *eating*.'

Lunch being over we drifted into the shade of the nearby olives and drowsed sleepily through the heat of the afternoon, while the sharp, soothing song of the cicadas poured over us. Occasionally one or other of us would rise, wander down to the sea and flop into the shallows for a minute before coming back, cooled, to resume his siesta. At four o'clock Spiro, who had been stretched out massive and limp, bubbling with snores, regained consciousness with a snort and waddled down the beach to relight the fire for tea. The rest of us awoke slowly, dreamily, stretching and sighing, and drifted down over the sand towards the steaming, chattering kettle. As we crouched with the cups in our hands, blinking and musing, still half-asleep, a robin appeared among the lilies and hopped down towards us, his breast glowing, his eyes bright. He paused some ten feet away and surveyed us critically. Deciding that we needed some entertainment, he hopped to where a pair of lilies formed a beautiful arch, posed beneath them theatrically, puffed out his chest, and piped a liquid, warbling song. When he had finished he suddenly ducked his head in what appeared to be a ludicrously conceited bow, and then flipped off through the lilies, frightened by our burst of laughter.

'They *are* dear little things, robins,' said Mother. 'There was one in England that used to spend hours by me when I was gardening. I love the way they puff up their little chests.'

'The way that one bobbed looked exactly as if he was bowing,' said Theodore. 'I must say when he . . . er . . . puffed up his chest he looked very like a rather . . . you know . . . a rather *outsize* opera singer.'

'Yes, singing something rather frothy and light . . . Strauss, I should think,' agreed Larry.

'Talking of operas,' said Theodore, his eyes gleaming, did I ever tell you about the last opera we had in Corfu?'

We said no, he hadn't told us, and settled ourselves comfortably, getting almost as much amusement from the sight of Theodore telling the story as from the story itself.

'It was . . . um . . . one of those travelling opera companies, you know. I think it came from Athens, but it may have been Italy. Anyway, their first performance was to be *Tosca*. The singer who took the part of the heroine was exceptionally . . . er . . . '*well developed*, as they always seem to be. Well, as you know, in the final act of the opera the heroine casts herself to her doom from the battlements of a fortress – or, rather, a *castle*. On the first night the heroine climbed up on to the

castle walls, sang her final song, and then cast herself to her
... you know ... her *doom* on the rocks below. Unfortunately
it seems that the stage hands had forgotten to put anything
beneath the walls for her to *land* on. The result was that the
crash of her landing and her subsequent ... er ... yells of
pain detracted somewhat from the impression that she was a
shattered corpse on the rocks far below. The singer who was
just bewailing the fact that she was dead had to sing quite ...
er ... quite *powerfully* in order to drown her cries. The heroine
was, rather naturally, somewhat upset by the incident, and so
the following night the stage hands threw themselves with
enthusiasm into the job of giving her a pleasant landing.
The heroine, somewhat battered, managed to hobble her way
through the opera until she reached the ... er ... final scene.
Then she again climbed on to the battlements, sang her last
song, and cast herself to her death. Unfortunately the stage
hands, having made the landing *too* hard on the first occasion,
had gone to the opposite extreme. The huge pile of mattresses
and ... er ... you know, those springy bed things, was so
*resilient* that the heroine hit them and then bounced up again.
So while the cast was down at the ... er ... what d'you call
them ... ah, yes, the *footlights* telling each other she was
dead, the upper portions of the heroine reappeared two or
three times above the battlements, to the mystification of the
audience.'

The robin, who had hopped nearer during the telling of the
story, took fright and flew off again at our burst of laughter.

'Really, Theodore, I'm sure you spend your spare time
making up these stories,' protested Larry.

'No, no,' said Theodore, smiling happily in his beard; 'if it
were anywhere else in the world I would have to, but here in
Corfu they ... er ... anticipate art, as it were.'

Tea over, Thedore and I returned to the lake's edge once
more and continued our investigation until it grew too
shadowy to see properly; then we walked slowly back to the
beach, where the fire Spiro had built pulsed and glowed like
an enormous chrysanthemum among the ghostly white lilies.
Spiro, having speared three large fish, was roasting them on a
grid, absorbed and scowling, putting now a flake of garlic, now
a squeeze of lemon-juice or a sprinkle of pepper on the delicate
white flesh that showed through where the charred skin was
starting to peel off. The moon rose above the mountains,
turned the lilies to silver except where the flickering flames
illuminated them with a flush of pink. The tiny ripples sped

over the moonlit sea and breathed with relief as they reached the shore at last. Owls started to chime in the trees, and in the gloomy shadows fireflies gleamed as they flew, their jade-green, misty lights pulsing on and off.

Eventually, yawning and stretching, we carried our things down to the boats. We rowed out to the mouth of the bay, and then in the pause while Leslie fiddled with the engine, we looked back at Antiniotissa. The lilies were like a snow-field under the moon, and the dark backcloth of olives was pricked with the lights of fireflies. The fire we had built, stamped, and ground underfoot before we left, glowed like a patch of garnets at the edge of the flowers.

'It is certainly a very ... er ... *beautiful* place,' said Theodore with immense satisfaction.

'It's a glorious place,' agreed Mother, and then gave it her highest accolade, 'I should like to be buried there.'

The engine stuttered uncertainly, then broke into a deep roar; the *Sea Cow* gathered speed and headed along the coastline, trailing the *Bootle-Bumtrinket* behind, and beyond that our wash fanned out, white and delicate as a spider's web on the dark water, flaming here and there with a momentary spark of phosphorescence.

# 17

# The Chessboard Fields

Below the villa, between the line of hills on which it stood and the sea, were the Chessboard Fields. The sea curved into the coast in a great, almost landlocked bay, shallow and bright, and on the flat land along its edges lay the intricate pattern of narrow waterways that had once been salt pans in the Venetian days. Each neat little patch of earth, framed with canals, was richly cultivated and green with crops of maize, potatoes, figs, and grapes. These fields, small coloured squares edged with shining waters, lay like a sprawling, multi-coloured chessboard on which the peasants' coloured figures moved from place to place.

This was one of my favourite areas for hunting in, for the tiny waterways and the lush undergrowth harboured a multitude of creatures. It was easy to get lost there, for if you were enthusiastically chasing a butterfly and crossed the wrong little wooden bridge from one island to the next you could find yourself wandering to and fro, trying to get your bearings in a bewildering maze of fig-trees, reeds, and curtains of tall maize. Most of the fields belonged to friends of mine, peasant families who lived up in the hills, and so when I was walking there I was always sure of being able to rest and gossip over a bunch of grapes with some acquaintance, or to receive interesting items of news, such as the fact that there was a lark's nest under the melon-plants on Georgio's land. If you walked straight across the chessboards without being distracted by friends, side-tracked by terrapins sliding down the mud banks and plopping into the water, or the sudden crackling buzz of a dragon-fly swooping past, you eventually came to the spot where all the channels widened and vanished into a great flat acreage of sand, moulded into endless neat pleats by the previous night's tides. Here long winding chains of flotsam marked the sea's slow retreat, fascinating chains full of coloured seaweed, dead pipe-fish, fishing-net corks that looked good enough to eat – like lumps of rich fruit cake – bits of bottle-glass emeried and carved into translucent jewels by the tide and the sand, shells as spiky as hedgehogs, others smooth, oval, and delicate pink, like the finger-nails of some drowned goddess. This was the sea-birds' country: snipe, oyster-catcher, dunlin, and terns strewn in small pattering groups at the edge of the sea, where the long ripples ran towards the land and broke in long curving ruffs round the little humps of sand. Here, if you felt hungry, you could wade out into the shallows and catch fat, transparent shrimps that tasted as sweet as grapes when eaten raw, or you could dig down with your toes until you found the ribbed, nut-like cockles. Two of these, placed end to end, hinge to hinge, and then twisted sharply in opposite directions, opened each other neatly; the contents, though slightly rubbery, were milky and delicious to eat.

One afternoon, having nothing better to do, I decided to take the dogs and visit the fields. I would make yet another attempt to catch Old Plop, cut across to the sea for a feed of cockles and a swim, and make my way home via Petro's land so that I could sit and exchange gossip with him over a water-melon or a few plump pomegranates. Old Plop was a large and ancient terrapin that lived in one of the canals. I had been trying to capture him for a month or more, but in spite of his age he was very wily and quick, and no matter how cautiously I stalked him when he lay asleep on the muddy bank, he would always wake up at the crucial moment, his legs would flail frantically, and he would slide down the mud slope and plop into the water like a corpulent lifeboat being launched. I had caught a great many terrapins, of course, both the black ones with the thick freckling of golden pin-head spots on them, and the slim grey ones with fawny-cream lines; but Old Plop was something I had set my heart on. He was bigger than any terrapin I had seen, and so old that his battered shell and wrinkled skin had become completely black, losing any markings they may have had in his distant youth. I was determined to possess him, and as I had left him alone for a whole week I thought it was high time to launch another attack.

With my bag of bottles and boxes, my net, and a basket to put Old Plop in should I catch him, I set off down the hill with the dogs. The Magenpies called 'Gerry! ... Gerry! ... *Gerry* ...' after me in tones of agonized entreaty, and then, finding I did not turn, they fell to jeering and cackling and making rude noises. Their harsh voices faded as we entered the olive-groves, and were then obliterated by the choir of cicadas whose song made the air tremble. We made our way along the road, hot, white, and as soft as a powder-puff underfoot. I paused at Yani's well for a drink, and then leant over the rough sty made from olive branches in which the two pigs lived, wallowing with sonorous content in a sea of glutinous mud. Having sniffed deeply and appreciatively at them, and slapped the largest on his grubby, quivering behind, I continued down the road. At the next bend I had a brisk argument with two fat peasant ladies, balancing baskets of fruit on their heads, who were wildly indignant at Widdle. He had crept up on them when they were engrossed in conversation and after sniffing at them had lived up to his name over their skirts and legs. The argument as to whose fault it was kept all of us happily occupied for ten minutes, and was then continued as I walked down the road, until we were separated by such a distance that we could no longer hear and appreciate each other's insults.

Cutting across the first three fields, I paused for a moment in Taki's patch to sample his grapes. He wasn't there, but I knew he wouldn't mind. The grapes were the small fat variety, with a sweet, musky flavour. When you squeezed them the entire contents, soft and seedless, shot into your mouth, leaving the flaccid skin between your finger and thumb. The dogs and I ate four bunches and I put another two bunches in my collecting bag for future reference, after which we followed the edge of the canal towards the place where Old Plop had his favourite mud slide. As we were drawing near to this spot, I was just about to caution the dogs on the need for absolute silence, when a large green lizard flashed out of a corn-patch and scuttled away. The dogs, barking wildly, galloped in eager pursuit. By the time I reached Old Plop's mud slide there was only a series of gently expanding ripples on the water to tell me that he had been present. I sat down and waited for the dogs to rejoin me, running through in my mind the rich and colourful insults with which I would bombard them. But to my surprise they did not come back. Their yelping in the distance died away, there was a pause, and then they started to bark in a chorus – monotonous, evenly spaced barks that meant they had found something. Wondering what it could be I hurried after them.

They were clustered in a half-circle round a clump of grass at the water's edge, and came gambolling to meet me, tails thrashing, whining with excitement, Roger lifting his upper lip in a pleased grin that I had come to examine their find. At first I could not see what it was they were so excited over; then what I had taken to be a rootlet moved, and I was looking at a pair of fat brown water-snakes, coiled passionately together in the grass, regarding me with impersonal silvery eyes from their spade-shaped heads. This was a thrilling find, and one that almost compensated for the loss of Old Plop. I had long wanted to catch one of these snakes, but they were such fast and skilful swimmers that I had never succeeded in getting close enough to accomplish a capture. Now the dogs had found this fine pair, lying in the sun – there for the taking, as it were.

The dogs, having done their duty by finding these creatures and leading me to them, now retreated to a safe distance (for they did not trust reptiles) and sat watching me interestedly. Slowly I manoeuvred my butterfly net round until I could unscrew the handle; having done this, I had a stick with which to do the catching, but the problem was *how* to catch two snakes with one stick? While I was working this out, one of them decided the thing for me, uncoiling himself unhurriedly and sliding into the water as cleanly as a knife-blade. Thinking that I had lost him, I watched irritably as his undulating length merged with the water reflection. Then, to my delight, I saw a column of mud rise slowly through the water and expand like a rose on the surface; the reptile had buried himself at the bottom, and I knew he would stay there until he thought I had gone. I turned my attention to his mate, pressing her down in the lush grass with the stick; she twisted herself into a complicated knot, and opening her pink mouth, hissed at me. I grabbed her firmly round the neck between finger and thumb, and she hung limp in my hand while I stroked her handsome white belly, and the brown back where the scales were raised slightly like the surface of a fir-cone. I put her tenderly into the basket, and then prepared to capture the other one. I walked a little way down the bank and stuck the handle of the net into the canal to test the depth, and discovered that about two feet of water lay on a three-foot bed of soft, quivering mud. Since the water was opaque, and the snake was buried in the bottom slush, I thought the simplest method would be to feel for him with my toes (as I did when searching for cockles) and, having located him, to make a quick pounce.

I took off my sandals and lowered myself into the warm water, feeling the liquid mud squeeze between my toes and stroke up my legs, as soft as ashes. Two great black clouds bloomed about my thighs and drifted across the channel. I made my way towards the spot where my quarry lay hidden, moving my feet slowly and carefully in the shifting curtain of mud. Suddenly, under my foot, I felt the slithering body, and I plunged my arms elbow-deep into the water and grabbed. My fingers closed only on mud which oozed between them and drifted away in turbulent, slow-motion clouds. I was just cursing my ill-luck when the snake shot to the surface a yard away from me, and started to swim sinuously along the surface. With a yell of triumph I flung myself full length on top of him.

There was a confused moment as I sank beneath the dark waters and the silt boiled up into my eyes, ears, and mouth, but I could feel the reptile's body thrashing wildly to and fro, firmly clasped in my left hand, and I glowed with triumph. Gasping and spluttering under my layer of mud, I sat up in the canal and grabbed the snake round the neck before he could recover his wits and bite me; then I spat for a long time, to rid my teeth and lips of the fine, gritty layer which coated them. When I at last rose to my feet and turned to wade ashore I found to my surprise that my audience of dogs had been enlarged by the silent arrival of a man, who was squatting comfortably on his haunches and watching me with a mixture of interest and amusement.

He was a short, stocky individual whose brown face was topped by a thatch of close-cropped fair hair, the colour of tobacco. He had large, very blue eyes that had a pleasant humorous twinkle in them, and crows' feet in the fine skin at the corners. A short, hawk's-beak nose curved over a wide and humorous mouth. He was wearing a blue cotton shirt that was bleached and faded to the colour of a forget-me-not dried by the sun, and old grey flannel trousers. I did not recognize him, and supposed him to be a fisherman from some village farther down the coast. He regarded me gravely as I scrambled up the bank, and then smiled.

'Your health,' he said in a rich, deep voice.

I returned his greeting politely, and then busied myself with the job of trying to get the second snake into the basket without letting the first one escape. I expected him to deliver a lecture to me on the deadliness of the harmless water-snakes and the dangers I ran by handling them, but to my surprise he remained silent, watching with interest while I pushed the writhing reptile into the basket. This done, I washed my hands and produced the grapes I had filched from Taki's fields. The man accepted half the fruit and we sat without talking, sucking the pulp from the grapes with noisy enjoyment. When the last skin had plopped into the canal, the man produced tobacco and rolled a cigarette between his blunt, brown fingers.

'You are a stranger?' he asked, inhaling deeply and with immense satisfaction.

I said that I was English, and that I and my family lived in a villa up in the hills. Then I waited for the inevitable questions as to the sex, number, and age of my family, their work and aspirations, followed by a skilful cross-examination as to why we lived in Corfu. This was the usual peasant way; it was not done unpleasantly, nor with any motive other than friendly interest. They would vouchsafe their own private business to you with great simplicity and frankness, and would be hurt if you did not do the same. But, to my surprise, the man seemed satisfied with my answer, and asked nothing further, but sat there blowing fine streamers of smoke into the sky and staring about him with dreamy blue eyes. With my finger-nail I scraped an attractive pattern in the hardening carapace of grey mud on my thigh, and decided that I would have to go down to the sea and wash myself and my clothes before returning home. I got to my feet and shouldered my bag and nets; the dogs got to their feet, shook themselves, and yawned. More out of politeness than anything, I asked the man where he was going. It was, after all, peasant etiquette to ask questions. It showed your interest in the person. So far I hadn't asked him anything at all.

'I'm going down to the sea,' he said, gesturing with his cigarette – 'down to my boat . . . Where are you going?'

I said I was making for the sea too, first to wash and secondly to find some cockles to eat.

'I will walk with you,' he said, rising and stretching. 'I have a basketful of cockles in my boat; you may have some of those if you like.'

We walked through the fields in silence, and when we came out on to the sands he pointed at the distant shape of a rowing-boat, lying comfortably on her side, with a frilly skirt of ripples round her stern. As we walked towards her I asked if he was a fisherman, and if so, where he came from.

'I come from here . . . the hills,' he replied – 'at least, my home is here, but I am now at Vido.'

The reply puzzled me, for Vido was a tiny islet lying off the town of Corfu, and as far as I knew it had no one on it at all except convicts and warders, for it was the local prison island. I pointed this out to him.

'That's right,' he agreed, stooping to pat Roger as he ambled past, 'that's right. I'm a convict.'

I thought he was joking, and glanced at him sharply, but his expression was quite serious. I said I presumed he had just been let out.

'No, no, worse luck,' he smiled. 'I have another two years to do. But I'm a good prisoner, you see. Trustworthy and make no trouble. Any like me, those they feel they can trust, are allowed to make boats and sail home for the week-end, if it's not too far. I've got to be back there first thing Monday morning.'

Once the thing was explained, of course, it was simple. It never even occurred to me that the procedure was unusual. I knew one wasn't allowed home for week-ends from an English prison, but this was Corfu, and in Corfu anything could happen. I was bursting with curiosity to know what his crime had been, and I was just phrasing a tactful inquiry in my mind when we reached the boat, and inside it was something that drove all other thoughts from my head. In the stern, tethered to the seat by one yellow leg, sat an immense black-backed gull, who contemplated me with sneering yellow eyes. I stepped forward eagerly and stretched out my hand to the broad, dark back.

'Be careful . . . watch out; he is a bully, that one!' said the man urgently.

His warning came too late, for I had already placed my hand on the bird's back and was gently running my fingers over the silken feathering. The gull crouched, opened his beak slightly, and the dark iris of his eye contracted with surprise, but he was so taken aback by my audacity that he did nothing.

'Spiridion!' said the man in amazement, 'he must like you; he's never let anyone else touch him without biting.'

I buried my fingers in the crisp white feathers on the bird's neck, and as I scratched gently the gull's head drooped forwards and his yellow eyes became dreamy. I asked the man where he had managed to catch such a magnificent bird.

'I sailed over to Albania in the spring to try to get some hares, and I found him in a nest. He was small then, and fluffy as a lamb. Now he's like a great duck,' the man said, staring pensively at the gull, 'fat duck, ugly duck, biting duck, aren't you, eh?'

The gull at being thus addressed opened one eye and gave a short, harsh yarp, which may have been repudiation or agreement. The man leant down and pulled a big basket from under the seat; it was full to the brim with great fat cockles that chinked musically. We sat in the boat and ate the shellfish, and all the time I watched the bird, fascinated by the snow-white breast and head, his long hooked beak and fierce eyes, as yellow as spring crocuses, the broad back and powerful wings, sooty black. From the soles of his great webbed feet to the tip of his beak he was, in my opinion, quite admirable. I swallowed a final cockle, wiped my hands on the side of the boat, and asked the man if he could get a baby gull for me the following spring.

'You want one?' he said in surprise; 'you like them?'

I felt this was understating my feelings. I would have sold my soul for such a gull.

'Well, have him if you want him,' said the man casually, jerking a thumb at the bird.

I could hardly believe my ears. For someone to possess such a wonderful creature and to offer him as a gift so carelessly was incredible. Didn't he *want* the bird, I asked?

'Yes, I like him,' said the man, looking at the bird meditatively, 'but he eats more than I can catch for him, and he is such a wicked one that he bites everybody; none of the other prisoners or the warders like him. I've tried letting him go, but he *won't* go – he keeps coming back. I was going to take him over to Albania one week-end and leave him there. So if you're sure you want him you can have him.'

Sure I wanted him? It was like being offered an angel. A slightly sardonic-looking angel, it's true, but one with the most magnificent wings. In my excitement I never even stopped to wonder how the family would greet the arrival of a bird the size of a goose with a beak like a razor. In case the man changed his mind I hastily took off my clothes, beat as much of the dried mud off them as possible, and had a quick swim in the shallows. I put on my clothes again, whistled the dogs, and prepared to carry my prize home. The man untied the string, lifted the gull up and handed him to me; I clasped it under one arm, surprised that such a huge bird should be so feather-light. I thanked the man profusely for his wonderful present.

'He knows his name,' he remarked, clasping the gull's beak between his fingers and waggling it gently. 'I call him Alecko.

He'll come when you call.'

Alecko, on hearing his name, paddled his feet wildly and looked up into my face with questioning yellow eyes.

'You'll be wanting some fish for him,' remarked the man. 'I'm going out in the boat tomorrow, about eight. If you like to come we can catch a good lot for him.'

I said that would be fine, and Alecko gave a yarp of agreement. The man leant against the bows of the boat to push it out, and I suddenly remembered something. As casually as I could I asked him what his name was, and why he was in prison. He smiled charmingly over his shoulder.

'My name's Kosti,' he said, 'Kosti Panopoulos. I killed my wife.'

He leant against the bows of the boat and heaved; she slid whispering across the sand and into the water, and the little ripples leapt and licked at her stern, like excited puppies. Kosti scrambled into the boat and took up the oars.

'Your health,' he called. 'Until tomorrow.'

The oars creaked musically, and the boat skimmed rapidly over the limpid waters. I turned, clasping my precious bird under my arm, and started to trudge back over the sand, towards the chessboard fields.

The walk home took me some time. I decided that I had misjudged Alecko's weight, for he appeared to get heavier and heavier as we progressed. He was a dead weight that sagged lower and lower, until I was forced to jerk him up under my arm again, whereupon he would protest with a vigorous yarp. We were half-way through the fields when I saw a convenient fig-tree which would, I thought, provide both shade and sustenance, so I decided to take a rest. While I lay in the long grass and munched figs, Alecko sat nearby as still as though he were carved out of wood, watching the dogs with unblinking eyes. The only sign of life were his irises, which would expand and contract excitedly each time one of the dogs moved.

Presently, rested and refreshed, I suggested to my band that we tackle the last stage of the journey; the dogs rose obediently, but Alecko fluffed out his feathers so that they rustled like dry leaves, and shuddered all over at the thought. Apparently he disapproved of my hawking him around under my arm like an old sack, ruffling his feathers. Now that he had persuaded me to put him down in such a pleasant spot he had no intention of continuing what appeared to him to be a tedious and unnecessary journey. As I stooped to pick him up he snapped his beak, uttered a loud, harsh scream, and lifted his wings above his back in the posture usually adopted by tombstone angels. He glared at me. Why, his look seemed to imply, leave this spot? There was shade, soft grass to sit on, and water nearby; what point was there in leaving it to be humped about the countryside in a manner both uncomfortable and undignified? I pleaded with him for some time and, as he appeared to have calmed down, I made another attempt to pick him up. This time he left me in no doubt as to his desire to stay where he was. His beak shot out so fast I could not avoid it, and it hit my approaching hand accurately. It was as though I had been slashed by an ice-pick. My knuckles were bruised and aching, and a two-inch gash welled blood in great profusion. Alecko looked so smug and satisfied with this attack that I lost my temper. Grabbing my butterfly net I brought it down skilfully and, to my surprise, enveloped him in its folds. I jumped on him before he could recover from the shock and grabbed his beak into one hand. Then I wrapped my handkerchief round and round his beak and tied it securely in place with a bit of string, after which I took off my shirt and wrapped it round him, so that his flailing wings were pinioned tightly to his body. He lay there, trussed up as though for market, glaring at me and uttering muffled screams of rage. Grimly I picked up my equipment, put him under my arm, and stalked off towards home. Having got the gull, I wasn't going to stand any nonsense about getting him back to the villa. For the rest of the journey Alecko proceeded to produce, uninterruptedly, a series of wild, strangled cries of piercing quality, so by the time we reached the house I was thoroughly angry with him.

I stamped into the drawing-room, put Alecko on the floor, and started to unwrap him, while he accompanied the operation raucously. The noise brought Mother and Margo hurrying in from the kitchen. Alecko, now freed from my shirt, stood in the middle of the room with the handkerchief still tied round his beak and trumpeted furiously.

'What on earth's that?' gasped Mother.

'What an *enormous* bird!' exclaimed Margo. 'What is it, an eagle?'

My family's lack of ornithological knowledge had always been a source of annoyance to me. I explained testily that it was not an eagle but a black-backed gull, and told them· how I had got him.

'But dear, how on earth are we going to *feed* him?' asked Mother. 'Does he eat fish?'

Alecko, I said hopefully, would eat anything. I tried to catch him to remove the handkerchief from his beak, but he was obviously under the impression that I was trying to attack him, so he screamed and trumpeted loudly and ferociously through the handkerchief. This fresh outburst brought Larry and Leslie down from their rooms.

'Who the hell's playing *bagpipes*?' demanded Larry as he swept in.

Alecko paused for a moment, surveyed this newcomer coldly, and, having summed him up, yarped loudly and scornfully.

'My God!' said Larry, backing hastily and bumping into Leslie. 'What the devil's *that*?'

'It's a new bird Gerry's got,' said Margo; 'doesn't it look *fierce*?'

'It's a gull,' said Leslie, peering over Larry's shoulder; 'what a whacking great thing!'

'Nonsense,' said Larry; 'it's an albatross.'

'No, it's a gull.'

'Don't be silly. Whoever saw a gull that size? I tell you it's a bloody great albatross.'

Alecko padded a few paces towards Larry and yarped at him again.

'Call him off,' Larry commanded. 'Gerry, get the damn thing under *control*; it's attacking me.'

'Just stand still. He won't hurt you,' advised Leslie.

'It's all very well for you; you're behind me. Gerry, catch that bird at once, before it does me irreparable damage.'

'Don't shout so, dear; you'll frighten it.'

'I like that! A thing like a Roc flapping about on the floor attacking everyone, and you tell me not to frighten it.'

I managed to creep up behind Alecko and grab him; then, amid his deafening protests, I removed the handkerchief from his beak. When I let him go again he shuddered indignantly, and snapped his beak two or three times with a sound like a whip-crack.

'Listen to it!' exclaimed Larry. 'Gnashing its teeth!'

'They haven't got teeth,' observed Leslie.

'Well, it's gnashing *something*. I hope you're not going to let him keep it, Mother? It's obviously a dangerous brute; look at its eyes. Besides, it's unlucky.'

'Why unlucky?' asked Mother, who had a deep interest in superstition.

'It's a well-known thing. Even if you have just the *feathers* in the house everyone goes down with plague, or goes mad or something.'

'That's peacocks you're thinking of, dear.'

'No, I tell you it's albatrosses. It's well known.'

'No, dear, it's peacocks that are unlucky.'

'Well, anyway, we can't have that thing in the house. It would be sheer lunacy. Look what happened to the Ancient Mariner. We'll all have to sleep with crossbows under our pillows.'

'Really, Larry, you do *complicate* things,' said Mother. 'It seems quite tame to me.'

'You wait until you wake up one morning and find you've had your eyes gouged out.'

'What nonsense you talk, dear. It looks quite harmless.'

At this moment Dodo, who always took a little while to catch up with rapidly moving events, noticed Alecko for the first time. Breathing heavily, her eyes protruding with interest, she waddled forward and sniffed at him. Alecko's beak flashed out, and if Dodo had not turned her head at that moment – in response to my cry of alarm – her nose would have been neatly sliced off; as it was she received a glancing blow on the side of the head that surprised her so much that her leg leapt out of joint. She threw back her head and let forth a piercing yell. Alecko, evidently under the impression that it was a sort of vocal contest, did his best to out-scream Dodo, and flapped his wings so vigorously that he blew out the nearest lamp.

'There you are,' said Larry in triumph. 'What did I say? Hasn't been in the house five minutes and it kills the dog.'

Mother and Margo massaged Dodo back to silence, and Alecko sat and watched the operation with interest. He clicked his beak sharply, as if astonished at the frailty of the dog tribe, decorated the floor lavishly, and wagged his tail with the swagger of one who had done something clever.

'How nice!' said Larry. 'Now we're expected to wade about the house waist deep in guano.'

'Hadn't you better take him outside, dear?' suggested Mother. 'Where are you going to keep him?'

I said I had thought of dividing the Magenpies' cage and keeping Alecko there. Mother said this was a very good idea. Until his cage was ready I tethered him on the veranda, warning each member of the family in turn as to his whereabouts.

'Well,' observed Larry as we sat over dinner, 'don't blame *me* if the house is hit by a cyclone. 'I've warned you; I can do no more.'

'Why a cyclone, dear?'

'Albatrosses always bring bad weather with them.'

'It's the first time I've heard a cyclone described as bad weather,' observed Leslie.

'But it's *peacocks* that are unlucky, dear; I keep telling you,' Mother said plaintively. 'I know, because an aunt of mine had some of the tail-feathers in the house and the cook died.'

'My dear Mother, the albatross is world famous as a bird of ill-omen. Hardened old salts are known to go white and faint when they see one. I tell you, we'll find the chimney covered with Saint Elmo's fire one night, and before we know where we are we'll be drowned in our beds by a tidal wave.'

'You said it would be a cyclone,' Margo pointed out.

'A cyclone *and* a tidal wave,' said Larry, 'with probably a touch of earthquake and one or two volcanic eruptions thrown in. It's tempting Providence to keep that beast.'

'Where did you get him, anyway?' Leslie asked me.

I explained about my meeting with Kosti (omitting any mention of the water-snakes, for all snakes were taboo with Leslie) and how he had given me the bird.

'Nobody in their right senses would give somebody a present like that,' observed Larry. 'Who is this man, anyway?'

Without thinking, I said he was a convict.

'A *convict*?' quavered Mother. 'What d'you mean, a convict?'

I explained about Kosti being allowed home for the weekends, because he was a trusted member of the Vido community. I added that he and I were going fishing the next morning.

'I don't know whether it's very wise, dear,' Mother said doubtfully. 'I don't like the idea of your going about with a convict. You never know what he's done.'

Indignantly, I said I knew perfectly well what he'd done. He killed his wife.

'A *murderer*?' said Mother, aghast. 'But what's he doing wandering round the countryside? Why didn't they hang him?'

'They don't have the death penalty here for anything except bandits,' explained Leslie; 'you get three years for murder and five years if you're caught dynamiting fish.'

'Ridiculous!' said Mother indignantly. 'I've never heard of anything so scandalous.'

226

'I think it shows a nice sense of the importance of things,' said Larry. 'Whitebait before women.'

'Anyway, I won't have you wandering around with a murderer,' said Mother to me. 'He might cut your throat or something.'

After an hour's arguing and pleading I finally got Mother to agree that I should go fishing with Kosti, providing that Leslie came down and had a look at him first. So the next morning I went fishing with Kosti, and when we returned with enough food to keep Alecko occupied for a couple of days, I asked my friend to come up to the villa, so that Mother could inspect him for herself.

Mother had, after considerable mental effort, managed to commit to memory two or three Greek words. This lack of vocabulary had a restrictive effect on her conversation at the best of times, but when she was faced with the ordeal of exchanging small talk with a murderer she promptly forgot all the Greek she knew. So she had to sit on the veranda, smiling nervously, while Kosti in his faded shirt and tattered pants drank a glass of beer, and while I translated his conversation.

'He seems such a *nice* man,' Mother said, when Kosti had taken his leave; 'he doesn't look a bit like a murderer.'

'What did you think a murderer looked like?' asked Larry – 'someone with a hare lip and a club foot, clutching a bottle marked POISON in one hand?'

'Don't be silly, dear; of course not. But I thought he'd look . . . well, you know, a little more *murderous*.'

'You simply can't judge by physical appearance,' Larry pointed out; 'you can only tell by a person's actions. I could have told you he was a murderer at once.'

'How, dear?' asked Mother, very intrigued.

'Elementary,' said Larry with a deprecating sigh. 'No one but a murderer would have thought of giving Gerry that albatross.'

# 18

# An Entertainment with Animals

The house was humming with activity. Groups of peasants loaded with baskets of produce and bunches of squawking hens, clusterd round the back door. Spiro arrived twice, and sometimes three times a day, the car piled high with crates of wine, chairs, trestle tables, and boxes of foodstuffs. The Magenpies, infected with the excitement, flapped from one end of their cage to the other, poking their heads through the wire and uttering loud raucous comments on the bustle and activity. In the dining-room Margo lay on the floor, surrounded by huge sheets of brown paper on which she was drawing large and highly coloured murals in chalk; in the drawing-room Leslie was surrounded by huge piles of furniture, and was mathematically working out the number of chairs and tables the house could contain without becoming uninhabitable; in the kitchen Mother (assisted by two shrill peasant girls) moved in an atmosphere like the interior of a volcano, surrounded by clouds of steam, sparkling fires, and the soft bubbling and wheezing of pots; the dogs and I wandered from room to room helping where we could, giving advice and generally making ourselves useful; upstairs in his bedroom Larry slept peacefully. The family was preparing for a party.

As always, we had decided to give the party at a moment's notice, and for no other reason than that we suddenly felt like it. Overflowing with the milk of human kindness, the family had invited everyone they could think of, including people they cordially disliked. Everyone threw themselves into the preparations with enthusiasm. Since it was early September we decided to call it a Christmas party, and, in order that the whole thing should not be too straightforward, we invited our guests to lunch, as well as to tea and dinner. This meant the preparation of a vast quantity of food, and Mother (armed with a pile of dog-eared recipe books) disappeared into the kitchen and stayed there for hours at a time. Even when she did emerge, her spectacles misted with steam, it was almost impossible to conduct a conversation with her that was not confined exclusively to food.

As usual, on the rare occasions when the family were unanimous in their desire to entertain, they started organizing so far in advance, and with such zest, that by the time the day of the festivities dawned they were generally exhausted and irritable. Our parties, needless to say, never went as we envisaged. No matter how we tried there was always some last-minute hitch that switched the points and sent our carefully arranged plans careering off on a completely different track from the one we had anticipated. We had, over the years, become used to this, which is just as well, for otherwise our Christmas party would have been doomed from the outset, for it was almost completely taken over by the animals. It all started, innocently enough, with goldfish.

I had recently captured, with the aid of Kosti, the ancient terrapin I called Old Plop. To have obtained such a regal and interesting addition to my collection of pets made me feel that I should do something to commemorate the event. The best thing would be, I decided, to reorganize my terrapin pond, which was merely an old tin wash-tub. I felt it was far too lowly a hovel for such a creature as Old Plop to inhabit, so I obtained a large square stone tank (which had once been used as an olive oil store) and proceeded to furnish it artistically with rocks, water-plants, sand, and shingle. When completed it looked most natural, and the terrapins and water-snakes seemed to approve. However, I was not quite satisfied. The whole thing, though undeniably a remarkable effort, seemed to lack something. After considerable thought I came to the conclusion that what it needed to add the final touch was goldfish. The problem was where to get them? The nearest place to purchase such a thing would be Athens, but this would be a complicated business, and, moreover, take time. I wanted my pond to be complete for the day of the party. The family were, I knew, too occupied to be able to devote any time to the task of obtaining goldfish, so I took my problem to Spiro. He, after I had described in graphic detail what goldfish were, said that he thought my request was impossible; he had never come across any such fish in Corfu. Anyway, he said he would see what he could do. There was a long period of waiting, during which I thought he had forgotten, and then, the day before the party, he beckoned me into a quiet corner, and looked around to make sure we were not overheard.

'Master Gerrys, I thinks I can gets you them golden fishes,' he rumbled hoarsely. 'Donts says anythings to anyones. You comes into towns with me this evenings, whens I takes your Mothers in to haves her hairs done, and brings somethings to puts them ins.'

Thrilled with this news, for Spiro's conspiratorial air lent a pleasant flavour of danger and intrigue to the acquisition of goldfish, I spent the afternoon preparing a can to bring them home in. That evening Spiro was late, and Mother and I had been waiting on the veranda some considerable time before his car came honking and roaring up the drive, and squealed to a halt in front of the villa.

'Gollys, Mrs Durrells, I'm sorrys I'm lates,' he apologized as he helped Mother into the car.

'That's all right, Spiro. We were only afraid that you might have had an accident.'

'Accidents?' said Spiro scornfully. 'I never has accidents. No, it was them piles again.'

'*Piles?*' said Mother mystified.

'Yes, I always gets them piles at this times,' said Spiro moodily.

'Shouldn't you see a doctor if they're worrying you?' suggested Mother.

'Doctors?' repeated Spiro, puzzled. 'Whats fors?'

'Well, piles can be dangerous, you know,' Mother pointed out.

'*Dangerous?*'

'Yes, they can be if they're neglected.'

Spiro scowled thoughtfully for a minute.

'I mean them aeroplane piles,' he said at last.

'*Aeroplane* piles?'

'Yes. French I thinks theys are.'

'You mean aeroplane *pilots*.'

'Thats whats I says, piles,' Spiro pointed out indignantly.

It was dusk when we dropped Mother at the hairdressers, and Spiro drove me over to the other side of the town, parking outside some enormous wrought-iron gates. He surged out of the car, glanced around surreptitiously, then lumbered up to the gates and whistled. Presently an ancient and be-whiskered individual appeared out of the bushes, and the two of them held a whispered consultation. Spiro came back to the car.

'Gives me the cans, Master Gerrys, and yous stay heres,' he rumbled. 'I wonts be longs.'

The be-whiskered individual opened the gates, Spiro waddled in, and they both tip-toed off into the bushes. Half an hour later Spiro reappeared, clutching the tin to his massive chest, his shoes squelching, his trouser legs dripping water.

'Theres you ares, Master Gerrys,' he said, thrusting the tin at me. Inside swam five fat and gleaming goldfish.

Immensely pleased, I thanked Spiro profusely.

'Thats all rights,' he said, starting the engine; 'only donts says a things to anyones, eh?'

I asked where it was he had got them; who did the garden belong to?

'Nevers you minds,' he scowled; 'jus' you keeps thems things hidden, and donts tells a soul about them.'

It was not until some weeks later that, in company with Theodore, I happened to pass the same wrought-iron gates, and I asked what the place was. He explained that it was the palace in which the Greek King (or any other visiting royalty) stayed when he descended on the island. My admiration for Spiro knew no bounds: to actually burgle a palace and steal goldfish from the King's pond struck me as being a remarkable achievement. It also considerably enhanced the prestige of the fish as far as I was concerned, and gave an added lustre to their fat forms as they drifted casually among the terrapins.

It was on the morning of the party that things really started to happen. To begin with, Mother discovered that Dodo had chosen this day, of all days, to come into season. One of the peasant girls had to be detailed to stand outside the backdoor with a broom to repel suitors so that Mother could cook uninterruptedly, but even with this precaution there were occasional moments of panic when one of the bolder Romeos found a way into the kitchen via the front of the house.

After breakfast I hurried out to see my goldfish and discovered to my horror, that two of them had been killed and partially eaten. In my delight at getting the fish, I had forgotten that both terrapins and water-snakes were partial to a plump fish occasionally. So I was forced to move the reptiles into kerosene tins until I could think of a solution to the problem. By the time I had cleaned and fed the Magenpies and Alecko I had still thought of no way of being able to keep the fish and reptiles together, and it was nearing lunch-time. The arrival of the first guests was imminent. Moodily I wandered round to my carefully arranged pond, to discover, to my horror, that someone had moved the water-snakes' tin into the full glare of the sun. They lay on the surface of the water so limp and hot that for a moment I thought they were dead; it was obvious that only immediate first aid could save them, and picking up the tin I rushed into the house. Mother was in the kitchen, harassed and absent-minded, trying to divide her attention between the cooking and Dodo's followers.

I explained the plight of the snakes and said that the only thing that would save them was a long, cool immersion in the bath. Could I put them in the bath for an hour or so?

'Well, yes, dear; I suppose that would be all right. Make sure everyone's finished, though, and don't forget to disinfect it, will you?' she said.

I filled the bath with nice cool water and placed the snakes tenderly inside; in a few minutes they showed distinct signs of reviving. Feeling well satisfied, I left them for a good soak, while I went upstairs to change. On coming down again I sauntered out on to the veranda to have a look at the lunch table, which had been put out in the shade of the vine. In the centre of what had been a very attractive floral centre-piece perched the Magenpies, reeling gently from side to side. Cold with dismay I surveyed the table. The cutlery was flung about in a haphazard manner, a layer of butter had been spread over the side plates, and buttery footprints wandered to and fro across the cloth. Pepper and salt had been used to considerable effect to decorate the smeared remains of a bowl of chutney. The water-jug had been emptied over everything to give it that final, inimitable Magenpie touch.

There was something decidedly queer about the culprits, I decided; instead of flying away as quickly as possible they remained squatting among the tattered flowers, swaying rhythmically, their eyes bright, uttering tiny chucks of satisfaction to each other. Having gazed at me with rapt attention for a moment, one of them walked very unsteadily across the table, a flower in his beak, lost his balance on the edge of the cloth, and fell heavily to the ground. The other one gave a hoarse cluck of amusement, put his head under his wing, and went to sleep. I was mystified by this unusual behaviour. Then I noticed a smashed bottle of beer on the flagstones. It became obvious that the Magenpies had indulged in a party of their own, and were very drunk. I caught them both quite easily, though the one on the table tried to hide under a butter-bespattered napkin and pretend he was not there. I was just standing with them in my hands, wondering if I could slip them back in their cage and deny all knowledge of the outrage, when Mother appeared carrying a jug of sauce. Caught, as it were, red-handed I had no chance of being believed if I attributed the mess to a sudden gale, or to rats, or any one of the excuses that had occurred to me. The Magenpies and I had to take our medicine.

'Really, dear, you *must* be careful about their cage door. You know what they're like,' Mother said plaintively. 'Never mind, it was an accident. And I suppose they're not really responsible if they're *drunk*.'

On taking the bleary and incapable Magenpies back to their cage I discovered, as I had feared, that Alecko had seized the opportunity to escape as well. I put the Magenpies back in their compartment and gave them a good telling off; they had by now reached the belligerent stage, and attacked my shoe fiercely. Squabbling over who should have the honour of eating the lace, they then attacked each other. I left them flapping round in wild, disorderly circles, making ineffectual stabs with their beaks, and went in search of Alecko. I hunted through the garden and all over the house, but he was nowhere to be seen. I thought he must have flown to the sea for a quick swim, and felt relieved that he was out of the way.

By this time the first of the guests had arrived, and were drinking on the veranda. I joined them, and was soon deep in a discussion with Theodore; while we were talking, I was surprised to see Leslie appear out of the olive-groves, his gun under his arm, carrying a string bag full of snipe, and a large hare. I had forgotten that he had gone out shooting in the hope of getting some early woodcock.

'Ah ha!' said Theodore with relish, as Leslie vaulted over the veranda rail and showed us his game bag. 'Is that your own hare or is it . . . um . . . a *wig*?'

'Theodore! You pinched that from Lamb!' said Larry accusingly.

'Yes . . . er . . . um . . . I'm afraid I did. But it seemed such a good *opportunity*,' explained Theodore contritely.

Leslie disappeared into the house to change, and Theodore and I resumed our conversation. Mother appeared and seated herself on the wall, Dodo at her feet. Her gracious hostess act was somewhat marred by the fact that she kept breaking off her conversation to grimace fiercely and brandish a large stick at the panting group of dogs gathered in the front garden.

Occasionally an irritable, snarling fight would flare up among Dodo's boy friends, and whenever this occurred the entire family would turn round and bellow 'Shut up' in menacing tones. This had the effect of making the more nervous of our guests spill their drinks. After every such interruption Mother would smile round brightly and endeavour to steer the conversation back to normal. She had just succeeded in doing this for the third time when all talk was abruptly frozen again by a bellow from inside the house. It sounded the sort of cry the minotaur would have produced if suffering from toothache.

'Whatever's the matter with Leslie?' asked Mother.

She was not left long in doubt, for he appeared on the veranda clad in nothing but a small towel.

'Gerry,' he roared, his face deep red with rage. 'Where's that boy?'

'Now, *now*, dear,' said Mother soothingly, 'whatever's the matter?'

'Snakes,' snarled Leslie, making a wild gesture with his hands to indicate extreme length and then hastily clutching at his slipping towel, 'snakes, that's what's the matter.'

The effect on the guests was interesting. The ones that knew us were following the whole scene with avid interest; the uninitiated wondered if perhaps Leslie was a little touched, and were not sure whether to ignore the whole incident and go on talking, or whether to leap on him before he attacked someone.

'What *are* you talking about, dear?'

'That bloody *boy's* filled the soddin' *bath* full of bleeding *snakes*,' said Leslie, making things quite clear.

'Language, dear, language!' said Mother automatically, adding absently, 'I do wish you'd put some clothes on; you'll catch a chill like that.'

'Damn great things like *hosepipes* . . . It's a wonder I wasn't bitten.'

'Never mind, dear, it's really my fault. I told him to put them there,' Mother apologized, and then added, feeling that the guests needed some explanation, 'they were suffering from sunstroke, poor things.'

'Really, Mother!' exclaimed Larry, 'I think that's carrying things too far.'

'Now don't *you* start, dear,' said Mother firmly; 'it was Leslie who was bathing with the snakes.'

'I don't know why Larry always has to interfere,' Margo remarked bitterly.

'Interfere? I'm not interfering. When Mother conspires with Gerry in filling the bath with snakes I think it's my duty to complain.'

'Oh, shut up,' said Leslie. 'What I want to know is, when's he going to remove the bloody things?'

'I think you're making a lot of fuss about nothing,' said Margo.

'If it has become necessary for us to perform our ablutions in a nest of hamadryads I shall be forced to move,' Larry warned.

'Am I going to get a bath or not?' asked Leslie throatily.

'Why can't you take them out yourself?'

'Only Saint Francis of Assisi would feel really at *home* here . . .'

'Oh, for heaven's sake be quiet!'

'I've got just as much right to air my views . . .'

'I want a *bath*, that's all. Surely it is not too much to ask . . .'

'Now, now, dears, don't quarrel,' said Mother. 'Gerry, you'd better go and take the snakes out of the bath. Put them in the basin or somewhere for the moment.'

'No! They've got to go right outside!'

'All right, dear; don't shout.'

Eventually I borrowed a saucepan from the kitchen and put my water-snakes in that. They had, to my delight, recovered completely, and hissed vigorously when I removed them from the bath. On returning to the veranda I was in time to hear Larry holding forth at length to the assembled guests.

'I assure you the house is a deathtrap. Every conceivable nook and cranny is stuffed with malignant faunae waiting to pounce. How I have escaped being maimed for life is beyond me. A simple, innocuous action like lighting a cigarette is fraught with danger. Even the sanctity of my bedroom is not respected. First, I was attacked by a scorpion, a hideous beast that dripped venom and babies all over the place. Then my room was torn asunder by magpies. Now we have snakes in the bath and huge flocks of albatrosses flapping round the house, making noises like defective plumbing.'

'Larry, dear, you do *exaggerate*,' said Mother, smiling vaguely at the guests.

'My dear Mother, if anything I am understating the case. What about the night Quasimodo decided to sleep in my room?'

'That wasn't very dreadful, dear.'

235

'Well,' said Larry with dignity, 'it may give *you* pleasure to be woken at half past three in the morning by a pigeon who seems intent on pushing his rectum into your eye . . .'

'Yes, well, we've talked quite enough about animals,' said Mother hurriedly. 'I think lunch is ready, so shall we all sit down?'

'Well, anyway,' said Larry as we moved down the veranda to the table, 'that boy's a menace . . . he's got beasts in his belfry.'

The guests were shown their places, there was a loud scraping as chairs were drawn out, and then everyone sat down and smiled at each other. The next moment two of the guests uttered yells of agony and soared out of their seats, like rockets.

'Oh, dear, *now* what's happened?' asked Mother in agitation.

'It's probably scorpions again,' said Larry, vacating his seat hurriedly.

'Something bit me . . . bit me in the leg!'

'There you are!' exclaimed Larry looking round triumphantly. '*Exactly* what I said! You'll probably find a brace of bears under there.'

The only one not frozen with horror at the thought of some hidden menace lurking round his feet was Theodore, and he gravely bent down, lifted the cloth and poked his head under the table.

'Ah ha!' he said interestedly, his voice muffled.

'What is it?' asked Mother.

Theodore reappeared from under the cloth.

'It seems to be some sort of a . . . er . . . some sort of a *bird*. A large black and white one.'

'It's that albatross!' said Larry excitedly. 'No, no,' corrected Theodore; 'it's some species of *gull*, I think?

'Don't move . . . keep quite still, unless you want your legs taken off at the knee!' Larry informed the company.

As a statement calculated to quell alarm it left a lot to be desired. Everybody rose in a body and vacated the table.

From beneath the cloth Alecko gave a long, menacing yarp; whether in dismay at losing his victims or protest at the noise, it was difficult to say.

'Gerry, catch that bird up immediately!' commanded Larry from a safe distance.

'Yes, dear,' Mother agreed. 'You'd better put him back in his cage. He can't stay under there.'

I gently lifted the edge of the cloth, and Alecko, squatting regally under the table, surveyed me with angry yellow eyes. I stretched out a hand towards him, and he lifted his wings and clicked his beak savagely. He was obviously in no mood to be trifled with. I got a napkin and started to try to manoeuvre it towards his beak.

'Do you require any assistance, my dear boy?' inquired Kralefsky, obviously feeling that his reputation as an ornithologist required him to make some sort of offer.

To his obvious relief I refused his help. I explained that Alecko was in a bad mood and would take a little while to catch.

'Well, for heaven's sake hurry up; the soup's getting cold,' snapped Larry irritably. 'Can't you tempt the brute with something? What do they eat?'

'All the nice gulls love a sailor,' observed Theodore with immense satisfaction.

'Oh, Theodore, please!' protested Larry, pained; 'not in moments of crisis.'

'By Jove! It does look savage!' said Kralefsky as I struggled with Alecko.

'It's probably hungry,' said Theodore happily, 'and the sight of us sitting down to eat was gull and wormwood to it.'

'*Theodore!*'

I succeeded at last in getting a grip on Alecko's beak, and I hauled him screaming and flapping out from under the table. I was hot and dishevelled by the time I had pinioned his wings and carried him back to his cage. I left him there, screaming insults and threats at me, and went back to resume my interrupted lunch.

'I remember a very dear friend of mine being molested by a large gull, once,' remarked Kralefsky reminiscently, sipping his soup.

'Really?' said Larry. 'I didn't know they were such depraved birds.'

'He was walking along the cliffs with a lady,' Kralefsky went on without listening to Larry, 'when the bird swooped out of the sky and attacked them. My friend told me he had the greatest difficulty in beating it off with his umbrella. Not an enviable experience, by Jove, eh?'

'Extraordinary!' said Larry.

'What he *should* have done,' Theodore pointed out gravely, 'was to point his umbrella at it and shout – "Stand back or I'll fire".'

'Whatever for?' inquired Kralefsky, very puzzled.

'The gull would have believed him and flown away in terror,' explained Theodore blandly.

'But I don't quite understand ...' began Kralefsky, frowning.

'You see, they're terribly *gullible* creatures,' said Theodore in triumph.

'Honestly, Theodore, you're like an ancient copy of *Punch*,' groaned Larry.

The glasses clinked, knives and forks clattered, and the wine-bottles glugged as we progressed through the meal. Delicacy after delicacy made its appearance, and after the guests had shown their unanimous approval of each dish Mother would smile deprecatingly. Naturally, the conversation revolved around animals.

'I remember when I was a child being sent to visit one of our numerous elderly and eccentric aunts. She had a bee fetish; she kept vast quantities of them; the garden was overflowing with hundreds of hives humming like telegraph poles. One afternoon she put on an enormous veil and a pair of gloves, locked us all in the cottage for safety, and went out to try to get some honey out of one of the hives. Apparently she didn't stupefy them properly, or whatever it is you do, and when she took the lid off, a sort of waterspout of bees poured out and settled on her. We were watching all this through the window. We didn't know much about bees, so we thought this was the correct procedure, until we saw her flying round the garden making desperate attempts to evade the bees, getting her veil tangled up in the rose-bushes. Eventually she reached the cottage and flung herself at the door. We couldn't open it because she had the key. We kept trying to impress this on her, but her screams of agony and the humming of the bees drowned our voices. It was, I believe, Leslie who had the brilliant idea of throwing a bucket of water over her from the bedroom window. Unfortunately in his enthusiasm he threw the bucket as well. To be drenched with cold water and then hit on the head with a large galvanized-iron bucket is irritating enough, but to have to fight off a mass of bees at the same time makes the whole thing extremely trying. When we eventually got her inside she was so swollen as to be almost unrecognizable.'

'Dreadful, by Jove,' exclaimed Kralefsky, his eyes wide. 'She might have been killed.'

'Yes, she might,' agreed Larry. 'As it was, it completely ruined my holiday.'

'Did she recover?' asked Kralefsky. It was obvious that he was planning a thrilling Infuriated Bee Adventure that he could have with his lady.

'Oh, yes, after a few weeks in hospital,' Larry replied carelessly. 'It didn't seem to put her off bees though. Shortly afterwards a whole flock of them swarmed in the chimney, and in trying to smoke them out she set fire to the cottage. By the time the fire brigade arrived the place was a mere charred shell, surrounded by bees.

'Dreadful, *dreadful*,' murmured Kralefsky.

Theodore, meticulously buttering a piece of bread, gave a tiny grunt of amusement. He popped the bread into his mouth, chewed it solidly for a minute or so, swallowed, and wiped his beard carefully on his napkin.

'Talking about fires,' he began, his eyes alight with impish humour, 'did I tell you about the time the Corfu Fire Brigade was modernized? It seems that the Chief of the fire service had been to Athens and had been greatly . . . er . . . *impressed* by the new fire-fighting equipment there. He felt it was high time that Corfu got rid of its horse-drawn fire engine and should obtain a new one . . . um . . . preferably a nice, shiny *red* one. There were several other improvements he had thought of as well. He came back here alight with . . . um . . . with *enthusiasm*. The first thing he did was to cut a round hole in the ceiling of the fire station, so that the firemen could slide down a pole in the correct manner. It appears that in his haste to become modernized he forgot the pole, and so the first time they had a *practice* two of the firemen broke their legs.'

'No, Theodore, I refuse to believe that. It couldn't be true.'

'No, no, I assure you it's perfectly true. They brought the men to my laboratory to be X-rayed. Apparently what had happened was that the Chief had not explained to the men about the pole, and they thought they had to *jump* down the hole. That was only the beginning. At quite considerable cost an extremely . . . er . . . large fire engine was purchased. The Chief insisted on the *biggest* and *best*. Unfortunately it was so big that there was only one way they could drive it through the town – you know how narrow most of the streets are. Quite often you would see it rushing along, its bell clanging

239

like mad, in the *opposite* direction to the fire. Once outside the town, where the roads are somewhat broader, they could cut round to the fire. The most curious thing, I thought, was the business about the very modern fire alarm the Chief had sent for: you know, it was one of those ones where you break the glass and there is a little sort of . . . um . . . telephone inside. Well, there was a great argument as to where they should put this. The Chief told me that it was a very difficult thing to decide, as they were not sure *where* the fires were going to break out. So, in order to avoid any confusion, they fixed the fire alarm on the *door* of the fire station.'

Theodore paused, rasped his beard with his thumb, and took a sip of wine.

'They had hardly got things organized before they had their first fire. Fortunately I happened to be in the vicinity and could watch the whole thing. The place was a garage, and the flames had got a pretty good hold before the owner had managed to run to the fire station and break the glass on the fire alarm. Then there were angry words exchanged, it seems, because the Chief was annoyed at having his fire alarm broken so *soon*. He told the man that he should have knocked on the door; the fire alarm was brand new, and it would take weeks to replace the glass. Eventually the fire engine was wheeled out into the street and the firemen assembled. The Chief made a short speech, urging each man to do his . . . um . . . duty. Then they took their places. There was a bit of a fuss about who should have the honour of ringing the bell, but eventually the Chief did the job himself. I must say that when the engine *did* arrive it looked very impressive. They all leapt off and bustled about, and looked very efficient. They uncoiled a very large hose, and then a fresh hitch became apparent. No one could find the key which was needed to unlock the back of the engine so that the hose could be attached. The Chief said he had given it to Yani, but it was Yani's night off, it seems. After a lot of argument someone was sent running to Yani's house, which was . . . er . . . *fortunately*, not too far away. While they were waiting, the firemen admired the blaze, which by now was quite considerable. The man came back and said that Yani was not at his house, but his wife said he had gone to the fire. A search through the crowd was made and to the Chief's indignation they found Yani among the onlookers, the key in his pocket. The Chief was very angry, and pointed out that it was *this* sort of thing that created a bad impression. They got the back of the engine open, attached the hose, and turned on the water. By that time, of course, there was hardly any garage left to . . . er . . . *put out.*'

Lunch over, the guests were too bloated with food to do anything except siesta on the veranda, and Kralefsky's attempts to organize a cricket match were greeted with complete lack of enthusiasm. A few of the more energetic of us got Spiro to drive us down for a swim, and we lolled in the sea until it was time to return for tea, another of Mother's gastronomic triumphs. Tottering mounds of hot scones; crisp, paper-thin biscuits; cakes like snowdrifts, oozing jam; cakes dark, rich, and moist, crammed with fruit; brandy snaps brittle as coral and overflowing with honey. Conversation was almost at a standstill; all that could be heard was the gentle tinkle of cups, and the heartfelt sigh of some guest, already stuffed to capacity, accepting another slice of cake. Afterwards we lay about on the veranda in little groups, talking in a desultory, dreamy fashion as the tide of green twilight washed through the olive-groves and deepened the shade beneath the vine so that faces became obscured in the shadow.

Presently Spiro, who had been off in the car on some mysterious expedition of his own, came driving through the trees, his horn blaring to warn everything and everyone of his arrival.

'Why *does* Spiro have to shatter the evening calm with that ghastly noise?' inquired Larry in a pained voice.

'I agree, I agree,' murmured Kralefsky sleepily; 'one should have nightingales at this time of day, not motor-car horns.'

'I remember being very puzzled,' remarked Theodore's voice out of the shadows, with an undertone of amusement, 'on the first occasion when I drove with Spiro. I can't recall exactly what the conversation was about, but he suddenly remarked to me, 'Yes, Doctors, peoples are scarce when I drive through a village." I had a . . . um . . . curious mental picture of villages quite empty of people, and huge piles of corpses by the side of the road. Then Spiro went on, "Yes, when I goes through a village I blows my horns like hells and scares them all to death."'

The car swept round to the front of the house, and the headlight raked along the veranda briefly, showing up the frilly ceiling of misty green vine leaves, the scattered groups of guests talking and laughing, the two peasant girls with their scarlet head-scarves, padding softly to and fro, their bare feet scuffing on the flags, laying the table. The car stopped, the sound of the engine died away, and Spiro came waddling up the path, clutching an enormous and apparently heavy brown-paper parcel to his chest.

'Good God! Look!' exclaimed Larry dramatically, pointing a trembling finger. 'The publishers have returned my manuscript again.'

Spiro, on his way into the house, stopped and scowled over his shoulder.

'Golly, nos, Master Lorrys,' he explained seriously, 'this is thems three turkeys my wifes cooked for your mothers.'

'Ah, then there is still hope,' sighed Larry in exaggerated relief; 'the shock has made me feel quite faint. Let's all go inside and have a drink.'

Inside, the rooms glowed with lamplight, and Margo's brilliantly coloured murals moved gently on the walls as the evening breeze straightened them carefully. Glasses started to titter and chime, corks popped with a sound like stones dropping into a well, the siphons sighed like tired trains. The guests livened up; their eyes gleamed, the talk mounted into a crescendo.

Bored with the party, and being unable to attract Mother's attention, Dodo decided to pay a short visit to the garden by herself. She waddled out into the moonlight and chose a suitable patch beneath the magnolia tree to commune with nature. Suddenly, to her dismay, she was confronted by a pack of bristling belligerent and rough-looking dogs who obviously had the worst possible designs on her. With a yell of fright she turned tail and fled back into the house as quickly as her short fat little legs would permit. But the ardent suitors were not going to give up without a struggle. They had spent a hot and irritating afternoon trying to make Dodo's acquaintance, and they were not going to waste this apparently heaven-sent opportunity to try to get their relationship with her on a more intimate footing. Dodo galloped into the crowded drawing-room, screaming for help, and hot on her heels came the panting, snarling, barging wave of dogs. Roger, Puke and Widdle, who had slipped off to the kitchen for a snack, returned with all speed and were horrified by the scene. If anyone was going to seduce Dodo, they felt, it was going to be one of them, not some scrawny village pariah. They hurled themselves with gusto upon Dodo's pursuers, and in a moment the room was a confused mass of fighting, snarling dogs and leaping hysterical guests trying to avoid being bitten.

'It's wolves! . . . It means we're in for a hard winter,' yelled Larry, leaping nimbly on to a chair.

'Keep calm, keep calm!' bellowed Leslie, as he seized a cushion and hurled it at the nearest knot of struggling dogs. The cushion landed, was immediately seized by five angry mouths and torn asunder. A great whirling cloud of feathers gushed up into the air and drifted over the scene.

'Where's Dodo?' quavered Mother. 'Find Dodo: they'll hurt her.'

'Stop them! Stop them! They're killing each other,' shrilled Margo, and seizing a soda siphon she proceeded to spray both guests and dogs with complete impartiality.

'I believe *pepper* is a good thing for dog-fights,' observed Theodore, the feathers settling on his beard like snow, 'though of course I have never tried it *myself.*'

'By Jove!' yelled Kralefsky, 'watch out . . . save the ladies!'

He followed this advice by helping the nearest female on to the sofa and climbing up beside her.

'Water also is considered to be good,' Theodore went on musingly, and as if to test this he poured his glass of wine with meticulous accuracy over a passing dog.

Acting on Theodore's advice, Spiro surged out to the kitchen and returned with a kerosene tin of water clasped in his ham-like hands. He paused in the doorway and raised it above his head.

'Watch outs,' he roared; 'I'll fixes the bastards.'

The guests fled in all directions, but they were not quick enough. The polished, glittering mass of water curved through the air and hit the floor, to burst up again and then curve and break like a tidal wave over the room. It had the most disastrous results as far as the nearest guests were concerned, but it had the most startling and instantaneous effect on the dogs. Frightened by the boom and swish of water, they let go of each other and fled out into the night, leaving behind them a scene of carnage that was breath-taking. The room looked like a hen-roost that had been hit by a cyclone; our friends milled about, damp and feather-encrusted; feathers had settled on the lamps and the acrid smell of burning filled the air. Mother, clasping Dodo in her arms, surveyed the room.

'Leslie, dear, go and get some towels so that we can dry ourselves. The room *is* in a mess. Never mind, let's all go out on to the veranda, shall we?' she said, and nodded sweetly. 'I'm so sorry this happened. It's Dodo, you see; she's very *interesting* to the dogs at the moment.'

Eventually the party was dried, the feathers plucked off them, their glasses were filled and they were installed on the veranda where the moon was stamping the flags with ink-black shadows of the vine leaves. Larry, his mouth full of food, strummed softly on his guitar, and hummed indistinctly; through the french windows we could see Leslie and Spiro both scowling with concentration, skilfully dismembering the great brown turkeys; Mother drifted to and fro through the shadows, anxiously asking everyone if they were getting enough to eat; Kralefsky was perched on the veranda wall – his body crab-like in silhouette, the moon peering over his hump – telling Margo a long and involved story; Theodore was giving a lecture on the stars to Dr Androuchelli, pointing out the constellations with a half-eaten turkey leg.

Outside, the island was striped and patched in black and silver by moonlight. Far down in the dark cypress-trees the owls called to each other comfortingly. The sky looked as black and soft as a mole-skin covered with a delicate dew of stars. The magnolia tree loomed vast over the house, its branches full of white blooms, like a hundred miniature reflections of the moon, and their thick, sweet scent hung over the veranda languorously, the scent that was an enchantment luring you out into the mysterious, moonlit countryside.

# The Return

With a gentlemanly honesty which I found hard to forgive, Mr Kralefsky had informed Mother that he had taught me as much as he was able; the time had come, he thought, for me to go to somewhere like England or Switzerland to finish my education. In desperation I argued against any such idea; I said I *liked* being half-educated; you were so much more *surprised* at everything when you were ignorant. But Mother was adamant. We were to return to England and spend a month or so there consolidating our position (which meant arguing with the bank) and then we would decide where I was to continue my studies. In order to quell the angry mutterings of rebellion in the family she told us that we should look upon it merely as a holiday, a pleasant trip. We should soon be back again in Corfu.

So our boxes, bags, and trunks were packed, cages were made for birds and tortoises, and the dogs looked uncomfortable and slightly guilty in their new collars. The last walks were taken among the olives, the last tearful good-byes exchanged with our numerous peasant friends, and then the cars, piled high with our possessions, moved slowly down the drive in procession, looking, as Larry pointed out, rather like the funeral of a successful rag-and-bone merchant.

Our mountain of possessions was arranged in the Customs shed, and Mother stood by it jangling an enormous bunch of keys. Outside in the brilliant white sunlight the rest of the family talked with Theodore and Kralefsky, who had come to see us off. The Customs officer made his appearance and wilted slightly at the sight of our mound of baggage, crowned with a cage from which the Magenpies peered malevolently. Mother smiled nervously and shook her keys, looking as guilty as a diamond smuggler. The Customs man surveyed Mother and the luggage, tightened his belt, and frowned.

'Theese your?' he inquired, making quite sure.

'Yes, yes, all mine,' twittered Mother, playing a rapid solo on her keys. 'Did you want me to open anything?'

The Customs man considered, pursing his lips thoughtfully.

'Hoff yew any noo clooes?' he asked.

'I'm sorry?' said Mother.

'Hoff yew any noo clooes?'

Mother cast a desperate glance round for Spiro.

'I'm sorry. I didn't quite catch . . .'

'Hoff yew any noo clooes . . . *any noo clooes?*'

Mother smiled with desperate charm.

'I'm sorry I can't quite . . .'

The Customs man fixed her with an angry eye.

'Madame,' he said ominously, leaning over the counter, 'do yew spik English?'

'Oh, yes,' exclaimed Mother, delighted at having understood him, 'yes, a *little*.'

She was saved from the wrath of the man by the timely arrival of Spiro. He lumbered in, sweating profusely, soothed Mother, calmed the Customs man, explained that we had not had any new clothes for years, and had the luggage shifted outside on to the quay almost before anyone could draw breath. Then he borrowed the Customs man's piece of chalk and marked all the baggage himself, so there would be no further confusion.

'Well, I won't say good-bye but only *au revoir*,' mumbled Theodore, shaking hands precisely with each of us. 'I hope we shall have you back with us . . . um . . . *very soon*.'

'Good-bye, good-bye,' fluted Kralefsky, bobbing from one person to the other. 'We shall so look forward to your return. By Jove, yes! And have a good time, make the most of your stay in old England. Make it a *real* holiday, eh. That's the ticket!'

Spiro shook each of us silently by the hand, and then stood staring at us, his face screwed up into the familiar scowl, twisting his cap in his huge hands.

'Wells, I'll says good-byes,' he began and his voice wavered and broke, great fat tears squeezing themselves from his eyes and running down his furrowed cheeks. 'Honest to Gods, I didn't means to cry,' he sobbed, his vast stomach heaving, 'but it's just like saying goodsbye to my own peoples. I feels you belongs to me.'

The tender had to wait patiently while we comforted him. Then, as its engine throbbed and it drew away across the dark blue water, our three friends stood out against the multi-coloured background, the tottering houses sprawled up the hillside, Theodore neat and erect, his stick raised in grave salute, his beard twinkling in the sun; Kralefsky bobbing and ducking and waving extravagantly; Spiro, barrel-bodied and scowling, alternately wiping his eyes with his handkerchief and waving it to us.

As the ship drew across the sea and Corfu sank shimmering into the pearly heat haze on the horizon a black depression settled on us, which lasted all the way back to England. The grimy train scuttled its way up from Brindisi towards Switzerland, and we sat in silence, not wishing to talk. Above our heads, on the rack, the finches sang in their cages, the Magenpies chuckled and hammered with their beaks, and Alecko gave a mournful yarp at intervals. Around our feet the dogs lay snoring. At the Swiss frontier our passports were examined by a disgracefully efficient official. He handed them back to Mother, together with a small slip of paper, bowed unsmilingly, and left us to our gloom. Some moments later Mother glanced at the form the official had filled in, and as she read it, she stiffened.

'Just look what he's put,' she exclaimed indignantly, '*impertinent* man.'

Larry stared at the little form and snorted.

'Well, that's the penalty you pay for leaving Corfu,' he pointed out.

On the little card, in the column headed *Description of Passengers*, had been written, in neat capitals: One travelling Circus and Staff.

'What a thing to write,' said Mother, still simmering, 'really, some people are *peculiar*.'

The train rattled towards England.